TRAVELLER'S GUIDE TO
BOTSWANA

Peter Comley has been living in Botswana since 1980, and has been guiding and conducting photographic safaris in all of Botswana's major tourist areas, as well as in Zimbabwe, Zambia, Namibia and South Africa. He has lead a wide range of specialist safaris, including anthropological, ecological, wildlife and bushlore tours. He is the author of various articles for wildlife magazines, and is a published wildlife photographer.

Salome Meyer joined Peter Comley in Botswana in 1985, when they opted for living in the wilds and started their own safari company offering a variety of special interest safaris. She is a registered member of the Field Guides Association of Southern Africa, has conducted many safaris and bushlore courses, and escorted Peter on numerous expeditions. A keen traveller and explorer with an eager fascination for the bush, she is now concentrating on developing her writing and photographic skills.

PHOTOGRAPHIC CREDITS

PETER COMLEY
SALOME MEYER

TRAVELLER'S GUIDE TO
BOTSWANA

NH
NEW
HOLLAND

ACKNOWLEDGEMENTS

Numerous people have, over the years, contributed either directly or indirectly, to the compilation of information in this book, and although there are too many to mention by name, our gratitude is extended to each and every one of them. In particular, we would like to thank Pete Smith for his patient help with the vegetation, Richard Randall for sharing his knowledge of birds and for access to his personal reference library, and Roy and Alison Ashby for their support and friendship. Mike Slogrove, Pat Carr-Hartley, Jonathan Gibson, Geoff Williams and Gavin Blair all freely shared their knowledge of Botswana with us. Nick Walker, the senior curator of the National Museum, Ilona Somerset, Alec Campbell and Neil Parsons provided valuable insights into present and future developments of the country's historical sites. We also wish to thank the Government of Botswana for their permission to write this book and the various departments for their assistance, particularly the Department of Wildlife and National Parks who answered our queries with friendly enthusiasm. We are grateful to the staff of Struik, particularly Christine Didcott, our editor, for their professionalism, and Afroventures who generously allowed us to use their photocopier. And to Django, we promise to make up for all the walks he so patiently missed out on.

This edition published in 1994 by New Holland (Publishers) Ltd
London • Cape Town • Sydney

Copyright © 1994 in text: Peter Comley and Salome Meyer
Copyright © 1994 in photographs: as credited on page 192
Copyright © 1994 New Holland (Publishers) Ltd

ISBN: 1 85368 333 7

New Holland (Publishers) Ltd
37 Connaught Street, London W2 2AZ

Project Manager: Christine Didcott
Editor: Linda Cilliers and Annlerie van Rooyen
Design and DTP make-up: Kevin Shenton
Cover Design: Neville Poulter
Cartographer: Angus Carr
Picture researcher: Kate Boswell
Indexer and proofreader: Ethné Clarke

Reproduction by Unifoto (Pty) Ltd
Printed and bound in Singapore by Tien Wah Press (Pte.) Ltd

Every effort has been made to enusure factual accuracy in this book. However, with the rapid changes that are taking place in Botswana, it is inevitable that information in this book will become outdated. The authors invite any comments or suggestions for future updates. Please write to:
The Editor, Traveller's Guide to Botswana, New Holland (Publishers) Ltd, PO Box 1144, Cape Town 8000.

Contents

PART ONE

AN INTRODUCTION TO BOTSWANA

Africa conjures up images of wide open grass plains and umbrella thorn trees; elephant, buffalo, giraffe and lion; sandy roads and open landrovers; sunshine and khaki clothes. Of course, it also holds the promise of adventure. Botswana is all that: the quintessential, slumbering old Africa.

It is a land unlike any other – a land of harsh contrasts, yet compelling beauty. The spirit of Botswana will captivate you and lure you back time after time. Here you will discover true wilderness, untamed by modern civilisation. A land of open spaces where you can travel alone for days without any sign of human activity. Wild animals live their lives alongside humans. Sun-drenched days cast their mesmerizing spell and the people of the land reciprocate with the relaxed and carefree nature that typifies Africa.

LEFT: *Tourists watching hippos at Linyanti.*
ABOVE: *Sunset over Guma Lagoon, Okavango.*

7

THE LAND

With an area of 581 730 square kilometres, Botswana is roughly the size of France, with a population now creeping past 1,3 million. Situated on the southern African plateau, it is a landlocked nation, bounded by South Africa to the south, Zimbabwe to the east, Namibia to the west and north, and with Zambia brushing the far north-east. It averages 950 metres above sea level and is more than 600 kilometres from the nearest coast. The Tropic of Capricorn cuts across the southern section of Botswana leaving the bulk of the country within the tropics. Huge contrasts are evident in the weather patterns where the energy-sapping summer heat gives way to bitingly cold nights in the desert. Cycles of drought follow rain in endless succession.

The most striking feature of the land is its flatness, as it is essentially a basin of rock, filled and levelled with Kalahari sand. It is an arid country. Eighty-four per cent of the land is

Okavango from the air, showing the system of islands and channels.

covered by dry, dun-coloured Kalahari sands and savanna scrub, to be broken only occasionally by the breathtaking wonders of the Okavango Delta, the Makgadikgadi Pans and Tsodilo Hills in the north. These natural phenomena, and the experience of a truly remote and unspoilt wilderness, are the magnets that attract visitors to Botswana.

Subtle changes in the scenery may be overlooked by the complacent traveller. Along the south-eastern boundary of the country, the stretches of white sands are replaced by red soils and rocky outcrops that break the flatness of the land. It is here that you come across the ephemeral rivers – dry one day and in raging torrent the next. The eastern rim is the only part free of Kalahari sands and this small section of land (15 per cent), is where 80 per cent of the population lives.

With the exception of very isolated outcrops and gently rolling dunes, the Kalahari horizon is almost completely unbroken. The shimmering expanses of the Makgadikgadi Salt Pans provide an awe-inspiring break from the relentless sameness of the Kalahari. These barren white pans eventually give way to waving grasslands that roll across the horizon.

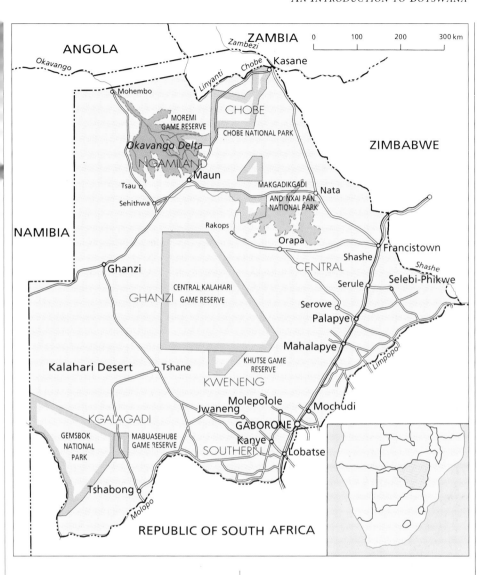

Beyond the grass plains are the patchy forests of the north. On breaking through the forests, one suddenly encounters the lush wonderland of the Okavango, right in the heart of the Kalahari, where, suddenly, earthy shades transform into brilliant greens and blues as the harsh landscape meets palm-fringed islands and water lilies floating gently on cool, clear waters.

Across this spectacular kaleidoscope, wild animals move in astounding profusion and variety. Here, too, contrasts are evident: some animals have adapted to a desert environment, while others have evolved to survive in the permanent waters of the Okavango. Botswana supports large concentrations of game, particularly in areas set aside as national parks and game reserves. Nearly 99 000 square kilometres of land is protected which represents an impressive 17 per cent of the total area of the country – one of the highest percentages in the world of land devoted to conservation.

WHAT TO EXPECT

Botswana is not a land that appeals to all. Approach it with an open mind and you will be amply rewarded. Life in the country is simple, with the emphasis on comfort, charm and the outdoors. The main tourist attraction is its wilderness, and visitors should make the most of this aspect, rather than expect sophisticated entertainment. Accommodation is generally comfortable, but not lavish.

Due to the remoteness of the tourist areas, operational costs are high and these are passed on to the visitor. Botswana is not an inexpensive destination. Neither is it formally structured and rigidly organised. Accept that your flight may be delayed, or that your favourite wine may not be available.

THE OKAVANGO DELTA AND OTHER RIVERS

In an arid land, water is the most precious of all commodities. Botswana is criss-crossed with a great number of rivers, but few of these hold any water at all. Even fewer guarantee a

year-round supply. No significant rivers rise on the Kalahari sand.

Today, only dry and desolate valleys remain where once there had been great rivers. Such are the Molopo and Nossob rivers in the southern Kalahari, Deception Valley and the Savuti Channel. In the entire country there are only two perennial rivers: the Okavango and the Chobe, both in the north. Others, like the Motloutse and the Limpopo that form the eastern border with South Africa, flow after the rains but, except for a few pools, are dry during the winter months.

The Okavango rises in Angola and enters the dry north of Botswana from the Caprivi as the third largest river in southern Africa. Here, its fast flow is suddenly checked by the thick mantle of Kalahari sand. Searching for an escape route, the river spreads out in a fan-shape on the desert floor, creating one of the largest inland deltas in the world, the Okavango Delta. Its waters spill over the desert to form over 15 000 square kilometres of floodplains, islands, and lagoons linked by a maze of fast-flowing channels. It provides food and water for scores of animals. Mammals, birds, reptiles, fish and insects all flourish in this tropical paradise. The vegetation, dominated by palms, papyrus and towering trees, has the greatest concentration of species in southern Africa, outside of the fynbos region of the Cape. This is the glittering gem of Botswana – a vast oasis set in a harsh desert.

ABOVE: *Blue wildebeest roam the Kalahari.*
LEFT: *Lush vegetation thrives in the permanent waters of the Okavango.*

INLAND DELTAS

Although the Okavango Delta is often described as unique because of its own individual ecology, it is by no means the only inland delta in the world. Others include the Niger Delta, the Kafue Flats of Zambia and the deltaic confluence of the Magdalena, San Jorge and Cauca rivers in Columbia which covers an area of 20 000 square kilometres. In Brazil an enormous delta of over 50 000 square kilometres is formed where the Amazon and Tapajos rivers meet.

Comprising 15 000 square kilometres, the Okavango is not the largest inland delta in the world. However, what makes the Delta unique is its location in an arid area, its special diversity of fauna and flora and the fact that it is the only major delta whose waters do not reach the ocean.

The Chobe River also rises in Angola, where it is known as the Kwando. It flows roughly parallel to the Okavango, along the northern boundary of Botswana and forms the lesser known, but equally beautiful, Linyanti Swamps. The Chobe creates conditions favourable for the famed elephant herds that rely on its waters during the dry winter season.

The Limpopo River valley forms the eastern boundary between Botswana and the Transvaal, in northern South Africa. It also defines the southern border of the Tuli Block, a wedge of land jutting between South Africa and Zimbabwe, where much of Botswana's agriculture

takes place. This is an attractively rugged part of Botswana and is unlike the rest of the country. The Limpopo cuts its way through granite outcrops that stand high above the valley and meanders through mopane, mashatu and acacia forests, sustaining a multitude of animals, both wild and domesticated.

The Tuli area is an archaeologist's dream. Some of Africa's most fascinating and important iron age settlements have been excavated along the Limpopo River system, illustrating its historical role in sustaining life. Among the ancient stone-walled remains are a number that date to and correspond with those of Great Zimbabwe to the north (AD 1250-1450).

At the crown of the Limpopo lies the Motloutse River, scene of the discovery of Botswana's first diamond by Dr Gavin Lamont in 1955 – an event which many years later led geologists to the diamond pipe at Orapa.

ABOVE: *Sandy roads are typical of Chobe National Park.*
LEFT: *Elephants drinking at the Serondela campsite, Chobe.*

ABOVE: *Dramatic cloud formations create a spectacular backdrop to the Kalahari plains.*
LEFT: *Rocky outcrops near Francistown.*

KALAHARI DESERT

The centre of Botswana is a hollow basin filled with sand that, over millennia, had been blown there by the wind. It now forms a vast flat plain covering 80 per cent of the country and extending southward into South Africa, westward into Namibia and north through Angola and Zambia to the equator. This is the Kalahari, one of the most extensive mantles of sand on earth, but not the largest desert.

The word 'desert' is a misnomer when applied to the elusive Kalahari. It conjures up images of red sand dunes sighing under the relentless sun, where its wizened people, eking out an existence, dance for rains that never come. The name is derived from the Sebgalagadi word *Kgalagadi*, meaning 'the great drying up' or 'the great thirst'. The Kalahari has been described as a desert, a thirstland and a sandveld. A true desert has no surface water and supports neither vegetation nor human activity; the Kalahari, however, is well-vegetated and the average rainfall is too high for it to be a true desert. But it retains no permanent surface water: life is sustained by the seasonal pans that sometimes hold a little with rain water and the subterranean streams that flow beneath the surface. In this way, it has supported the San for thousands of years.

What might have been a boring and interminably flat stretch of sand covered by scrub is broken by enormous grassy plains, forests, dune fields stabilised by vegetation, numerous white clay pans, dry fossil valleys and isolated rocky outcrops. Because of its aridity, thick sands, size and inaccessibility, much of the Kalahari remains wilderness, inhabited by animals adapted to live in this environment and hardy people who understand its vagaries and who can eke out a living from its dry soils.

PANS

One of the most common physical features in Botswana is the large number of pans etched across the landscape. These are closed basins, a few of which sometimes hold summer rains well into the winter months and are often the sole providers of surface water for man and beast in the most arid of areas. They vary in size from a few metres or a few hundred metres across, to dry lake beds several kilometres wide. Most are bare, shallow hollows with dune systems on the south-western side, a result of the prevailing north-easterly winds.

The smaller pans play a role in nurturing and determining the movement and migration of wildebeeste. In addition, those which are rich in minerals, such as nitrogen and phosporous, add greatly to the mineral intake of the resident wildlife. For the rest, though, the pans feature only marginally in the habits of the plains game, which follow the rainfall, and, in winter, obtain their moisture from plants and from the dew (they feed nocturnally, from about midnight to dawn).

RIGHT: *Fish and tawny eagle at Makgadikgadi.*
BELOW: *Vast grass plains stretch across the Makgadikgadi Pans.*

The pans of the Makgadikgadi are entirely different. They once formed the centre of the great Lake Makgadikgadi. This was the largest lake in Africa at the time, but it has been dry for the past two millenia and more.

Today, Makgadikgadi consists of two large salt pans, Sowa and Ntwetwe, and a number of smaller pans. Combined, these are the size of Wales. After substantial rains, the pans partially fill with water. Flamingoes and other waders flock down from East Africa to breed in this temporary aquatic paradise. The grassy plains that encircle the salt pans provide food for large numbers of browsing animals which, in turn, attract many predators.

The pans contain a seemingly unlimited supply of soda ash, which is now being mined on the eastern edge of Sowa Pan.

As the great lake dried, it left behind smaller isolated lakes such as the Mababe Depression of the Savuti region, Nxai and Kudiakam Pans and Lake Ngami. All of these have also dried up, but may fill with water seasonally and attract migrant species.

HILLS AND DUNES

There are no mountains in Botswana; even rocky outcrops are uncommon and quite striking when they do occur. Apart from those of the eastern hardveld, there are hardly any other hills in Botswana. On the periphery of the Kalahari, there is a gradual transition from sandveld to hardveld with an increasing presence of hills, low escarpments and the fault-lines of the northern river system.

Isolated hills, or *Inselbergs*, most rising up to only 150 metres above the surrounding plains are restricted to the middle Kalahari where they were formed from a variety of rocks. The

Game-viewing drives are popular in Moremi Game Reserve.

most well-known examples of *Inselbergs* are the Tsodilo Hills (400 metres) in the western Kalahari and the Seven Hills of Savuti. Substantial ranges of hills also overlook the Kalahari in the vicinity of Serowe. The only other features that break the flatness are sand dunes, sand ridges and petrified dunes, many of which may easily be mistaken for hills.

Over thousands of years, Botswana has experienced periods of aridity, followed by spells of high rainfall. As a consequence of the dry periods, the country is dotted with dune fields.

Although sand-ridges also form prominent features on the landscape, they are not dunes, but rather the edges of the once great Lake Makgadikgadi. Many a traveller has come to know the slog and grind of crossing the Magwikwe sandridge between Moremi and Savuti!

GAME RESERVES AND NATIONAL PARKS

Botswana's major attractions are its untouched open spaces, unspoiled wilderness and its wildlife. Both Tanzania and Kenya offer greater numbers of game, but the true wilderness experience belongs to Botswana. The government fully realises this and has taken the

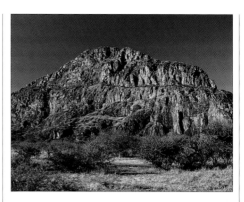

ABOVE: *The Tsodilo Hills rise out of the flat landscape of the north-western Kalahari.*
BELOW: *The baobab – a common sight in many parts of Botswana.*

decision to conserve the aspect of Botswana that is responsible for its appeal through its low-volume high-cost tourism policy. The country has half a dozen huge reserves.

The importance of conserving the natural heritage is echoed in the words of President Masire: 'The Kalahari, semi-arid and without streams, is very different from the Okavango Delta. Yet, both are valuable natural resources and both can be sensitive to misuse. Both could be destroyed through ignorance, haste or greed. It is our privilege to use them, but it is our duty to conserve them for the future.'

The main draw card for tourists is the Okavango Delta. A large proportion of the Delta is not conserved as a national park. Moremi Game Reserve, which covers the eastern section of the Delta, is the only formally protected part of the Okavango, although much of the rest is afforded some protection as wildlife management areas. These wildlife management areas, which are controlled by the Department of Wildlife and National Parks, have been set aside for utilisation of wildlife, which at present is understood to mean hunting – both private and commercial.

Chobe National Park, the third largest of the parks, is situated in the far north-eastern corner of the country. It is well-known for its great elephant and buffalo herds, although a wide diversity of other mammals is also found here. Chobe is distinctly different from Moremi and has habitat ranging from woodland forests to the dry Savuti marsh.

Another northern reserve is the Makgadikgadi and Nxai Pan National Park, comprising the formerly separate Nxai Pan area and the great basins of the Makgadikgadi complex. This dryland reserve is very different in character from Moremi and Chobe. Makgadikgadi comprises flat landscapes of tall, waving grass, groves of palm trees and a section of the salt pans. In contrast, Nxai Pan embraces two large,

flat and open grass-covered pans which are dotted with acacia-canopied ground.

Central Kalahari Game Reserve (the country's largest reserve), Khutse Game Reserve, Gemsbok National Park – second largest of the parks – and Mabuasehube Game Reserve are all set in the Kalahari and are relatively undeveloped and inaccessible.

At 120 000 hectares, the North-east Tuli Game Reserve, which comprises Tuli and Mashatu game reserves and various private farms, is the largest private game reserve in southern Africa. With rocky hills, sandstone outcrops and rivers, it is very different to the rest of Botswana. It is famous for having the largest herd of elephants in the world to roam a private reserve.

Manyalanong Game Reserve protects a Cape vulture colony, while Gaborone Game Reserve and Maun Game Reserve provide a taste of wildlife for townsfolk. These are all small (under 5 square kilometres in size).

VEGETATION

Given the flatness of the land and the fact that 84 per cent of the country is covered by Kalahari sands, one would not expect much variation in the vegetation. For much of Botswana this is true, but despite the uniformity of the savanna bushveld that covers most of the landscape, subtle changes are noticeable.

The whole of the south-western part of the country is scrub and woodland savanna, with thinly spread bushes covering the undulating sands. Changes in sand colour, from deep red in the extreme south-west to oranges, yellows and pale greys in the north, indicate a corresponding change in bush density or composition. Each one of these striking colours reflects the underlying parent rock and as each rock has its own characteristic mineral composition the vegetation growing in each soil type is distinctively different.

The Makgadikgadi Pans themselves are largely barren, though there are vegetated ridges and 'islands', surrounded by grassland plains with rows of palms lining the horizon.

Much of the rest of the country consists of the typical tree savanna of Africa – mature acacias set in fields of waving grasses or stunted scrub. However, enormous areas of grey loamy soils, towards the north, are covered by mopane forest, a strong species that denies sustenance to all but the hardiest ground cover.

The red soil of the eastern hardveld may have supported open grassland, but overgrazing, dating as far back as the 11th century, has weakened the grass structure and permitted hardy thorn bushes to encroach, forming impenetrable thickets in places.

In the north-east lie the mixed deciduous forests that consist mostly of hardwoods, the Zambezi teak (*Baikiaea plurijuga*) being the most common. This area has been protected by the establishment of five forest reserves under the control of the Department of Forestry. Logging is permitted, under licence, within the reserves. The timber is mostly exported to South Africa for use in the building and furniture industries. Unfortunately, despite the fact that slow-growing hardwoods are being harvested, there is no re-planting programme and this does not augur well for the long-term viability of the industry.

The Okavango changes all the rules. The juxtaposition between desert and water wonderland is apparent in the dense vegetation. More than a thousand species of plants, ranging from permanently submerged and floating aquatic plants to water-loving grasses and sedges fringing the edges of the channels; from riparian forests to dryland scrub and savanna, all combining to turn the Delta into Africa's largest and most attractive oasis. The contrast between the lush Okavango and the surrounding bush is never greater than during the dry winter months. The neutral brown and grey tones of leafless shrubs and dried grasses give way to a dazzling spectrum of greens that are generated by innumerable aquatic and riparian plants. Shades of emerald, lime and jade are mirrored by the still, azure waters.

FAUNA

Botswana boasts 164 species of mammals. These include the 'big five': lion, leopard, buffalo, elephant and the very occasional rhino, though these have been poached almost to the point of regional extinction. The country owes its diversity of mammals to the divergent types of habitat. The gemsbok, for example, needs little moisture to survive and finds life comfortable in the Kalahari, while the sitatunga spends its life waist-deep in water in the Okavango. Certain antelope species, such as red lechwe and puku are confined to the northern Botswana and Kafue (Zambia) wetlands.

Over 550 species of birds exist in Botswana and this, too, reflects the variation in habitat. Some of the larger birds include the ostrich, kori bustard and secretary birds, while splashes of vivid colour are provided by the carmine bee-eaters, lilacbreasted rollers and the elusive Narina trogon. Rare or endangered birds include the slaty egret, wattled crane, Pel's fishing owl, and the Cape vulture.

Reptiles and amphibians are extremely plentiful (157 species of reptiles and 38 of amphibians). Of the 72 species of snakes,

Lion are often seen on the roadside.

15 are highly venomous and seven are considered potentially deadly. But rest assured, black mambas, spitting cobras, boomslang, puff adders and night adders are rarely encountered. Crocodiles, monitor lizards and pythons – the largest of the snakes and the only one that is on the conserved species list – are commonly seen throughout the year, while flap-knecked chameleons, as well as the leopard and Kalahari tortoises are usually spotted only in the summer months.

There are over 70 species of fish, which are confined to the permanent waters of the Okavango and the Chobe Rivers and to a lesser extent the Limpopo River. The most important angling fish are tigerfish, bream, catfish (or barbel), pike and carp.

CLIMATE

Botswana has a dry, semi-arid climate that is reasonably consistent. The northern two-thirds of the country lies within the tropics, but due to the land's altitude and its distance from the oceans, the climate is more temperate than tropical. The weather is influenced by prevailing high and low pressure cells that dominate the sub-continent and exert a major influence on the rain-bringing winds.

The winter months, from May to August, are dry and cloudless, with the days generally warm and the nights cold. Day and night temperatures vary considerably, particularly in the less vegetated desert regions. Day-time temperatures of 27 °C can drop to below freezing at night. With the arrival of a cold front, temperatures may plummet suddenly. These cold snaps, caused by Atlantic lows, usually last for a few days. Should you be caught on a game drive in an open vehicle at such times, you may be left wondering what had happened to your safari to sunny Botswana!

Early summer is usually hot with little relief from rain. Temperatures in September to November can soar to 40 °C during the day and cool off to 17 °C at night.

The rainy season is normally between December and April, although early rains, from September onwards, are not unusual. Rain arrives suddenly in the form of short and intense thunderstorms that may be very localised. Torrential rain may fall in one place, while another, only a few kilometres away, will remain

ABOVE: *Heavy summer rains flood the Nata to Kasane road.*
BELOW: *An aerial view of Maun.*

authorities have initiated a 'drought-watch' programme; rainfall is carefully monitored and drought relief systems initiated well in time to avoid the all-too-common scenes of starvation witnessed in other parts of Africa.

CITIES AND TOWNS

Most of Botswana's larger towns and villages are located on either side of the main north-south road, which follows the eastern contour of the country. The eastern corridor has always been more accessible and habitable, with water more freely available than in the arid Kalahari. Scatters of San and other hardy peoples have managed to make a home in the harsh inner sanctum of the Kalahari. Other than the settlements in the east, some villages and small towns are huddled around the Okavango Delta, the Chobe River and in the Kalahari.

The two major centres, the capital of Gaborone, in the south-east near the South African border, and Francistown in the east, are both expanding rapidly – and indeed they are probably the fastest growing centres in Africa.

At the time of Botswana's independence, Gaborone was no more than a small, rural village, selected as capital because of its location near water in Botswana (the old administrative capital, Mafikeng, was outside the border) and the rail line to South Africa and Zimbabwe. It has subsequently grown into a modern capital with an ever- improving infrastructure, international hotels, good restaurants and well-stocked shops.

Francistown was the site of a 1870s gold rush and then grew into the trading centre of the north. In the early 1980s, it was overtaken by Gaborone as Botswana's largest town.

Maun, in the north, is the main centre of the tourist industry. It is rapidly changing from a rugged frontier settlement to a complacent middle-sized town. Kasane on the Chobe River is the other main tourist centre serving the north of the country.

bone dry. Zebra and wildebeest herds, in particular, follow the thunder showers to take advantage of the water and fresh growth. The average rainfall is 450 millimetres per annum, with the highest figures recorded in the north-east of the country and a gradual decrease to below 300 millmetres in the south-west. Similarly, humidity decreases from east to west and from north to south. During the dry winter months, when humidity is at its lowest, it often drops to 30 below per cent.

Throughout the country, potential evapo-transpiration (the loss of moisture through evaporation and transpiration by plants) far exceeds the rainfall. This means that agriculture without irrigation is only viable in some years (about six seasons out of ten), even during the wet months. Many rural people subsist on meagre crops of sorghum and maize.

Droughts occur on an almost regular cyclical basis, with the southern part of the country being most susceptible to drought. The

PEOPLE

Definition by ethnic group is frowned upon in Botswana and, under the constitution, all citizens are regarded equal. As a result, remarkable unity has been achieved. People throughout the country regard themselves as Batswana (the people of Botswana) first, then as Bayei, Batawana, Hambukushu, Bakwena, Bakalanga, Basubiya, European and so on.

BATSWANA

Botswana means 'land of the Batswana' and, indeed, the Batswana character is clearly evident in the peaceful, pragmatic attitude to political and social life in the country. The astuteness of the guiding fathers must be appreciated when one examines the wisdom and strength of character with which these people managed to maintain the integrity of their institutions when other, more powerful tribes capitulated under the firepower of white colonisation. The level-headedness of the national leaders is reflected even at village level, where the elders control daily village life through the tribal court, or *kgotla*.

Colonial partitioning paid little heed to tribal boundaries and, as a result, three-quarters of the Batswana now live in South Africa. In spite of this, the remaining Batswana form the country's most populous grouping by far and constitute about half of the population. The ancestry of the Batswana can be traced back to the mid-14th century, when the offspring of a Kwena chief, Malope, who is thought to have lived in the hilly Magaliesberg region close to present-day Pretoria, left with some followers to settle around what is now the Zeerust area of the western Transvaal. Over the decades drought, overgrazing and other catalysts prompted these forebears of the Batswana to split again, the offshoots moving away, merging with other Sotho peoples and

sometimes even rejoining their parent tribes (*merafe*) in a protracted and complex process of fission, migration and fusion from which, after three centuries, eight identifiably coherent groups emerged. The other Batswana groups are the Batawana, the Bakgatla, the Barolong, the Balete and the Batlokwa.

The language spoken by the Batswana is Setswana. There is a dialectical difference between regions, but not so great that people have any difficulty in communicating. Being the national language, it is spoken by the vast majority of Botswana's citizens.

Historically, the leadership structure of a tribe, or *morafe* (singular) consisted of a *kgosi* (the chief or leader and a member of the royal family), his family members and their servants. The royal family was normally situated in the centre of the *morafe*. The *kgosi* was the ultimate authority and had considerable rights and obligations. He was responsible for dispensing justice and law, providing defence, bringing rain, giving health, controlling the wealth and dispensing gifts. In return, he

ABOVE: *Rural butcher in Rakops, Kalahari.*
BELOW: *A meeting of the tribal court* (kgotla) *in Maun to discuss the future of the Delta.*

Cattle are considered an important asset in rural Batswanan society.

devoted all his time to the tribe and was constantly on hand to help people with their problems. He retained control of his armies by placing close members of his family at the head of every regiment. Hunting was a communal affair ordered by the *kgosi* and often required the services of many people, although the meat so procured belonged to him for distribution. Today, although many of the *kgosi*'s powers have been assumed by the State, he still plays a central role in community life, dispensing justice, defending traditions and ensuring the well-being of his people.

The Batswana are predominantly a pastoral society. Traditionally, wealth lies in the ownership of cattle, which play a pivotal role in determining the status of the individual and of the *morafe*. Many laws and traditions revolve around cattle ownership and the transfer of these animals between families. The *kgosi* had the power to take cattle for misdemeanours and was entitled to redistribute the confiscated beasts. This was used to maintain discipline and to ensure obedience to the leaders. Families were careful not to lose their cattle, as cattle separated the rich from the poor. A man's family was required to transfer a *bogadi* (dowry) of cattle to his bride's family for marriage. A man would therefore marry his cousins knowing that when his children in turn married their cousins, the cattle given for his wives would come back to him. To a large extent, this system of marrying cousins has now broken down, although *bogadi* is still transferred to the bride's father.

Individual ownership of tribal land was not recognised and a person was granted only use of the land. Once the person had left the land, another was able to apply for its use. This was the traditional system, which no longer functions. A person can now be granted user-rights, which can be as security against loans or sold.

The Batswana evolved a system of social security through the extended family – now in a state of decline – whereby all related members of a family have rights and duties of support. A working person may be responsible for the support of over ten other persons. If a worker has a family that is not working, the bulk of his salary can go to supporting them.

Urbanisation has had a major effect on the social and cultural life of the Batswana. With the rapid urban growth, the influence of the tribal system is diminishing, fuelling the crime rate and introducing Batswana youth to many of the social problems inherent in western urban living. In many cases, the extended family system is breaking down and causing problems for those at home who are dependent on financial support from the employed members of the family.

SAN

Better known to most as Bushmen, the name San is preferred by modern writers, as the word 'Bushmen' is deemed both racist and sexist.

Moving southwards from Central Africa, the San probably settled in Botswana about 25 000 to 40 000 years ago. They were hunter-gatherers, the men being responsible for the provision of meat, while women gathered the fruits and tubers that formed the bulk of their diet. The San lived in small bands of no more than 80, as the arid desert regions could not support large groups of people. Private possessions were few, as everything had to be carried along as they moved from one water source to the next. Although they have a leadership structure, many decisions were taken by the whole group. Fights were rare and disagreements were quickly and amicably settled; co-operation was essential for survival in the harsh conditions.

The San believed that everything was part of a greater scheme and had an equal right to existence. Man had no special standing in nature and no right to kill indiscriminately. Hunting was an activity that carried not only honour, but also the duty of sharing with others, as it represented spiritual unification with the dead animal.

For them, there were two gods – one good, but removed from the mundane, and the other an evil meddler who took on human form. A trance dance is still commonly practised and is executed for healing purposes and to fend off evil and to contact the spirit world.

Modern-day San must confront similar problems to those faced by other aboriginal peoples. Traditional society is disintegrating as competition from dominant cultures increases. The San want to retain their own style and standard of living, but pasturalists have encroached on their traditional lands and they can no longer lead the life they understand and value. The breakdown of ancient ways has caused many social problems such as poverty, alcoholism and unemployment, as well as a standard of living that falls far short of the national average.

Schools have been built in villages where the supply of water and drought-relief food entices the San to stay. Western education has introduced a desire for material goods that had never before been part of the San culture. The remote areas offer little employment, and there is a steady move to the bigger towns in search of work.

KHOI

Of the same racial and linguistic group as the San, the Khoi (commonly known as Hottentots) are distinguished from their cousins by a generally more settled lifestyle, by their greater preoccupation with ownership of cattle – and by the precepts and social structures these elements have helped create. Their cattle-owning ancestors were probably living in northern Botswana just over two millenia ago. Later Khoi groups – the Nama – filtered in from Namibia in the west, most notably during the German colonial wars of the early 1900s, many of them to settle around Bokspits in the extreme south-west, and in Matsheng in the northern Kgalagadi district.

BAKALANGA

The Bakalanga is the second largest population group in the country and have also fallen victim to the artificial colonial boundaries. The boundary between Zimbabwe and Botswana split the Bakalanga into two groups, with most of the country's Bakalanga living in

San using traditional hunting weapon.

Ovaherero women in typical Victorian-style dress, modelled on those worn by the wives of early missionaries.

Being a proud, determined and pastoral people, they rebuilt their herds and are now major cattle owners. Among these people, a man who does not own his own beasts has no standing in society and is even expected to become a servant of a cattle owner.

Traditionally, they worshipped their ancestors. Records of ancestors and their burial grounds were passed on orally from generation to generation. Although not as important as the tribal ancestors, they also believed in a higher being. Today the old religion is hardly ever practised and has generally been replaced by Christianity.

Some Ovaherero object to having their photographs taken on religious grounds. First ask permission to photograph them.

the Francistown region. Although they own cattle and goats, they are primarily agriculturalists to whom the tilling of the land plays an important role in their customs and religion. Cattle ownership among Bakalanga does not afford the individual the same prestige as it does the Batswana; usually only the chief kept cattle for the common good of the tribe. As a result of historical turmoil, groups of Bakalanga are to be found as far afield as Maun, Palapye, Serowe, Mahalapye and Mochudi.

OVAHERERO

The Ovaherero nation is split into three main groups: the Herero who live mostly in Namibia, the Mbanderu who mainly live in Botswana and the Ovahimba who live in northern Namibia and Angola. Although the majority of these people are in fact Mbanderu, the name 'Herero' is far more widely known.

Many Ovaherero are relative newcomers who fled from a war of extermination perpetrated against them by the Germans in 1904/1905. They settled in the area to the west of the Okavango and in the south, particularly in the Lake Ngami region. They had lost all their possessions and had to work as servants for the Batawana.

BAYEI

Bayei men will be your polers if you undertake a traditional mokoro safari in the Okavango. These friendly, peaceful people found refuge in the Okavango while moving away from the Mababe area to avoid both the slave-hunters from Angola and the Balozi people of the upper Zambezi floodplains, who were expanding their territorial authority. They have occupied the periphery of the Delta since the end of the 18th century. Those who lived in the tsetse-fly infected areas of the Delta subsisted on fish, while the cattle herds were kept on the non-infested fringes.

HAMBUKUSHU

The Hambukushu shared many of the hardships of the Bayei and were driven westwards from southern Zambia to the main Okavango River where they tilled the land along its banks. The last major influx of Hambukushu arrived from southern Angola as refugees during the Angolan civil war of the 1970s. They settled in the Etsha region along the western fringe of the Okavango and are regarded as master basket weavers.

ABOVE: *Traditional Hambukushu baskets, showing the distinctive geometric patterning that has made them a sought-after curio.*
RIGHT: *Bayei mokoro poler in the Delta.*

BAKHALAGARI

Possibly the earliest of the black people to settle in Botswana who are still living there. They moved west from South Africa and had almost encircled the Kalahari by 1700. Harsh living conditions and encroachment on their land by stronger tribes reduced their numbers by about 80 000, mostly in the Kalahari region, and today many have been assimilated by the other, more dominant groups.

BASUBIYA

The people who live in the Chobe enclave settled there in the early 18th century before building a powerful empire that included the Bayei and the Hambukushu. They are agriculturalists who, unlike the Bayei of the floodplains, plough the dry lands. They plant their crops in late winter, after the flood has receded, to take advantage of the moist soil.

WHITES

The white community can be separated into two groupings – those who live in Botswana on a permanent basis, often as citizens; and expatriates who work there on a short-term contract (usually two years) and who plan to move on again. Among the former are people who identify deeply with the country. The expatriates, who mostly hail from Europe and the United States, offer skills not available within Botswana and without whom the country could not have progressed as rapidly. Financially attractive packages are available to these skilled foreigners who are mainly employed by the government, aid agencies and large companies. As the level of education rises, less reliance on such outside skills will become inevitable.

HISTORICAL BACKGROUND

Evidence of early human remains and stone tool-making exists throughout eastern Botswana. Rock art dating back more than 2 000 years was left by the San and it seems likely that they have lived in Botswana for at least 25 000 years.

Bantu-speakers began moving down from the north in slow migrations that began well before the first millenium, adopting an iron-age technology along the way to become productive and prosperous by 500 BC. They were forest farmers to begin with, but in due course acquired cattle and sheep. By the 19th century these 'black people' had long been living peacefully throughout the country.

However, things were soon to change. In the early 19th century a wave of wars known

23

as the Difaqane swept the subcontinent, the later ones influenced by Boer Trekker movement from the coastal Cape, by the explosive expansion of Shaka's Zulu empire, and by the arrival of Mzilikazi, founder of the Ndebele nation in the Batswana-occupied region of the western Transvaal. The Batswana scattered, seeking refuge among friendly tribes and it was to be 20 years before they were to return to their land.

Hunters, traders and missionaries started arriving in Botswana in 1806. The industrial revolution in Europe had created a need for new markets and raw materials. This precipitated a later rush for Africa from traders seeking concessions for their governments. Moreover, guns – and a new method of hunting – had been introduced to the Batswana, who had realised the value and power of firearms after a handful of Boers had been able to rout the omnipotent Ndebele in the 1830s.

Even the best hunters struggled to make a living in South Africa, the game having been so depleted. They turned their attention to the unexplored north and introduced guns, a new method of hunting to the Batswana. The game soon dwindled, unable to withstand the relentless slaughter.

Missionaries were to play a major role in the lives of the Batswana, acting as mediators in disputes with other white men and bringing to the country a religion which today is central to many Batswana lives.

In 1836, some 20 000 Boers left the Cape to avoid British officialdom and settled in the land north of the Vaal River. Helped by the Batswana, they resisted and then defeated Mzilikazi's Ndebele, and laid claim to the land. However, it was traditional Botswana territory. They had been uprooted by Mzilikazi, who then regarded it as his. After the Boers had driven off Mzilikazi, the Batswana found that the land they had previously occupied was no longer theirs and that they were only allowed to stay on as labourers on the Boer farms.

This set the scene for land clashes between Boer and Batswana which still persist in South Africa today. As a result of constant raids and Boer expansion, the Batswana came to hate and fear them and turned to the British, whom they considered the lesser of two evils.

Southern Africa had been a troublesome region for the British. Wars against the indigenous people and squabbles with the Boers were costing money and prestige. Britain had no desire to further increase their commitment in the area. The Germans, however, were set to establish themselves in Namibia and the fear existed that they would cast their eyes eastward, blocking the road to the promising Ndebele concessions in Zimbabwe. Reluctantly, Britain decided to annex another vast area; this time at minimal cost.

In March 1885, a protectorate was declared over Bechuanaland and the borders of present day Botswana was thus defined. The area to the south of the Molopo River, part of the present-day northern Cape region, became a Crown Colony and was known as British Bechuanaland. The area to the north, present-day Botswana, was to remain largely independent but under protection from the Boers in the south and the Ndebele in the north-east. Cecil John Rhodes, chairman of the British South Africa Company (BSAC), was determined to include the Bechuanaland Protectorate into Rhodesia and manoeuvred himself into position for the takeover of the Protectorate.

Britain was ready to hand over the Protectorate to Rhodes when Batswana chiefs Khama, Bathoen and Sebele went to England in 1895 to plead their case. Their distrust of Rhodes was deep, following clashes Khama had with him when the two allied against the Ndebele. The harsh treatment of those living in Rhodesia increased their efforts to keep their land out of his control. In their negotiations they managed to persuade the colonial secretary to keep their three reserved territories under Crown protection. It was the British government's intention, though, to cede the 'Kalahari' and the proposed railway 'strip' running up the eastern region (to Rhodesia) to the BSAC, but even this concession to Rhodes's aspiration was shortly to be withdrawn (after the fiasco of the Jameson Raid).

LEFT: *Sir Charles Rey, Commissioner of the Bechuanaland Protectorate from 1929-1937.*
RIGHT: *Sir Seretse Khama, first president of Botswana.*

The chiefs' triumphal return was followed a month later on 29 December 1895 by the Jameson Raid – an ill-timed and poorly executed plan by Rhodes to overthrow the Boers in the Transvaal Republic. Dr Jameson, a trusted confidant of Rhodes, launched the raid with the intention of triggering an uprising by the non-Boers in the Transvaal. Jameson and his party were captured by President Kruger's commandos before they reached Johannesburg and Rhodes, quite rightly, received much of the blame, which effectively ended his expansion plans.

The British continued to administer the Protectorate for the next 70 years – years of slow progress against the background of security and peace. Sir Charles Rey was among several notable administrators of this period. A vibrant go-getter, he introduced dramatic changes in many areas. He increased the power of the administration and appointed an economic consultant, who proposed various surveys which were aimed at improving the cattle ranching industry, dredging the Okavango Delta and moving the capital to within the Protectorate's borders.

Rey fought vigourously for increased British finance and eventually succeeded. In eight years, he more than doubled school attendance; increased expenditure twofold; raised attendance at out-patient hospitals by more than eight times and improved the infrastructure in all areas. He was also the first to propose that a national park be established in the Chobe region. Some twenty years were to elapse before a similar infusion of funds and drive occurred.

By 1955, British policy had begun to alter course considerably. Plans were made for independence for the Protectorate, and legislation was passed to effect this. The Protectorate was granted internal self-government in 1965 and the Republic of Botswana became completely independent on 30 September 1966, under the new president, Sir Seretse Khama.

BOTSWANA TODAY

GOVERNMENT

'....our new nation, economically poor but developing, with our four objectives of rapid economic growth, social justice, economic independence and sustained production. We are dedicated to improving the lot of our people in the rural areas and we are dedicated to creating more employment for our people. But we intend to conserve our resources wisely and not destroy them. Those of us who happen to live in the 20th century are no more important than our descendants in centuries to come.'

(Hon Sir QKJ Masire, President of Botswana)

Botswana is an independent, stable and harmonious republic with universal franchise for all citizens over 21 in a multi-party democracy.

The government is styled on the Westminster system with an executive president as head of state and government. The president is elected by 34 members of the one-house National Assembly (parliament) for a term of five years. He selects his 15 cabinet ministers from the Assembly and appoints a vice-president.

Legislative power within Botswana lies with the National Assembly. The House of Chiefs, which is not part of the legislature, is composed of eight tribal chiefs of the main tribes plus seven other members, and is the equivalent of the British House of Lords. It has the constitutional function to advise the National Assembly on proposed bills affecting land use, social customs and so forth, however their recommendations have no force in law.

For administrative purposes Botswana is divided into nine districts – Kweneng, Northwest, Ghanzi, Central, North-east, Kgatleng, Southern, South-east and Kgalagadi. Each of these disticts is represented by a District Commissioner, under whom the *dikgosi* fall and who is responsible for the planning and implementation of the various district development programmes.

LEGAL SYSTEM

Botswana's constitution has remained essentially unaltered since independence. That, combined with its uncompromising commitment to full democracy, makes it a rarity in modern Africa.

The system of justice can be divided into two sectors. The court of appeal, the high court and the magistrate's courts function within statutory law and the Roman-Dutch common law. The high court is situated in Lobatse, while magistrate's courts are located throughout the country.

The customary courts are traditional chiefs' courts that preside over the complex tribal laws of the Batswana people, and also hear criminal cases. The courts can be seen in most villages and may be identified by the half circle of up-right poles beneath a shady tree. They provide a forum where local disputes may be resolved. Their jurisdiction is limited to petty theft, minor assault, verbal abuse, matrimonial squabbles, land disputes and those common conflicts which affect the daily harmony of the tribe. Punishment is usually meted out as verbal censure, which carries with it social disgrace, or, in more severe cases, lashes given in public and up to six months' imprisonment.

Botswana has two police forces – the Botswana Police Force responsible for national law enforcement, and the tribal police who enforce local customary laws.

THE ECONOMY

Botswana's economic progress since independence has been one of the few success stories on the African continent. Twenty-five years ago, the country was one of the 20 poorest nations in the world. Today, it is considered the wealthiest non-oil producing country in Africa.

This remarkable growth happened during a time when much of the continent was battling with African socialism which saw prosperous economies slide into poverty. At the same time, Botswana was surrounded by countries at war with themselves. To the east, the long Rhodesian war spilled over into Botswana.

After its resolution in late 1979, civil war increased in Namibia to the north and west of Botswana. In South Africa matters were hardly better, with military raids into Gaborone by the South African Defence Force during the 1980s.

Two prolonged and serious droughts in the 1970s and 1980s caused enormous losses of livestock and demanded major food aid programmes in remote rural areas. Yet, despite these obstacles, Botswana remained a haven of peace in turbulent Africa: through sound government, adherence to a free-market economy and fortuitous mineral discoveries, the country has achieved notable success.

As a British Protectorate, Botswana had been largely neglected by the British administration and the incoming government of Sir Seretse Khama had very little infrastructure on which to launch a sound economy in 1966. By 1991, the Gross Domestic Product was P7 billion (US$ 3,5 billion) and the economy had been growing at 13 per cent annually. Gaborone had developed into a city with 140 000 inhabitants. *(Botswana Review of Commerce and Industry*, 1992)

An internationally linked microwave telephone system now stretches to Maun, Ghanzi, Kasane and all the major towns in the southeastern belt. Tarred roads abound in most of the larger towns and reach the entire length of the country, from the old capital of Mafokeng in South Africa to Kasane and Shakawe in the extreme north. More tarred roads are inching their way across the desert. Once remote centres are being linked, causing inevitable changes to lifestyles.

Potable water is supplied in most rural villages and electricity generated within the country is distributed in the major towns.

Foreign exchange reserves are, in per capita terms, one of the highest in the world and are sufficient to pay for 26 months of imports. Economic growth can be ascribed to mineral and beef exports, tourism and donor aid.

Diamond-sorting building in Gaborone. Approximately one third of the diamonds mined in Botswana are of gem quality.

MINING AND INDUSTRY

Diamonds are by far the single most important source of income for Botswana. The discovery of diamonds in 1967, after a protracted search of twelve years, dramatically changed the pace of development in Botswana. There are three diamond mines, Jwaneng in the southern Kalahari, and Orapa and Letlhakane in the central Kalahari, whose combined earnings have accounted for approximately 77 per cent of the total export earnings and 45 per cent of the GDP. These mines are jointly owned by De Beers Mining Company and the Botswana Government. In 1989 diamond exports totalled US$ 1,41 billion. By value of diamonds, Botswana is the biggest producer in the world, with an annual output of 15 million carats. (Botswana Review of Commerce and Industry, 1992)

A copper/nickel mine at Selebi-Phikwe produces and exports copper. However, as a result of the suppressed copper and nickel price on the international market, the mine ran into massive debt from which it is currently struggling to recover.

27

LEFT: *Sunflowers flourish in the rich black soil near Pandamatenga.*
ABOVE: *A mokoro excursion is a highlight of any visit to the Okavango Delta.*

In 1991 a soda ash plant was opened at Sowa Pan at a cost of US$ 320 million. The plant is to produce 350 000 tons of soda ash per year, earning US$ 60 million annually in exports. Soda ash is used in the manufacture of both flat and container glass and it is expected that it will lead to the creation of new industries such as glass manufacturing. In addition, 600 000 tons of salt worth US$ 17 million per year will be produced as a by-product. (*Botswana Review of Commerce and Industry, 1992*)

Botswana has vast reserves of low-grade coal in the eastern areas around Palapye and Mahalapye. This coal is used to supply power to all the major centres in the east through power stations situated at Selebi-Phikwe and at Morupule near Palapye. There are also indications of natural gas and oil deposits which could have far-reaching implications for the country, if they prove to be substantial.

Gold mines still operate in the Francistown area, but deposits are small and not of importance to the national economy.

At independence there was no industry at all in the country. Few believed that Botswana would be in able to enter the world economy with no infrastructure, no market economy and an insufficiently trained population. Today, 25 years later, Botswana has begun to produce a wide range of industrial and commercial goods, including textiles, non-ferrous metal fabrications, vaccines, solar power units, vehicle spares, televisions, computers and electronic equipment, shoes, concrete, canned meats and chemical and pharmaceutical products. Botswana also produces its own soap, candles, flour, maize meal, beer and soft drinks. Motor vehicle assembly plants and foundries casting in aluminium and iron increase the industrial base while bakeries provide fresh bread to all the major centres.

AGRICULTURE

Erratic rainfall during the summer months makes agriculture very difficult. About 70 per cent of the population grow crops, but repeated droughts and the attractions of urban life impede the already problematic crop production. Due to a harsh climate and poor soils, less than 5 per cent of the country is suitable for cultivation. Crops of bananas, citrus, cotton, legumes and wheat are produced in the Limpopo Valley and along the Chobe River. Grain and sunflowers were planted in Pandamatenga, but owing to a succession of droughts, floods and rodent plagues this project has met with little success.

Botswana imports 200 000 tons of grain and 30 000 tons of fresh fruit and vegetables annually. Extensive efforts to improve the agricultural output have met largely with failure and the idea of food self-sufficiency is being replaced by the concept of food security, that is, growing cash crops for export, while importing staples from neighbouring countries blessed with a kinder climate.

Animal husbandry has been practised in Botswana for about 2 000 years and is an integral part of the Batswana culture. In 1986 half of all households (both rural and urban) owned cattle. In many communities a man's status is judged by the number of cattle he owns, and dowries transferred for brides are still calculated in terms of cattle. At the time of independence, beef exports were the mainstay of the fledgling economy, but in recent years the value of beef exports has accounted for less than 4 per cent of total exports. The cattle population is over 2,6 million and exceeds the human population by more than two to one. The Ghanzi district in the central Kalahari, which was settled by Afrikaans-speaking farmers during the early 1900s, is divided into 6 000-hectare privately owned farms, and it is here that much of the country's export beef is produced.

In recent years, dairy produce has been on the increase, while the country is almost self-sufficient in chickens. Botswana's two million goats, although regarded as poor man's cattle, play an important role in the provision of meat and milk.

Skins and hides have been exported from Botswana for many years and game products have always played a valuable role in providing income to the rural population. Originally, game products came from hunting wild animals, but as this resource dwindled, farming of these animals has gained popularity. A number of game farms have been established on freehold land and many more cattle farmers are adding game, particularly antelope and zebra, to their livestock.

Three crocodile farms, the largest in Maun and the others in Kasane and the Tuli Block, have attempted to earn foreign exchange through the export of live crocodiles and their highly valued skins and meat. Unfortunately, as had been the case with ostrich farming, bureaucratic and marketing problems have hindered success.

Fish farming is being developed privately at Guma Lagoon in the Western Okavango, while the Department of Fisheries has for some time had plans to launch a large scale fish farming enterprise in the Delta. The Ministry of Agriculture, through its bee-keeping unit, is researching and encouraging the practise of bee-keeping by the small entrepreneur.

Commercial logging is conducted only in the northern forest reserves.

TOURISM

The major tourist centres in Botswana are the Okavango Delta, Moremi Wildlife Reserve, Chobe National Park and the Tuli Block. Some 17 per cent of Botswana has been protected as game reserves and national parks. This figure excludes the extensive hunting concessions which abut the parks and are allocated to the four main hunting companies. These areas are for the exclusive use of the concessionaires who may utilise the land for either hunting or photographic safaris. Under the present system these concessions are renewed on an annual basis but once the new land use plan has been instituted longer tenures will be offered.

There are more than 50 recognised safari operators in Botswana, providing 40 per cent of all employment in the undeveloped north. The value of tourism is uncertain, but estimated to be in excess of US$ 50 million a year.

Botswana has adopted a low-volume, high-cost policy for tourism. This should establish it as one of the few countries in the world to offer tourists true wilderness areas well into the 21st century. Provided the temptation for short-term reward as opposed to long-term objectives is resisted and a policy of non-interference in the parks is maintained, Botswana's wildlife will become increasingly valuable. As a self-sustaining asset, it should be able to provide the country with foreign exchange long after the diamond reserves have been exhausted.

GETTING AROUND BOTSWANA

For the most part Botswana is a flat arid country, scantily covered by grasslands and rugged woodland savanna. Huge tracts have no surface water, with the exception of the Okavango Delta and the rivers to the north and east, which make this Botswana's prime tourist destination. Movement around the country can be difficult and frustrating for the visitor intent on exploring the wilder regions; distances are huge; rural roads are often indistinct or in a state of disrepair; and to get to a particular destination often involves travel by four-wheel drive vehicle, light aircraft or boat. Finding your own way through the Okavango swamplands can be especially problematic; fly-in safaris are recommended.

LEFT: *Game-viewing vehicles transport visitors to remote wilderness areas.*
ABOVE: *Many of the roads in Botswana are untarred, but easily navigable.*

HOW TO GET THERE

BY AIR

Botswana is becoming increasingly accessible with direct international scheduled flights from Europe and Africa and daily connections to the world via Johannesburg (South Africa) and Harare (Zimbabwe). There are also regular scheduled flights to Maun from Windhoek (Namibia) which connect with flights to Europe. Air Botswana flies to ten African states but does not yet undertake intercontinental flights. Their destinations are Bulawayo, Dar-es-Salaam, Entebbe, Harare, Johannesburg, Lilongwe, Lusaka, Manzini, Maseru, Nairobi, Victoria Falls and Windhoek. Internally, Air Botswana flies to Francistown, Gaborone, Kasane, Maun, Selebi-Phikwe and Tuli Lodge.

Most of the air charter companies for the tourist industry are based in Maun. There is an air charter company operating out of Kasane (see page 181). It is also possible to charter planes out of Johannesburg, Gaborone and Windhoek. Most lodges in the Okavango have their own airstrips, as this provides the easiest access to the area. Check that an air transfer to the lodge of your choice is included as part of your travel package when making a booking.

BY RAIL

Botswana Railways offer a daily train service from Gaborone via Francistown to Bulawayo in Zimbabwe and a weekly overnight service to Johannesburg (see page 178).

BY ROAD

Botswana is connected to all four of her neighbours, Namibia, Zimbabwe, Zambia and South Africa, by tarred road, except for the Ghanzi-Windhoek road to Namibia, which is now under construction. A four-wheel drive is not essential for this road, but the surface is badly corrugated. For details on border posts and their opening hours, see page 178.

Many visitors to Botswana opt for the convenience of fly-in safaris.

TRAVEL WITHIN BOTSWANA

ON ARRIVAL

If you are joining an organised safari, or if you have booked through a tour operator, you will be met at the airport by one of their representatives or your guide, who will either take you directly on safari or to your place of accommodation, or assist you in transferring directly to your waiting charter plane. Be sure to advise him/her of your exact time and mode of arrival.

If you are on a do-it-yourself tour of Botswana, courtesy transport may be arranged with the lodge or hotel where you will be staying. Vehicles may be hired in Gaborone, Francistown, Maun or Kasane. A list of car rental agencies is provided on page 180. However, not all the companies are represented at the airports, and it is advisable to arrange this in advance. Taxis are in limited supply in Maun. Although they are more plentiful in Gaborone and Francistown, do not expect them to be lined up outside the airport waiting for tourists to arrive, as their main source of income is local trade. And prepare yourself for a hair-raising experience: not only are they notorious hell-drivers, but you could land up with 15 or more other people piled into the vehicle with you. Public transport facilities are not available from the airports. See pages 171 for more detailed information.

Chobe Game Lodge – an exclusive resort hotel located within Chobe National Park.

TRAVELLING WITHIN BOTSWANA

The roads within Botswana have had a recent face-lift and all the main arterial routes will soon be tarred. Travellers to Maun who remember the bone-shattering drive from Nata will be delighted to know that they are now able to complete the journey in comfort on a newly tarred road.

In general, the un-tarred roads of the eastern hardveld are navigable by two-wheel drive vehicles, while those in the Kalahari Sandveld areas require four-wheel drive. A four-wheel drive is essential for all the national parks and game reserves, although not essential for Serondela. This will depend entirely on your driving skills and your experience of driving in sandy conditions. For further information, see page 180.

SAFARI OPTIONS

The safari industry in Botswana has burgeoned over the last 15 years. Today, it is relatively large and sophisticated, accommodating many distinct types of travellers, to whom several safari styles are available. These may range from the silver candelabra, sunken bath and private swimming pool option, to the most basic rugged outdoor experience. Holiday arrangements and preparations will be dictated by the kind of safari you opt for.

A distinction is made between photographic and hunting safaris. In local parlance the term 'photographic safari' refers to any non-hunting safari. Thus, you may be on a photographic safari even if you do not possess a camera. Photographic safaris attract three groups of travellers: those who prefer to join an organised safari through a safari or tour operator; do-it-yourselfers who prefer to go it alone; and backpackers.

SAFARI AND TOUR OPERATORS

Here, you may choose between the relative comfort and luxury of an established lodge, or a mobile camping safari. Though mobiles are generally rather more rugged than lodges, you will be surprised how comfortable and lavish facilities on top-of-the-line mobile safaris are.

LODGES AND HOTELS

Camping is not everyone's idea of having fun and you may prefer to stay at lodges or hotels on your journey through Botswana. Once you have selected the lodges you want to visit, you have to decide how to reach them. You could

Meru tents offer a degree of comfort without intruding on the wilderness experience.

fly by charter plane (normally included in package deals) or by helicopter; alternatively, you may drive or go by boat, depending on where they are situated. If none of the available packages suit you, then a safari may be tailored to your specific requirements.

Tips on Selecting a Lodge Safari

Selecting a lodge from all the possible options can be extremely confusing. A good starting point is to look at the price. All the lodges in Botswana are expensive, but there is a great difference from the top to the bottom of the range. However, price is not always indicative of the relative difference in standards. Some factors you should take into consideration are:

Size: Many lodges are small and offer personalised service and attention as opposed to a 'conveyor-belt' style of operation.

Location: Seasonal game viewing, environmental diversity, proximity to other lodges, villages and/or cattle posts, as well as travel costs to the lodge should all be considered. If you have chosen a package safari, make sure that you will be able to enjoy the greatest possible diversity of environments during the time you have available.

Accommodation and service: Lodge accommodation varies from luxurious walk-in tents (based on the East African Meru style) to rustic chalets made of natural materials or modern, air-conditioned rooms. Service ranges from participatory to fully catered. Decide what you expect from your holiday before booking.

Guides: The quality of the guides used by the lodges will determine how much you gain from your bush experience. Each operator claims the finest guides, but a good basis for selection is by word of mouth recommendation. Ask the company to tell you in advance who your guide will be and what experience he or she has. You may request the services of a particular guide.

What is included in the price: Some lodges offer fully inclusive rates, while others offer meals, excursions, drinks, transport to and from the lodge and game park fees as optional extras. Make sure you know what is included.

MOBILE SAFARIS

The early overland expeditions of explorers like Livingstone, Baines and Anderson were the forerunners of the present-day mobile safari. These organised camping safaris are based on the concept of being totally self-contained and flexible, to allow you to follow seasonal game movements and migrations. With the added benefit of the safari being conducted by a professional guide, this is a popular way to experience Botswana. There are three levels of mobile safaris: exclusive, middle-market and economy camping.

Exclusive Mobile Safaris

The ultimate safari dream takes place in true Hemingway style – a small group of good friends surrounded by a team of well-trained staff and the luxury of the finest equipment. The top-of-the range mobile safaris are the most exclusive and expensive safaris on offer. Added logistics, preparation and organisation all contribute to the higher price. This is much more than an ordinary camping safari. There are extra vehicles to carry equipment such as beds, tables, linen, crockery and cutlery, refrigerators, mess, kitchen, shower and toilet tents. A large contingent of staff is needed to take care of all the camp chores and to break, move and set up new camps in time for your arrival. Fully inclusive rates are normally offered. For those who enjoy a reasonable degree of comfort without wanting to sacrifice the feeling of being part of the bush, this is the perfect option. Operators offering safaris within this bracket include: Kitso Safaris, Soren Lindstrom Safaris, Capricorn Safaris, Crocodile Camp Safaris, Kalahari-Kavango Safaris, Okavango Wilderness Safaris and Peter Comley Safaris.

Middle-market Mobile Safaris

As a compromise between the expense of the up-market safari and the discomfort of the cheaper options, these are the most popular safaris in Botswana. What equipment is provided and what chores you are expected to do vary among safari operators. You are usually expected to participate in the camp work, although some operators priced in this category employ staff to service the camp fully.

Equipment also varies considerably. It is best to compare exactly what the various operators are offering before selecting your safari. The experience and knowledge of guides differ widely in this category. If you demand the services of an experienced guide you should ensure that this has been arranged by your safari company before confirming your trip. Operators that generally organise safaris within this category include Afroventures, Crocodile Camp Safaris, Karibu Safaris, Okavango Wilderness Safaris, Gavin Blair Safaris, Chanouga Safaris, Go Wild, Kalahari-Kavango

Safaris, Penduka Safaris, Papadi, Penstone Safaris, Discover Botswana, Botswana Safaris, Koro Safaris, Nata Lodge Safaris and Sitatunga Safaris.

Economy Mobile Safaris

The bottom-of-the-range mobile safari offers an inexpensive and no-fuss opportunity to see the country. However, be prepared for considerable discomfort: you will probably be sleeping on the ground in a small and cramped tent, eating off your lap and sitting on camping stools. You will be expected to participate in all the camp chores such as cooking, erecting tents, washing up, collecting water and loading vehicles. You might have to supply your own sleeping bag and mattress, eating utensils or even your own tent. Operators in this category include Drifters, Papadi, Africa-in Tours and Safaris, Gamerovers, Island Safaris and Gametrails.

Tips on Selecting a Mobile Safari

Is the company a licensed operator? Check that your choice of safari operator is licensed to operate in Botswana. A number of illegal companies work in the country and if you select one of them, you run the risk of being turned away at park gates – an experience that could ruin your holiday.

Guide: Perhaps the most important aspect of a mobile safari is your guide. He or she is your constant companion and mentor and is responsible for every aspect of your safari, including your safety.

You should ensure that you are informed about who your guide is and what his/her experience and knowledge is *before* booking your safari. Experience and expertise of the guides from most of the larger companies fluctuate significantly. Also make sure your guide is licensed to run a safari.

Do you see the best of each area? Although a company may claim to take you to visit the best areas, check whether this is in fact the

Visitors who choose an economy safari are expected to participate in day-to-day camp tasks.

35

case. For instance, find out whether you will boat or fly into the Delta, or whether you will drive. If you drive, you may not get to see the best areas. Also check how many days will be spent travelling to wilderness areas on a main road. Much of this time can be considered lost and wasted.

Equipment: Check the vehicle. When joining a group, find out how many people are to travel in a vehicle and whether everyone will have a window seat. If the vehicle is enclosed, establish whether it has a game hatch from where everyone can have a good view of the surroundings and the wildlife.

Participatory safaris: You are expected to help with the chores. This may mean setting up your own tent, being involved in all the kitchen and camp chores, collecting firewood and water and so on. Too many chores can detract from your holiday, while the option of no chores does increase the cost of your safari.

What is included in the price? Find out whether your safari is fully inclusive or whether there are hidden extras such as a food kitty, drinks, game park fees, accommodation and flights, whether you provide your own camping equipment and so on.

PRIVATE SAFARI AND VEHICLE HIRE

Botswana's rural and bush areas have little in the way of road signs and no maps to keep up with the ever-changing dirt tracks. Even well-used tourist roads are poorly signposted, as many an intrepid explorer has found, to his embarrassment and to the amusement of the

people of Maun, when heading out for Savuti and unwittingly ending back in town after a two-day circular route.

Although many novices successfully negotiate Botswana's rural areas on their own, it is advisable to have at least one person in the party who has either been to Botswana before or who has experience of the African bush. If you decide to do without the services or assistance of a professional guide, it will be in your interests to be correctly prepared before venturing out of town.

It is possible to hire a four-wheel drive vehicle if you do not have one (see page 180). Assume that four-wheel drive is necessary for all excursions off the main roads, unless you have established reliably that this is not so. With the exception of the main roads between Kasane and Serondela, a four-wheel drive is required for all the national parks, as well as for most of the other places of interest. See page 179 for further information.

Essentials on a Private Safari
Vehicle
- Comprehensive tool kit
- Puncture repair kit, spare tube, tyre levers, tyre pump and gauge, hi-lift jack.
- Vehicle spares: points, plugs, condenser, fuel filters, fuel pump, fuel line, radiator hoses, radiator leak repair fluid, wheel bearings, brake and clutch kits, fan belt, regulator, fuses, globes, electric cord, jump leads, soft baling wire, engine oil, gearbox oil, brake and clutch fluid, coil, rotor arm, distributor cap, assorted bolts, nuts, screws, etc., workshop manual (with trouble-shooter guide), tow rope, spade, sand mats, spare set of keys, warning triangle, anti-freeze, funnel, spare shock absorbers and spring blades.

Take all of these items with you, even if you do not know how to use them. They might be of use to someone stopping to help you, or to someone else stranded along the way.

Some people prefer the flexibility of a do-it-yourself safari.

First aid

- Suggested first aid kit: (Ask any chemist, doctor, the AA or the Red Cross to assist you.)
- Broad spectrum antibiotic tablets; anti-histamine and cortisone (under medical supervision for snakebite treatment); antiseptic lotion; bandages; butterfly sutures; crepe and gauze; catgut and needle; cotton wool; burn ointment; anti-histamine cream; calamine lotion; colds and flu tablets; throat lozenges, cough mixture and vitamin C; diarrhoea tablets; eye ointment; headache tablets; malaria prophylactics; painkillers; plasters; sunburn lotion; syringes and injection needles; talcum powder; sulpher powder; nasal decongestant.
- First aid manual
- Snakebite kit: Only for use by trained medics (see page188).

Direction

- Maps: Maps and aerial photographs may be obtained from the Department of Surveys and Lands, Private Bag 0037, Gaborone. See page 180 for details.
- Compass: Do not use a compass to go off-road; there are vast open spaces where a breakdown can mean death. However, a compass is useful to confirm direction.
- *Visitors' Guide to Botswana,* Main and J and S Fowkes (Southern Books, 1993), is available at most book stores. This book gives specific directions to places of interest.

Safety measures

- Water: Allow 5 litres of water per person per day for drinking and cooking.
- Extra water will be needed for personal use and ablutions. Always carry sufficient water to tide you over in case of an emergency, or until rescue may reasonably be expected. In a well-used area, three days' supply should be sufficient, while in the more remote areas

Campers should ensure that they are properly equipped when camping in remote areas.

in the Kalahari you may not see another vehicle for weeks.
- Food: Take sufficient food to provide for the longest possible emergency. Pack according to pre-planned menus, and always take extra tinned food for unforeseen circumstances.
- Survival handbooks: Several of these are available on the market. Select one that is applicable to local conditions.
- Matches and firelighters: Take an adequate supply and keep them dry and sealed. Also take a lighter.
- Fuel: Most hired vehicles are fitted with long-range fuel tanks. If not, take extra fuel along in canisters. Check that all of these are full and allow for sufficient fuel for the journey, as well as for emergencies. Fuel consumption varies from vehicle to vehicle. The terrain and style of driving will also affect consumption and you should establish how much fuel will be required before setting out.

A large cool-box with ice is very useful to keep supplies cold and fresh if you do not have a refrigerator. (See *Advisories* at the end of every section for details on where to obtain ice.) In summer, if water is plentiful, it is wise to place a wet towel or blanket over the cool-box or

fridge (**not** over the chimney of gas fridges) to prevent the container from getting hot.

Foods that travel and last well on safari include: any tinned, dehydrated, air dried or dry goods, packets of soup, cereals, rusks, nuts, dried fruits and biltong (dried meat). Rye bread lasts longer than any other. Always keep perishables in steel trunks, not cardboard boxes. Fresh supplies such as cabbages, potatoes, onions, carrots, gem squash (or any type of pumpkin), oranges, tangerines (naartjies) and apples travel best. Wrap all fruits and vegetables individually in newspaper and pack them tightly between further layers of paper or cardboard – even tomatoes can last two to three weeks like this. Do not pack perishables with tins or bottles.

Backpackers

Official government policy is to attract high-cost, low-volume tourism. This makes inexpensive backpacking relatively difficult.

Entrance to the national parks is costly and most backpackers find that they cannot afford to spend much time game viewing in the parks. However, low cost options are sufficient to attract a constant stream of backpackers to the tourist regions of the north. Options for budget-conscious travellers include: avoiding the national parks and reserves and the game lodges; visiting areas in the Okavango that fall outside Moremi Wildlife Reserve or doing a boat trip (offered by all the lodges in Maun) into the lower Delta; visiting the Makgadikgadi Pans outside the reserve via Gweta and Nata; or by joining an overland safari, or part thereof, from London to Cape Town (or *vice versa*). Most backpackers normally team up with others and pool financial resources to hire a vehicle (with or without a guide), a boat or even to charter a plane. For low-cost accommodation options, see page 179.

Hitch-hiking in Botswana is not dangerous and is commonly practised by the locals. The greatest danger probably lies in the driving skills of the person offering you a ride! Due to the relatively low density of traffic on many roads, a lift can take a long time in coming.

Patience and a good book will help. To date it is still quite safe for anybody, even a woman on her own, to hitch-hike throughout the country. Hitch-hiking into the national parks is not easy or advised as most people touring the parks are normally fully laden with their own camping gear with little space left for extras. It is customary to contribute either towards the fuel expenses and/or food and refreshments *en route*.

SPECIAL INTEREST SAFARIS

A wide range of special interests are catered for in Botswana. If you do not find what you are looking for in this chapter, it does not mean that it cannot be done. These interests may be pursued on their own, or they may be combined with other activities, or simply worked into the itinerary of a standard safari. You are bound to find a safari operator among those listed, who would be willing to accommodate your special request. Contact addresses and telephone numbers for all operators included in this section are listed in the *Visitor's Digest* on page 182.

Elephant Safaris

Riding on the back of an African elephant against the spectacular backdrop of the Okavango is, for many people, a fantasy come true. Randall Jay Moore, an American biologist, brought circus-trained African elephants from the United States and based them on an island in the Okavango. The camp was named after the star bull of the troupe, Abu, who has become internationally famous for his roles in Hollywood productions. Abu's Camp is situated on the Xhenega River in the south western Okavango, about an hour's drive from Pom-Pom airstrip.

Each of the four adult elephants used for the rides is fitted with a *howdah* (comfortable seat), seating two guests and a *mahout* (professional elephant trainer), while the nine younger elephants tag along. The other animals habitually ignore these elephants, which allows you to get very close to them, as well as to the wild elephants in the area, who have displayed no

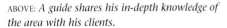

ABOVE: *A guide shares his in-depth knowledge of the area with his clients.*
ABOVE RIGHT: *Horseback safaris offer the rider a different perspective on the bush.*
BELOW: *Field scientist monitoring wild dog behaviour in SanTaWani.*

hostility towards their trained cousins. A rifle is taken along for protection, but has never had cause to be used.

Five comfortable tents with private showers and toilets provide accommodation at a base camp from where daily excursions take place. Elephant-back safaris last a minimum of four days with morning and afternoon rides of a few hours each. For variety you can also choose game drives, mokoro rides, foot safaris and fishing. Bookings may be made through Ker & Downey Safaris.

Horseback Safaris

The thrill of riding a horse into the middle of a herd of zebra or giraffe is unforgettable. Horse trails are conducted in the wetlands of the Okavango and in the salt pans of Makgadikgadi. A combination of the two safaris would give horse riders a good contrast of environments.

The safari horses in the Okavango are based at Guma Lagoon, although the horses are moved into the central Delta before your arrival. Fully serviced camps are set up and grooms are on hand to care for the horses. A rifle is taken on safari for your protection. A minimum of four and a maximum of 12-day safaris for groups or individuals are available. English saddles are used, but you may bring your own.

Riders must be sufficiently experienced to be able to post to the trot.

The Makgadikgadi trails are operated from Gweta Rest Camp. They offer fully catered three- to seven-day trips, as well as morning and evening rides. Only experienced riders are allowed to participate and English saddles are used. A cross-country course is being planned at the moment. The length of the safari will determine how many base camps are to be used. Distances covered vary and depend on what there is to see as well as the ability and endurance of the riders, but may be decided upon in advance.

Eco-safaris

With environmental awareness on the rise, an increasing number of travellers demand more ecological information than is traditionally offered by the tourist industry. Specialist guides cater for this need. They will accompany you on the safari of your choice, whether you want the luxury of a lodge safari or the exercise of a walking trail. With their in-depth knowledge of the land and its people, they will ensure that during your stay in Botswana you

ABOVE: *The Panhandle is renowned for the superb fishing opportunities it offers.*
LEFT: *The African jacana is commonly seen amongst the water lilies of the Delta.*

will gain a sound appreciation of the ways of its people and wildlife.

These safaris may include joining official field researchers at work on projects as diverse as a study on the behaviour of wild dogs or plant research. You may request that a specific topic such as survival skills or bushlore is concentrated on.

There are no fixed departure dates for these safaris, as they are all customised to suit your individual requirements.

Bird-watching Safaris

Home to more than 550 species of birds and a solid tourist infrastructure, Botswana offers the opportunity for excellent bird-watching safaris. Many of the active professional guides will astound you with their knowledge of and ability to spot and identify bird life. However, if bird-watching is of more than a passing interest to you, then you should make sure in advance that your guide is a competent birder or a specialist guide. Alternatively, you may join a specialist bird-watching safari, under the guidance of renowned ornithologists such as Ken Newman, Geoff Lockwood and Peter Steyn. These safaris are run by Okavango Wilderness Safaris or Karibu Safaris and operated with fixed departure dates. Both camping or lodge safaris are offered. You could also request an individually-tailored birding safari, led by an expert.

If you are planning your own birding safari, make sure that you visit as many habitats as possible. A route that will offer you a good cross-section of habitats includes the Panhandle, Moremi Wildlife Reserve, Savuti, Serondela and the Makgadikgadi Pans.

Fishing Safaris

Fishing is popular in the Okavango Delta and in the Chobe and Boteti rivers. The lodges of the northern Okavango all cater for fishing, as do the fishing camps on the Boteti. Chobe Safari Lodge is the centre of the fishing activities in Kasane.

The Chobe and upper Okavango are prime areas for tiger-fishing between August and February. A note of caution, however: the larger fish species breed in the upper Delta at this time of the year and sport fishing may have a detrimental effect on the breeding population.

Barbel (catfish) and bream (tilapia) may be caught with a line in the Okavango, Boteti, Limpopo and Chobe rivers, while fly-fishing is offered in Kasane by Chobe Fishing Safaris and Nxamaseri Fishing Safaris. For more information on fishing in the Okavango see pages 58, 60, 64, 72, and in Chobe see page 111.

Fishing in the Okavango is affected by flood levels and conditions, water temperatures and seasons, which all vary from year to year and from one part of the Delta to another. Check with your operator before planning your dates,

Mokoro trail viewed from the air.

and make sure he/she has a sound knowledge of this subject and is not merely trying to sell you a safari.

Fishing tackle is supplied at most lodges, but keen fishermen should bring their own fly rods with plenty of extra lures and steel trace, and your favourite spinners.

Mokoro Trails

Mokoro (a dug-out canoe) trails are synonymous with the Okavango. To visit the Delta without having at least attempted a ride in a mokoro is to have missed an essential part of your holiday. All the lodges in the seasonally flooded areas, together with those in the game areas of the permanent Delta, provide mokoro rides as standard fare for their clients.

If you want to do an extended mokoro trail, there are several ways of going about it. Both Oddballs and Gunns' camps will provide you with a poler and his mokoro and you can set off with him for as many days as you like. You will need to take all your own and your poler's provisions. Equipment can be hired from the camps, if necessary. Island Safari Lodge and Crocodile Camp, both in Maun, will organise your mokoro safari on a similar basis.

Providing your own equipment and dealing with a language barrier may intimidate you, so if the idea of a mokoro safari appeals but the prospect of roughing it does not, you may do this safari in a more comfortable manner with a professional guide. Contact Hartley's Safaris, Okavango Wilderness Safaris, Transokavango or a specialist guide.

Filming and Photographic Safaris

The fact that all non-hunting safaris are termed photographic safaris may be confusing to the serious photographer. If photography and filming are of special interest to you, it is essential to ensure that your guide is familiar with the requirements and techniques of professional photography. Many professional guides are outstanding at spotting animals, but have little understanding of the needs of a photographer.

If you are joining an organised group safari, check that you will be able to photograph from any seat in the vehicle and find out how many people will be on safari with you. The more people there are, the poorer your view will be and the more vehicle movement you will have to contend with. There is also the chance that someone in your party may object to sitting quietly at a pan or waterhole waiting for some action! Video photographers should ensure that batteries can be charged by the operator.

If you can afford to hire a specialist guide/photographer for a private safari with vehicles equipped to take photographs, you will be more likely to achieve the results you desire. See *Photography*, page 186 for a list of recommended equipment.

Boat safaris enable the visitor to view wildlife at close quarters.

Canoe Safaris

Canoe safaris are very limited because of the logistics involved in returning the canoes to the starting point, as well as the competition posed by mekoro and will be done on special request only. These safaris are led by specialist guides and full equipment and camp staff are taken along. Safaris by canoes driven by small outboard-engines have been tried in the past, but are non-operational at present.

Boat Safaris

If you are looking for a relaxed safari, filled with sunshine, fishing, walking and basic camping on remote islands, you will enjoy exploring the Okavango on a boat trip. There are no scheduled departures, as all boat safaris are individually tailored – so you can plan your safari to fit in with the time you have available. Contact Transokavango or Dan Rawson for boat safaris in the Okavango.

If you are a keen fisherman, spend more time in the north and perhaps go up the Panhandle. For a birding or game viewing safari, it would probably be best to stay in the seasonally flooded area, which has larger islands on which to walk. However, for an overall impression of the Okavango and to give yourself the best opportunity to see the more elusive sitatunga and Pel's fishing owl, you will need to venture into the permanent Delta. Once the floods pass the Xo Flats, the water levels drop and make it difficult to get through by boat and you may be required to push it. It is possible that access may soon be denied to boats where the Boro River forms the boundary with Moremi. Once that happens, all boating safaris will have to start and operate only within the northern reaches of the Okavango.

Houseboat Safaris

Houseboat safaris are operated on the Panhandle only. You can hire the houseboats complete with driver/guide for any length of time you desire.

ABOVE TOP: *Game guides study animal tracks on a walking trail in the Okavango.*
ABOVE: *Motorbike safaris make the vast spaces of the Makgadikgadi Pans more accessible.*
RIGHT: *Houseboat on the Chobe River.*

The houseboat based at Drotsky's Cabins, has sleeping bunks on board. Provisions are your own responsibility but should you run short of anything, the lodge has a shop. Fishing and bird watching are among the main activities on offer.

Walking Trails and Hiking
Botswana has no official, inexpensive, unguided hiking trails of the type commonly found in Europe and South Africa. Nevertheless, there are superb areas for walking in the wild, with the Okavango at the top of the list. Walks are normally conducted on various islands in the Delta.

Most foot trails in the Okavango are operated as part of mokoro excursions, although Mombo Camp offers straight guided walking trails without mokoro. Most lodges in game areas conduct shorter or longer game walks, provided they are situated *outside* the national parks. Under no circumstances is walking allowed within the parks and reserves, with the exception of Chief's Island in Moremi. Mashatu Game Reserve in eastern Botswana is privately owned and so is able to offer guided walking trails.

Motorbike Safaris
Three- and four-wheeler motorbike trails on the Makgadikgadi Pans are operated out of Gweta Rest Camp. This is a very exciting way to see one of the most remote areas in Botswana. The bikes can skim over the soft surface of the pans where it would be impossible to go by vehicle. Camp is erected on the shore of the Makgadikgadi Pans and exploratory trips are taken to different areas. This is an ideal way to find the flamingoes that visit the Pans in such great numbers after good rains. If you are adventurous, this is a superb addition to your Botswana safari.

A bird's-eye view of the myriad waterways of the Okavango Delta.

Small groups of up to seven people are catered for. There are no scheduled departures and all safaris are individually tailored to suit your requirements.

Fly-in Safaris

Safaris are individually tailored and you may set off from any point in southern Africa, but usually from Johannesburg. They can also include attractions beyond Botswana's borders. These safaris are very personalised and generally use the most comfortable lodges. Your pilot is also your guide, who will accompany you on your flying safari between lodges. However, check that this is the case. If you merely charter a plane while on safari, the pilot is under no obligation to take care of you at lodges and is unlikely to have any in-depth wildlife knowledge.

Helicopter Safaris

With its ability to hover, a helicopter is an ideal way to see and photograph game. Helicopters play an important role in game management, as they are perfect for anti-poaching action. They are also used to reach Game Department officials on the ground quickly, in case of a suspected outbreak of disease. However, the disadvantage for tourists is that helicopters have restricted landing rights in game areas.

Game flights or transfers by helicopter are available from Maun and Kasane (see page 181).

Ethnic Safaris

Botswana's government follows a strict policy against racial discrimination. As a result, safaris focusing on one racial group, such as the San, are now frowned upon. In future, this will effectively outlaw anthropological safaris.

However, scheduled and tailored safaris to visit the San, witness their way of life and gain special knowledge of the land and survival techniques in a desert environment are still available through Penduka Safaris.

Hunting Safaris

Since the 1960s, professional hunting has been a popular activity in large areas of the country and has played a major role in stimulating the tourist industry in Botswana.

Hunting is certainly a controversial issue and, in recent years, the industry has come under attack internationally from a growing lobby of critics, who maintain that local hunting ethics do not conform to international norms. Attempts are now in progress to introduce both codes of conduct and an examination system for apprentice hunters. On home ground, the industry is locked in a struggle for land in competition with the growing photographic industry.

There are, of course, valid reservations about the effect of hunting on the age and sex structure of various species and of its overall effect on the ecology. However, in their defence, hunting companies point out that by offering a controlled alternative to hunters, they have been responsible for preserving large areas of wilderness. While attracting foreign exchange into Botswana, the industry has also created employment for people in remote areas, whose skills would not have equipped them for urban employment. The first photographic lodges were built by hunting companies, who were also responsible for the early air charter companies.

Although still a controversial issue, hunting is winning new converts to its cause. It now has a large support base among modern conservationists and is likely to play a major role in wilderness areas in the foreseeable future.

If nothing else, hunting is an expensive business. To bag a lion, leopard, buffalo and an assortment of other game on a two-week hunt will set you back some US$ 25 000!

There are three major big-game hunting companies – Safari South, Hunters Africa and Vira Safaris – and a bird hunting outfit – Bird Safaris – in Botswana. Three are based in Maun and one in Kasane. Each receives concession areas where they may hunt and each area is allocated a certain number of licences per species. You may book either directly with a professional hunter, who then negotiates with the company for a licence, or with the company, who in turn hires a professional hunter to conduct the safari.

As a hunting client, you specify the trophies you want and this often determines the duration of the safari. To hunt a lion usually requires a minimum of two weeks.

Animals on the hunting list include lion, leopard, buffalo, crocodile, zebra, spotted hyaena, warthog, ostrich, and most of the antelope species. Elephant hunting was suspended in 1984 and despite local pressure to reintroduce it, elephants have remained off the list to date. Sitatunga, aquatic antelope that reside in the Okavango Delta and the Linyanti swamps, are highly prized for their rarity value.

The following species are conserved by law and may not be shot: aardwolf, antbear (aardvark), black-footed cat, brown hyaena, cheetah, civet, giraffe, elephant, hippopotamus, honey badger, klipspringer, mountain reedbuck, night ape (bush baby), oribi, otter, pangolin, puku, roan antelope, rock hyrax (dassie), rhinoceros, sable antelope, serval, Sharpe's grysbok (Sharpe's steenbok), grey rhebok, waterbuck and yellow-spotted dassie. Penalties for poaching these animals are harsh and strictly applied.

Bird Shooting

This is permitted under licence and a number of people add bird shooting to their photographic or hunting safari. Bird Safaris operates a camp at Lake Ngami and hunt mostly doves and game birds. When the lake fills up, water fowl are also available. There is concern that birds are being killed at an unsustainable rate, as there is no limit on how many may be killed by a hunter. Controls are being considered.

Almost all birds in Botswana are protected, and the law stipulates which birds may be hunted, for example, ducks, geese and pigeons. Birds conserved by law include the Kori bustard, Stanley's bustard, Narina trogon, Pel's fishing owl, secretary bird, spoonbill, and all the species of the following; buzzards, cranes, eagles, egrets, falcons, flamingoes, goshawks, harriers, herons, ibises, jacanas, kites, pelicans, sparrowhawks, storks and vultures. Penalties for poaching these birds are harsh.

Giraffe – one of Botswana's conserved species.

PART TWO

EXPLORING BOTSWANA

In Botswana, tourism centres on wildlife. The country encompasses a hugely diverse variety of habitats, which are home to an astounding array of animal and bird life. The vast arid expanse of the Kalahari provides a huge contrast with the lush abundance of the beautiful Okavango Delta. The shimmering flatness of the Makgadikgadi Pans is far removed from the sheer rock faces of Tsodilo Hills. Yet each of these areas has its own unique beauty and offers a wealth of exciting possibilties and adventures for travellers. The opportunity to enjoy a true wilderness experience captivates many visitors and lures them back to this land of compelling beauty.

LEFT: *Mokoro trail in the Okavango.*
ABOVE: *Hippo – a common resident of the Delta.*

THE OKAVANGO DELTA

Set like a jewel in the middle of the Kalahari desert, the Okavango Delta is Africa's largest and most beautiful oasis – an isolated paradise surrounded by a hostile environment. It is Botswana's prime wildlife location, with palm-fringed and thickly wooded islands, lush green vegetation, translucent waters and an exceptional range of bird and animal life. But the real attraction of the Okavango is tranquillity; its true spirit, one of harmony.

The Cubango, as the Okavango is known in Angola, rises on the Benguela Plateau, an extremely wet region with a rainfall of between 1 200 millimetres and 1 500 millimetres a year, which is also the source of six other rivers including the Zambezi, Chobe and Cunene. The Cubango flows first east and then south for 1 300 kilometres, gathering more water on its way before entering Botswana at Mohembo. It is the third largest river in southern Africa and brings with it some 11 billion cubic metres of water every year.

The Panhandle is the top section of the river and is quite distinctive from the rest of the Delta. It was given this name because, seen from the air, it resembles the handle of a pan, the Delta forming the pan itself. The river is trapped between two parallel fault lines running south-east, about 15 kilometres apart and forcing the main Okavango River to meander between them for the next 95 kilometres. Papyrus banks line the single major channel, which splits only occasionally to form navigable loops.

Villages are dotted along both sides of the Panhandle and life, not surprisingly, revolves completely around the river. Cattle, agriculture, fishing and harvesting wild foods are the mainstays of life for the villagers.

THE PERMANENTLY FLOODED ZONE

The permanently flooded zone comprises the Panhandle and the top section of the Delta – its southern boundaries being indicated by the transition from wild date palms (*Phoenix reclinata*) and papyrus banks (*Cyperus papyrus*) to real fan palms (*Hyphaene petersiana*) and phragmites reeds (*Phragmites mauritianus*). The visitor will find that in general there is less game but better fishing in this area than in the lower reaches of the Delta.

The mighty Okavango, unlike all the other rivers sharing the Benguela Plateau as their source, is not destined to empty its contents into the oceans: it spends itself on the arid flatness of the Kalahari, creating a unique inland delta.

What happens to the Okavango as it leaves the Panhandle has been aptly compared to water being poured down an inverted funnel. Water surges down the spout and fans out into an arc as it is confronted by the increased gradient, caused by one of the fault lines running perpendicular to the river. The arc represents the beginning of the Delta.

Here, the river slows down, dropping an enormous amount of silt in its own path. It is estimated that the amount of silt deposited into the Delta every year varies from 600 000 to over a million tonnes. The exact age of the Delta is unknown, but this must represent a considerable accumulation of silt, and siltation must eventually lead to the Delta choking itself as the basin slowly fills up. As more and more silt is deposited, the waters must increasingly spread out in search of a gradient, however gentle, to flow down.

This factor plays a major role in determining the dynamic hydrology of the Delta. Major changes occur as a result of channels changing direction or blocking up completely. (See *The Swamp Book*, Murray-Hudson, Forrestor and Cherry. Southern Books, 1989.) A good example is Lake Ngami at the bottom end of the Thaoge River, the main source of the lake and one of the three main rivers into which the Okavango splits, the other two being the Nqogha and Boro rivers.

When Livingstone first saw Lake Ngami in 1849, he described it as being 120 kilometres in circumference and over 2 metres deep in most places. This enormous lake dried up when the Thaoge became blocked with papyrus. As a result, the water had to change its flow to find a new channel. In this instance, it created a new one. What used to be a shallow floodplain was turned into the Nqogha River, which today carries a large proportion of the Delta's water in an easterly direction. This river also seems destined to change direction soon, as there is a significant bunding (the build-up of silt) is discernible in its middle reaches. If this damming occurs and the river changes course, the eastern section of the Delta may once again be deprived of water, with the Santantadibe River flowing through Maun as in days gone by.

These major changes seem to occur about once a century; it was that long ago that the Thaoge was a major river.

THE SEASONALLY FLOODED ZONE

The seasonally flooded area, which lies beyond the permanent waters, comprises the lower half of the Delta and extends from roughly the centre of the Delta down to Maun in the south and from the Thaoge River in the west to the Khwai River in the east. Great concentrations of game are attracted to the flooded grasslands during winter.

After the arrival of the annual rains from the Angolan uplands, the lower rivers flood their banks and fill the adjacent floodplains. This provides large feeding areas for fish and leaves behind fresh green grass for game once the waters recede.

THE ANNUAL FLOOD

Botswana receives its annual rainfall during the summer months, with a peak between December and March. The water levels of the Delta may rise considerably, depending on how heavy the rains are.

It is the flood from Angola, however, that is the major determinant of the water levels and the breeding ecology of many of the animals living in the Delta. Although the term flood invokes an image of violent and destructive forces, the annual flood is gentle – first, almost imperceptibly raising the water level of the permanent waters of the north and then slowly spilling over the vast floodplains of the Delta. Rains that fall in Angola from September onwards usually reach Shakawe only around February and the rest of the Panhandle around March.

Simultaneously, while the waters are rising in the northern part of the Delta, they are falling in the south, causing floodplains to dry and river levels to drop substantially. Fish are forced into the low rivers or get trapped in drying pools, providing a feast for anglers. Once the flood has passed through the Panhandle, the water level starts to drop there again, while it rises further south. The long awaited and much discussed flood normally reaches Maun between June and July.

This constant cyclical motion of water rising in the north while falling in the south, and then rising in the south and dropping in the north causes an annual wave action that has far-reaching consequences for the ecology of the Delta. In winter, when the surrounding countryside is drying up, the Delta has abundant water and food attracting vast numbers of animals. They move away to pristine grasses again when the rain falls in summer. Water birds move from the Delta to rain-filled pans in summer, to return to the Delta when the pans have dried up.

There are 1 078 recognised plant species in the Delta, giving it a species density 7 times higher than that in the rest of southern Africa and 50 times higher than that of Europe. There is only one plant endemic to the Okavango – an inconspicuous terrestrial yellow orchid that is normally hidden among the sedges and grasses along the water chanels. It is non-descript and grass-like in appearance and dies down every year when the flood recedes, to lie in wait for the next wave of water. Discovered by and named after Pete Smith, Maun's recognised authority on plants of the Okavango, this orchid is found only in the northern Okavango and Panhandle region.

Whether it is summer rain or winter floods, water is always entering the Delta; it is this aquatiac bundance that allows many plants to remain evergreen.

Lush vegetation lines the waterways of the Delta.

THREATS TO THE DELTA WETLANDS

Globally, wetlands are under threat from human activity and the Okavango is no exception. In a sense, it is its own worst enemy: containing nearly 90 per cent of the surface water in a very arid country with an ever-increasing demand for water, most of the Okavango's water simply evaporates with no tangible benefit to a thirsty land.

Only 3 per cent of the water that enters Botswana at Mohembo reaches Maun and some 2 per cent seeps into the sands to restore the ground-water levels. The remainder evaporates or is lost through transpiration; little wonder, then, that authorities look to this apparently abundant and wasted resource for the country's future water needs. While Botswana does not have any natural deep lakes, the volume of water flowing into the Okavango Delta every year is enough to support an industrialised country. It is hardly surprising, then, that the government would want to exploit this resource for the supply of water to the dry interior.

Historically, a number of attempts have been made to tame and utilise the waterways of the Delta. To date, none of them have been successful. A government project known as the Southern Okavango Integrated Water Development Project, whereby a 40-kilometre stretch of the Boro River would be dredged and various dams built to catch the resulting increased outflow, has been suspended because of public outcry and the findings of an international environmental impact study.

In Namibia, plans are afoot for a canal from the Okavango to the Namibian interior, which will syphon off water to supplement that country's water supply. Further north, planned irrigation projects that had been delayed by the civil war in Angola, are likely to draw off further water from the Okavango before it reaches Botswana.

Apart from excessive water being drained from it, other dangers threaten the Okavango. The increase in population in and around the Delta has caused increased resource utilisation by both man and livestock. The number of cattle using the Delta is in the region of 300 000, with stocking double the sustainable rate in many places. Inevitably, vegetation has deteriorated and will continue to do so under this onslaught. Palm trees which provide wine, palm hearts and basket-making materials are under serious threat in both the south and the west. This is likely to have serious social repercussions, as baskets often provide the sole source of income to some communities.

Tourism on a relatively large scale is new to the Delta and has been responsible for the over-utilisation and the subsequent destruction of its delicate ecology. New areas are opened up and new lodges and villages are mushrooming, along with the accompanying noise pollution from planes and outboard engines. An increased demand for mekoro has resulted in many large trees being felled.

In the past, the tsetse fly prevented man and his livestock from encroaching onto Delta territory. However, through years of aerial spraying, this natural protector has all but been eradicated, allowing access to cattle. The impact of annual dumping of poisons into the Delta has not been fully researched, but effects on the insect and fish population are inevitable and, given their importance throughout the food chain, this must affect bird, mammal and fish populations.

In 1958 there was an outbreak of foot-and-mouth-disease in Botswana and no meat could be exported. The buffalo fence and a series of other veterinary fences, totalling 3 000 kilometres, were built to prevent contact and act as quarantine buffer zones between domestic cattle and buffalo, who are regarded as potential carriers of the disease. This was done in compliance with the strict import regulations of the European Community, which buys 50 per cent of Botswana's beef. However, the fences blocked the paths of migratory animals to their dry-season water sources and many animals died of starvation. The buffalo fence, contrary to its original purpose, has protected the Okavango Delta from being devastated by man and his stock. Government now wants to extend the buffalo fence across the western and northern Okavango, giving rise to yet another controversial issue. While acknowledging that the fence to the south does prevent cattle influx, conservationists have asked, unsuccessfully, that the fence be re-aligned to allow continued seasonal movement of sable, buffalo and elephant in that region.

Those who live in this paradise have seen its fragile nature and all fear man's interference in its ecology. The country's need for water and the fact that it will have to yield some of its resources to national benefit is well understood; the challenge is to ensure that no more is used than is sustainable in the long term.

A proposal by the International Union for the Conservation of Nature that the Delta become a world heritage site will afford it international protection and, if accepted, could be particularly important in negotiating water take-off rights from beyond her borders.

Digging out a mokoro – a traditional skill passed down from generation to generation.

THE PANHANDLE

The Okavango, on its final stretch as a single entity before it fragments into innumerable smaller rivers and streams, shows little variation. As a deep fast-flowing river it winds its way through endless papyrus banks for almost one hundred kilometres. There are far fewer islands in this section than further south and generally they are no bigger than a termite mound with just enough space for a single palm tree. Birding is excellent, but this is generally not the area to visit in search of game. Fishing, especially for tigerfish, is good during the early summer months. The whole area is well populated with villages lining both banks of the river.

SHAKAWE

Shakawe is a fishing resort, the main village along the Panhandle and gateway to Namibia. Situated on the western bank of the Okavango River, it is renowned for its splendid fishing and birding.

Very basic supplies are available, but little in the way of fresh produce is on offer. Fresh

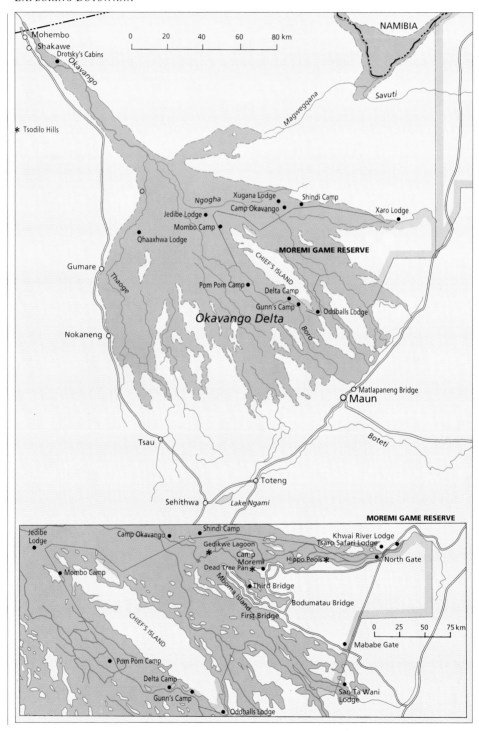

bread is available. There is no petrol on sale and the nearest filling station is at Bagani in the Caprivi and at Etsha 6 on the way to Maun. There are no hospitals or garages and spare parts are not available.

Several lodges and campsites offer accommodation in the area. Refer to *Advisory, The Panhandle*, page 90 for details.

Places of interest in and around Shakawe include:

The mokoro terminal behind the bakery is an interesting sight for visitors. Rows of mekoro and boats are parked here while their owners go shopping.

Carmine bee-eaters nesting on the riverbanks (see page62).

Tsodilo Hills A day trip to visit this interesting landmark (see *Western Kalahari*, page 150) can be arranged through Drotsky's Cabins and Shakawe Fishing Lodge.

Mahango Game Reserve On the Namibian side of the border this small but well-stocked and very pleasant reserve has a good selection of game, including elephant and large herds of

RIGHT: *Not only tourists use the ubiquitous mokoro.*

BELOW: *Seen from the air, the Okavango River meanders across the floodplains.*

sable, and is well worth a visit. A few kilometres beyond the reserve are the Popa Falls in the Okavango River. Attractive rapids rather than falls, these are not in themselves worthy of a great diversion.

GETTING THERE
By air

All the lodges south of Shakawe have their own airstrips. Shakawe has a landing strip which serves the three lodges in the area Drotsky's Cabins, Shakawe Fishing Lodge and Xaro Lodge. If you land there, you must make sure that you are expected and will be met at the airstrip, as all the lodges are at least 5 kilometres away with no means of communication with the airstrip.

By road

The 370-kilometre road from Maun to Sha-kawe is tarred as far as Sepupa (this will be completed by mid-1995).

From Maun, the road heads west past To-teng to the Ovaherero town, Sehitwa. Barred corrugated iron buildings stand as ghostly re-minders of a more prosperous era when Ngami could still be called a lake and Sehitwa was a flourishing town. Now, in its death throes, Ngami receives water from the Okavango Delta only in years of exceptional rains. From Sehitwa, the road branches north past the vil-lages of Tsau and Nokaneng. Beyond Noka-neng the road passes through acacia woodland to the village of Gumare which, due to its central location, was chosen as the site for the region's small hospital. Traditional baskets, made from the fronds of the vegetable ivory or real fan palm may be bought cheaply from the local weavers, and most passers-by will be able to direct you to one of the weaver's huts.

Strung out between Gumare and Sepupa are the thirteen settlements of Etsha. They were established for Hambukushu refugees, who resettled in the area about 1969. This was the second wave of refugees to flee war-torn Ango-la, the first having escaped the hostile Lozi tribe during the last decade of the 18th cen-tury. Only Etsha 6, which has petrol and a shop well stocked with dry goods, and Etsha 13 are of any size. This is the centre of the basket weaving industry as the Hambukushu, who are master weavers, brought their craft with them.

Maps will lead you to believe you are travel-ling along the edge of the Okavango, but you will not be even vaguely aware of its existence except around the quaint village of Sepupa, set on a high rise amidst riverine trees.

All the lodges are set south of Shakawe, but not all are clearly signposted. The road to Xaro Lodge should not be attempted without a four-wheel drive. It is advisable to leave your vehicle elsewhere and boat to Xaro. Drotsky's Cabins and Shakawe Fishing Lodge can be reached in a two-wheel drive vehicle.

The distance between Shakawe and Mo-hembo on the Namibian border is 15 kilo-metres. At Mohembo, a ferry will transport vehicles to the eastern side of the Pan-handle. The Namibian town of Rundu is 230 kilometres from Shakawe on a gravel road, which is suitable for two-wheel drive vehicles. The road to Katima Mulilo in eastern Caprivi (315 kilometres from Shakawe) is being up-graded and is due to be tarred soon.

By water

Shakawe is accessible from Maun by water but because of the distances involved and the maze of channels to be negotiated, you must go on an organised boat safari with a know-ledgeable guide and have a week or more to spare. Contact either Trans-Okavango or a spe-cialist guide (see page 182). Boat transfers from Shakawe to the respective lodges may also be arranged (see *Safari Operators*, page 182).

ABOVE: *Those travelling by road from Maun to Shakawe will pass through the small settlement of Sepupa.*
LEFT: *A ferry at Mohembo provides transport across the river.*

FISHING BIRDS OF THE OKAVANGO

Slaty Egret

This rarest heron in the world, the slaty egret occurs in the Okavango, the Chobe and Lake Bangweulu in Zambia, though the only existing breeding records are from the Okavango. A resident, they forage singly or in small groups of up to eight birds throughout the Delta, usually feeding in mid-afternoon in shallow, preferably falling, waters. Look for the yellow legs and slightly rufous throat to distinguish them from the black egret with which it is easily confused.

Pel's Fishing Owl

A rare and elusive species which attracts bird-watchers from around the globe in the hope of a sighting or a photograph, this large ginger-coloured owl preys on fish in open water at night and often roosts in the thick foliage of the African mangosteen (*Garcinia livingstonei*) by day. Tigerfish and bream are among its favourite prey, which it grasps with its especially adapted toes. The Okavango is home to the largest population in Africa, with sightings becoming more common the further north one goes, the Panhandle being the prime spot. They also occur along the Chobe, the Thamalakane and Boteti rivers, and may be seen all year round – often during the day while roosting, at dusk or dawn or at night with a spotlight, when they fish from a prominent perch above the water.

Pel's Fishing Owl

African Skimmer

This elegant bird, bearing an uncanny resemblance to the Concord, may be seen skimming over the water with its lower mandible scraping the surface. Skimmers, which are the size of large terns, have a bright orange-red bill which is yellow tipped and a black back with white underparts. They are intra-African migrants who arrive in the Panhandle in July and nest on the sandbanks until December. They are best seen from boats during this period but care should be taken not to approach too closely as these wary birds will abandon their nests if disturbed. Boats should be driven with care at all times to avoid bow-waves washing over their nests.

WHAT TO SEE AND DO

Activities in the Panhandle centre on the water, not on game, as elsewhere in Botswana.

Bird-watching

The Panhandle is one of the finest birding areas in the country with its contrasting habitats, permanent water and a riverine forest that is immediately surrounded by arid Kalahari woodland. Over 400 bird species occur in and around the Panhandle, with a number of species using the Okavango as their only breeding area in southern Africa. The Cape parrot and blackfaced babbler are found nowhere elsewhere in the country. Pennantwinged nightjar may be seen around the cultivated lands at dusk or dawn. Boat trips at night could reveal blackcrowned and whitebacked night herons.

All the lodges in Shakawe offer excellent opportunities to photograph the colourful carmine and whitefronted bee-eaters that nest in the towering sandbanks in September and October. Carmine bee-eaters visit the Okavango from early September to March after which they migrate as far as Gabon in North Africa. They are often seen hawking large flying insects from perches over the water.

Wildlife

Man has been living along the Panhandle in relatively high numbers for generations, with the result that game numbers are low. Only aquatic animals such as the hippo, crocodile and nile monitor, as well as secretive antelope including the bushbuck and sitatunga have survived. Occasionally, lonely bulls or small herds of elephant may wander through the area. Walks in the area are scenic and relaxing. Vehicles are unsuitable for game viewing in this area because the remaining game is confined to the thick vegetation around the river and to the papyrus beds in the river itself.

Should you wish to view game from the air, you can make prior arrangements to extend your flight to Shakawe to include this. There are no air-charter companies based in Shakawe and, unless there is a plane in the area, the cost of bringing one in from Maun is exorbitant.

The World of Water

Because activities in the Panhandle are focused on the water, fishing, birding and general boating are the main interests. All the lodges have boats, and sunset or sunrise cruises by either boat or pontoon offer top-notch photographic opportunities.

An exciting excursion, and one that can be considered a must, is a spotlit night ride on a boat. Night rides are available either regularly, or on request from the lodges. On these rides, you may have the privilege of getting wonderfully close views of sleeping bee-eaters and kingfishers. It is also a fine opportunity to spot night herons and Pel's fishing owl, while the red reflection of crocodiles' eyes alert you to how many of these reptiles there really are. If you are lucky, a young croc may be hauled onto the boat for closer inspection. Sitatunga leave their papyrus sanctuaries under the cloak of darkness and are often spotted in the open at night.

Although the local form of transport is the mokoro, tourists are best advised not to attempt canoe or mokoro trips themselves on the deep, fast-flowing open river with its hippos and crocodiles. Rather utilise the skills of the local fishermen who are experienced in handling this craft.

A three-hour boat ride downstream from Shakawe will take you to Red Cliffs – a solitary red sand dune which, although rather low-lying, affords the only vantage point along this stretch of water.

Fishing

The Panhandle is considered the best fishing area in Botswana and is renowned for its tigerfish. Bream and catfish also offer excellent sport-fishing.

Over eighty species of fish have been identified in the Okavango, but rarely will more than one-fifth of this number be found in the same community. Generally, three or four species tend to dominate in a particular location where they may be ideally suited to the ecology of that habitat.

Fish in the Okavango, like other southern African fish, breed in the summer months when the water is warm and water levels rise due to summer rains. However, in the Okavango the water level falls in the summer months due to receding floods. At this time of year food resources diminish instead of increase and potential breeding areas become exposed. This results in lower fish populations than would be expected.

The most important ecological determinant of the distribution of species in the Delta is the permanence of water and whether it is static or in flow. Tigerfish, for example, occur only in permanent, swift-flowing waters in the upper Delta, whereas pike, on the other hand, prefer the backwaters and the slower flowing rivers of the lower Okavango.

Between September and December of each year, fishermen from around the world are attracted to a remarkable phenomenon known as the Barbel Run. With the drying up of the floodplains, the smaller fish are forced to leave

AQUATIC ANTELOPE OF THE OKAVANGO

When startled, the sitatunga will bound toward deeper water and submerge itself.

A sighting of one of these retiring and elusive creatures is a highlight for many visitors to the Delta. Patience and silence are vital ingredients if you are to be successful in finding these animals, who are perfectly adapted to their watery worlds.

Sitatunga

A close relative of the bushbuck and the kudu, the sitatunga is the most aquatic of all antelope. Found in swamps from the Sudan in the north to the Okavango in the south, a sighting of a sitatunga is highly prized due to its secretive and nocturnal habits. It spends its days in thick papyrus beds, emerging only under cover of darkness to feed on the open plains and in the forests. Its hooves are elongated – nearly twice the length of other antelope the same size – and splayed wide to enable it to outrun predators in swamp conditions, but this adaption renders them clumsy and slow on land. Its long coat is water repellent to enable it to spend long hours in the water, and when alarmed, it will submerge itself almost completely leaving only its nostrils above the water. Both a browser and a grazer, the sitatunga favours flowering plants and will leave the water to graze, entering riparian forests to browse on woody vegetation. The males are chocolate brown and have spiralled horns similar to the kudu, while the females are unhorned and a lighter shade of brown.

From the air it is easily identified as a dark brown, usually solitary, antelope lying in thick papyrus or partly submerged in water. On land they are most often sighted on *silent* dawn and dusk mokoro rides, although walks on the island fringes may also be rewarding.

Red Lechwe

The lechwe is second only to the sitatunga as the most aquatic antelope and although they share many similar adaptations, it is more closely related to the reedbuck. The red lechwe, one of three subspecies, occurs in the Okavango and along the Chobe River. Like the sitatunga, the lechwe has widely splayed and elongated hooves which make it clumsy on land and it too has to rely on water as a refuge from predators.

Lechwe are often confused with impala which they superficially resemble. The lechwe, however, is a stockier animal with powerful, raised hindquarters that slope down to the front shoulder. They have light bellies and lack the characteristic black markings of the impala.

Lechwe are always found either on seasonally flooded grass plains or feeding in water up to their bellies. They graze on grasses near the water's edge and on sedges that grow in shallow waters. Although they live near water they seldom drink during the cool, dry winter, but slake their thirsts regularly as the temperature rises.

ABOVE LEFT: *Kavango tribespeople on their way to market.*
ABOVE: *Harvesting water lilies.*
LEFT: *Reeds fringe many of the Delta's watery thoroughfares.*

their favoured areas and enter the larger rivers and lagoons. Catfish, or barbel as they are known locally, congregate in their thousands in well-organised hunting packs that may extend for several kilometres in the main rivers to follow the small fish. The water froths and bubbles as the catfish thrash about in their feeding frenzy. The commotion attracts other predators such as tigerfish and birds – egrets, herons, cormorants, darters, white storks, pied and giant kingfishers – and crocodiles lie in wait on the river bottom to feed on the barbel themselves. This path of carnage provides an unforgettable and unique spectacle as it moves inexorably upstream.

Vegetation
Papyrus lines the waterways, leaving only a thin ribbon of water to meander through its lush greenery. Islands are few and small. The river banks are lined with tall forests generally made up of the African mangosteen, wild date palms and African ebony or jackal-berry (*Diospyros mespiliformis*), often the most majestic tree in the Delta with its black bark and dark crown towering above the other trees and its

shade sought-after by man and beast alike. Kiaat (*Pterocarpus angolensis*), much favoured for the manufacture of mekoro and African curios, are found in the savanna around the Panhandle and can be identified by their large and distinctive seed case with harsh bristles in the centre of the round papery pod.

Plant communities and their distribution are strongly influenced by, and are indicators of, the ecosystem to which they belong. Papyrus and the wild date palm generally occur in permanently flooded zones and the end of their range indicates the start of seasonally flooded areas.

The People
The entire area provides a glimpse into the way of life in rural Botswana. Women catching fish with the traditional Kavango baskets or making weirs on the floodplains to trap fish are a common sight. Ox-drawn sleighs, donkeys carrying Ovaherero women in full Victorian regalia, reed and thatch homesteads with pumpkins on the roof, basket and reed mat weaving and wine making are but few of the interesting things to see. On the western riverbank, picturesque Shakawe and Sepupa lie directly on the water, and on the eastern bank Seronga overlooks a deep translucent lagoon. The other villages are less attractively situated, but they are as steeped in traditional culture.

ACCOMMODATION

Drotsky's Cabins

Owned and run by Jan and Eileen Drotsky, a delightful couple who make all feel welcome, the lodge is 5 kilometres from Shakawe and set high on the banks of the Okavango River in the shade of beautiful trees. Activities focus on the water so if you are keen on fishing or boating, you'll find plenty to enjoy. If you require transport from Shakawe to the lodge, pre-arrange this with Merlin Services (Tel/fax: 660-571) in Maun, who will radio your request ahead as the lodge does not have a telephone.

Features:

• Accommodation in thatched A-frame chalets and tents • Curio shop
• New restaurant and a bar • Large shaded area for camping • Night boat rides
• Self-contained pontoons and Leisure Liner houseboats for private hire on an hourly or daily basis • Day trips to Tsodilo Hills
• Fishing tackle and boat hire
• Outstanding birding

RIGHT: *Chalets at Drotsky's Cabins – an attractive garden setting.*
BELOW: *Shakawe Fishing Lodge, famed for its excellent fishing and bird-watching.*

Nxamaseri Fishing Camp

Operated by Falcon Africa, this remote yet comfortable lodge is set on an island in the Nxamaseri Channel and the most practical way to reach it is by air, followed by a short boat-ride. An angler's and bird-lover's delight, this area supports almost 80 species of fish and an astounding array of bird life, including the Delta's largest concentration of fish eagle.

Features:

• Accommodation in brick and thatched chalets • *En suite* facilities • Excellent fishing in season • Superb birding

Shakawe Fishing Lodge

Owned by Barry and Elaine Price, but now under independent management, this is the most established camp in the Shakawe region.

Large trees provide welcome shade in the campsite at Drotsky's Cabins.

It is situated 10 kilometres south of Shakawe on the Okavango River; transport from Shakawe to the lodge must be arranged in advance through Travel Wild (Tel/fax: 660-493). There are fine opportunities for fishing and birdwatching, for which the camp is famed.
Features:
• Accommodation in Meru tents and thatched chalets • *En suite* ablution facilities • Swimming pool • Bar and restaurant • Curio shop • Day trips to Tsodilo Hills and Nxamasere Valley

Xaro Lodge
Set on a sweep in the river downstream of the other two lodges, this luxury tented camp is managed independently and caters for prebooked visitors, rather than walk-in trade. Like other lodges in the area, it caters for the keen angler and also offers river cruises and light aircraft flights over the region.
Features:
• Accommodation in Meru tents
• *En suite* facilities • Curio shop • Swimming pool • Superb birding • Fishing and boating • Trips to Tsodilo Hills

Public campsites
As this area lies outside the national parks, there are no government campsites; however, there are campsites at Drotsky's Cabins and Shakawe Fishing Lodge. Both boast clean facilities with hot water and lodge amenities are open to campers.

CENTRAL OKAVANGO
(PERMANENTLY FLOODED)

As the Okavango River leaves the constricting fault lines of the Panhandle, it spreads out across the flat, sandy land to create the spectacular Okavango Delta. The upper reaches of the Delta are permanently flooded and although the water level does fluctuate, the seasonal difference is not significant enough to affect the vegetation.

This part of the Delta is quite different to the Panhandle, with huge lagoons, narrow winding waterways, floating islands and innumerable small permanent islands; however, the deep waters, enormous stretches of papyrus and dense riverine vegetation are reminiscent of the Panhandle. As the islands are larger, with their perimeters edged by a narrow strip of woodland, there is a greater diversity of game, particularly in the east, but the concentration of bird life is lower than in the Panhandle. There are villages on the western fringe and a large village at Jedibe but in general, fewer people inhabit this part of the Delta than elsewhere. Cattle are to be found in increasing numbers on the Delta's western side and consequently the buffalo fence – the name afforded to the veterinary fence which separates livestock from game in the south of the Delta – is being extended further north to prevent additional cattle encroachment.

GETTING THERE
By air
The only practical way to reach the lodges in this region is by air – they all have their own landing strips. Most of the flights originate from Maun and take between 20 minutes and an hour, depending on how far north you travel. Flights from Kasane into the Delta are longer, usually taking around an hour and a half to two hours.

By road
It is possible, seasonally, to get to Qhaaxhwa Lodge and Guma Lagoon Lodge on the

ABOVE: *Sunset casts a gentle glow over the Okavango's tranquil waters.*
RIGHT: *Walking on a floating island.*

western side, and Mombo Camp, Xugana Lodge and Shindi Camp on the eastern side, by road. Contact the lodges involved if you wish to do this, as permission is required. To go to Guma or Qhaaxhwa you will need to pick up a guide in either Etsha 6 or Etsha 13. Most villagers will be prepared to help but you will need to negotiate a fee and return transport arrangements. There is no standard amount charged, so ask around if you feel the price is too high. Some guides will be prepared to walk back but will require compensation for this. Be prepared to drive through thick sand and water. Unless the water is very low at Qhaaxhwa, you will be obliged to leave your car on the mainland and cross to the island by boat. Provided you lock your vehicle, its contents should be safe left unattended.

By water

All the lodges are accessible by power boat, except for Qhaaxhwa, where the channels that lead to it have clogged up completely, but due to the distances and time involved a water transfer is impractical except as part of a boat safari. See *Safari Operators*, page 182.

WHAT TO SEE AND DO

A fascinating phenomenon that occurs in this part of the Okavango is the large floating peat islands. Over the years, peat builds up and becomes thick enough to bear a person's weight. Some islands are big enough to support herds of lechwe who reside there permanently. To walk on a surface that moves in waves underfoot is a rather disconcerting experience, but soon most people succumb to the temptation of jumping up and down to see how big a 'land wave' they can produce. A word of caution: be careful not to try this on a weak spot, as you could find yourself thigh deep in mud when your weight breaks through the layer of grass.

61

ABOVE LEFT: *Wild dogs are one of the region's more commonly seen predators.*
ABOVE: *Nile crocodiles make swimming particularly dangerous after their winter fast.*
LEFT: *An African fish eagle swoops above the water in search of prey.*

on the inhabited western fringe of the Delta, where, as a result of hunting and poaching, there is very little game left though lechwe and bushbuck are spotted occasionally.

The hippo population in this area is lower than one would expect. This is possibly because there is little grass on the small islands that make up the bulk of the region's land mass. Historically, a great deal of hunting pressure has been exerted on hippo in the Delta and although this is banned today, their numbers have not yet recovered.

There is something very special about walking freely among animals on an island in a remote wilderness, and this is certainly one of the highlights in the area. Game walks are offered by all the lodges on the islands in their immediate vicinity. The customary routine is to do a boat or mokoro ride to an island where you disembark then walk around the island to see which animals are resident or might have swum across and temporarily inhabit the island. All animals can and do swim from island to island and you might be lucky enough to witness some crossing the water.

Game drives are only available at Mombo and Shindi, during which leopard, African wildcat, civet, genet and hyaena may be seen. Night drives are also permitted at both camps.

Wildlife

In the late winter months, the area around Mombo Camp boasts some of the finest game viewing in the Delta with vast herds of buffalo and other herbivores attracting the large predators. Wild dogs and spotted hyena are regularly encountered.

Shindi, Xugana and Camp Okavango share similar habitats that support a reasonable variety of game. Sitatunga are regularly sighted at these three camps, as well as at Jedibe and Qhaaxhwa. Qhaaxhwa has a look-out bar for wonderful sunrise views and the occasional glimpse of hippo, crocodile, lechwe and otter, as well as cattle grazing on the island directly across the lagoon. Guma and Qhaaxhwa are

Game-viewing flights over Chief's Island in the southern Okavango, pre-arranged from Maun, are very rewarding in terms of the over-all numbers and the different species of animals sighted. Animals commonly spotted are elephant, large herds of buffalo, giraffe, lechwe, impala, kudu, waterbuck, tsessebe, wildebeest, zebra, baboon, warthog and hippo.

Horse safaris are also available in the central Okavango for experienced riders and last for a minimum of four days. See *Safari Options*, page 39 for details.

Bird-watching

Many visitors to the central Delta are disappointed by the apparent lack of abundant bird life. There are not as many birds as one may expect because the habitat here is quite homogeneous, mainly comprising deep water and small, densely foliaged islands. The water figs (*Ficus verruculosa*) normally house darters, reed cormorants, openbilled and marabou storks. The reedbanks are home to a variety of herons and their close relatives – the little bitterns and the egrets – also abound. Malachite and pied

No visit to the Okavango would be complete without a relaxing ride in a mokoro.

kingfishers, as well as little bee-eaters and fish eagles are always present. Walks on islands may flush out African snipe or Pel's fishing owl. The westernbanded snake eagle is normally a difficult bird to find, but can be seen still-hunting around Qhaaxhwa Island.

The World of Water

All the lodges have boats to take visitors out on daily excursions. Some of the lodges will offer night rides, but that is largely dependent on current camp management.

Mokoro Excursions

One of the most peaceful and relaxing things you may ever do is to be gently poled in a mokoro through the endless, winding channels of the Okavango by a person who is master of his environment. This is also the best possible way to sneak up on the elusive sitatunga who will dash back into the tall papyrus at the first sight of man. The mokoro, a dug-out canoe (mekoro is plural), is the traditional mode of transport in the Okavango. It was introduced to the Delta in the mid-1700s by the Bayei, who had learnt the craft of fashioning mekoro for the deep waters of the Zambezi River. This art is the domain of certain families

who have passed down the skill from generation to generation. Mekoro are carved by hand with an adze from only the largest hardwood trees such as *mukwa* (kiaat). The *ngashi*, a 3-metre long pole with a cleft base to allow traction on the sandy bottoms of the waterways, is carved from the silver terminalia (*Terminalia sericea*), because its long thin branches are strong and flexible. With the increased demand for mekoro brought about by tourism the hardwood trees have been depleted and any tree is used nowadays. In the interests of conservation and comfort, many of the lodges in the north of the Delta now use fibreglass canoes. Some of the larger mekoro carry up to five people, although the norm is three. An experienced poler makes the process of negotiating the narrow channels seem both effortless and simple; however, for the uninitiated, progress in the flat bottomed, front-heavy and unstable vessel can be a nightmare of ever-increasing circles.

As a passenger, the secret of a mokoro ride is to sit as low as possible and relax. Do not try and counter-balance as this could upset the balance and rhythm of your poler.

Xugana, Jedibe, Shindi and Camp Okavango all offer half-day or full day mokoro excursions. Because it is not situated on the water, Mombo does not offer excursions from the main camp, but does so using fly-camps (a pre-erected camp with simple facilities).

Fishing
Fishing can be first rate in this part of the Delta, and tigerfish as well as bream, catfish and pike are caught in the permanent Delta. But if fishing is the main purpose of your trip, then insist that your travel agent gets in touch with the camp manager to check the current conditions before you set out. It is better to postpone your journey than be disappointed. In general, the best fishing occurs from October to January.

Vegetation
Papyrus is the most common plant in this area and, because they feed on the papyrus heads, this is the place where you are most likely to

see sitatunga. Another good spot is among the Miscanthus grass with its cylindrical spiky leaves, which occurs in thick tussocks in shallow flooded areas.

Riverine forests dominate the fringes of the islands. Some of the most conspicuous of the trees are the yellow-trunked sycamore figs (*Ficus sycomorus*), strangler figs (*Ficus thonningii*), and sausage trees (*Kigelia africana*) with their velvety maroon flowers and large, heavy fruits plopping down in the dust during the heat of the day. These fibrous fruits, not edible to man, are devoured by baboons, giraffe, elephant and cattle.

The People
The people living at Jedibe are mostly Bayei, while those living on the western bank near Guma and Qhaaxhwa are predominantly Hambukushu. Traditionally, the Bayei are fishermen while the Hambukushu, who also fish, are more dependent on agriculture. You may come across fishing nets in the water or on islands, with row upon row of drying racks for the fish.

ACCOMMODATION
Camp Okavango
Set on an island outside Moremi Wildlife Reserve, everything about this de luxe camp reflects attention to detail; silver and crystal add style to gourmet meals, which are served by gaily clad and well-trained staff. Activities are focused on the water with mokoro rides, fishing, boating and photographic trips available. A speciality of this camp is the frequent sitatunga sightings which are made from fibreglass canoes. Most guests fly in from either Maun or Kasane, as the camp is not accessible by road; alternatively, you can enjoy a relaxing 3-hour boat trip from Camp Moremi, which is operated by the same organisation. Many guests like to spend time at each camp.
Features:
- Accommodation in luxurious Meru tents
- Private facilities • Well-stocked bar
- Fishing and boating • Bird-watching – especially woodland species around the lodge

Guma Lagoon

Set on one of the largest and most attractive lagoons in the Delta, this camp run by Geoff and Nookie Randal offers access to the fine fishing areas around Etsatsa. The area offers excellent fishing (the Panhandle is only a 40-minute boat ride away), as well as a range of other activities including bird-watching, mokoro trails and walks on islands. A pioneer fish farm with the double goal of restocking this part of the Delta, as well as being commercially viable, is in operation at the lodge. Although Guma Lagoon is accessible by road from Maun, many guests choose to fly in. The camp is not within any national park or reserve.

Features:
• Accommodation in chalets and tents
• *En suite* facilities • Horse trails operate from here • Game-viewing walks

Jedibe Island Camp

Deep in the heart of the Delta, this popular and attractive lodge is situated on an island amid a maze of deep streams. Jedibe offers guests a

An elegant evening's dining at Mombo Camp.

water experience of limpid lagoons, floodplains and aquatic plant and animal life. Enjoy being poled in a mokoro, catching a tigerfish or sighting a red lechwe while walking on one of the many palm-fringed islands. Two fly-camps, accessible by mokoro, add to the diversity of experience that this lodge offers. It is outside any reserve or national park.

Features:
• Accommodation in Meru tents • Private facilities • Birding and fishing • Boat and mokoro excursions

Mombo Camp

This remote and popular tented camp is situated just outside Moremi Wildlife Reserve on Mombo Island, to the north-west of Chief's Island. It is set under large, shady trees with a raised bar/lounge overlooking the floodplain. A fly-camp, some distance from Mombo main camp, is used as an overnight stop on walking safaris or for the more adventurous clients. In comparison to its sister camp, Jedibe, Mombo offers a more land-based experience.

Dense concentrations of animal life, including all the large predators as well as wild

BLOOMS ON THE WATER

The day lily.

There are a number of different types of water lilies in the Delta, of which the day lily (*Nymphaea nouchali var caerulea*) and the larger creamy-white flower with a yellow centre, the night lily (*Nymphaea lotus*), are the most abundant. The colours of the day lily, erroneously called the blue lily, range from baby blue and purple to pink and white. They are more delicate than the robust night lily and have smooth-edged green leaf-pads that often flip over in the wind to show their maroon undersides.

The night lily with its large and serrated leave-edges generally occurs in the northern reaches of the Okavango as it prefers faster flowing and deeper water. The flowers of the day lily usually open mid-morning and close mid-afternoon, while the night lily normally opens in late afternoon to close again at midnight, a factor to bear in mind if you want to photograph them. The bulbous rhizomes of both these lilies are held in high regard by the local people, who use them as a potato substitute in stews to impart a delicate, slightly astringent flavour. Unfortunately the plant has to be destroyed in the harvest. Snow lilies (*Nymphoides indica*), smaller and more delicate than the day lily, spread over the water's surface and prefer dappled light.

dog, elephant and buffalo, occur in this isolated region. Bird life is also prolific – waterbirds, such as the yellowbilled stork, are especially common.

Participate in game-viewing drives and explore nearby Moremi. Walking trails in the company of an experienced guide allow you to get close to nature.

Features:
- Accommodation in Meru tents
- *En suite* facilities • Elevated bar
- Game- and night drives • Walking trails

Qhaaxhwa Lodge

This lodge overlooking the beautiful Qhaaxhwa Lagoon is possibly the most attractively situated in the country, with a quaint bar elevated over the water. It is part of the large Gametracker organisation which was recently taken over by the prestigious Orient Express group, hence service and facilities are of a very high standard.

Birding in the area is excellent, and guests can also enjoy mokoro trips, fishing, boating and walking. This lodge is not within the boundaries of any national park.

Features:
- Accommodation in reed chalets
- *En suite* facilities • Boat and mokoro excursions • Elevated bar • Fishing and bird-watching

Shindi Camp

This comfortable camp built on a small island in the north-western Delta offers a splendid combination of dry-land and water activities, and is not within a reserve. It is renowned for its excellent birdlife – particularly its abundance of waterbirds – and is a photographer's delight.

Features:
- Accommodation in Meru tents • Game drives • Superb birding and heronries
- Bush walks • Boating

Xugana Lodge

This lodge, superbly placed on the picturesque Xugana Lagoon, is renowned for its high standard of service. Although the owners specialise in photographic safaris, a wide range of other activities are also available including bird-watching, rewarding angling, cruises on the lagoon and bush walks. It is not within a national park.

Features:
• Accommodation in raised wooden chalets • *En suite* facilities • Game drives • Superb birding and fishing • Boating

Public campsites
There are no official campsites in this region. The only way to camp in this part of the Delta is by going on a mokoro safari (see page 41).

BELOW: *Guests depart on a mokoro excursion from Gunn's Camp.*

BOTTOM LEFT: *A purple heron blends with the surrounding vegetation.*

BOTTOM RIGHT: *A four-wheel drive is highly recommended for travel in the Delta.*

TOP RIGHT: *Little bee-eaters roost in communal harmony at night.*

SOUTHERN OKAVANGO
(SEASONALLY FLOODED)

The lower part of the Delta is distinctly different in appearance from the northern section and the Panhandle. The islands here, of which Chief's Island is a perfect example, are much bigger than the ones further north. They are large Kalahari sandveld tongues that jut deep into the Delta and support vegetation and animals more typical of the dry deciduous woodlands towards Savuti. These islands are fringed by a wide belt of floodplain grassland. This area is subject to more radical seasonal changes than the permanently flooded zones. The floods arrive from Angola around April after the rainy season, when the pans are beginning to dry up, and the floodplains fill with water. Miraculously, the vegetation of short, dry grass changes almost overnight and the landscape is dominated by water lilies and other aquatic flowers. Fish come swarming into the newly filled plains in search of feeding areas, attracting storks, herons and kingfishers,

An elephant enjoys a water fig on the river's edge.

and animals move closer to the water provided by the floods.

By the time the rains are due again, the flood is spent and the floodplains are drying out. Fish move back into the main channels and trigger the start of the Barbel Run (see page 56). With the new rains, the animals disperse and the cycle starts over again.

MAUN

Known as a remote, hard-living, dusty frontier town, Maun is in the process of losing these aspects of its character that made it famous. Gateway to the Delta and Moremi Wildlife Reserve, Maun was established in 1915 as the tribal capital of the Batawana. Today, as a result of its proximity to the Okavango, it is the centre of the tourist industry and most safari companies are based there. Most of the work force is employed either directly or through service industries by the tourist trade. The town reflects its reliance on tourism as activity grinds to a halt when the visitors disappear in the late summer months. Built on the banks of the Thamalakane River, Maun means 'place of the short reeds'. It has changed

face drastically over the last few years and now boasts tarred roads in and around the town, streetlights, paved sidewalks and modern shopping complexes with specialised stores.

One hotel is situated in the town centre and six lodges (of which two have been closed since 1992) on the outskirts, each set on the banks of the Thamalakane River. There is also a campsite some ten kilometres from Maun. Refer to the *Advisory* on page 90 for details.

Maun Fresh Produce is the largest supermarket in town and provides most of the region with its fresh produce and food supplies. It was upgraded and enlarged in 1991 and is extremely well-stocked. Most basic items can be found in town. There are two curio shops at the airport, which is located away from the centre of the town. The Mall houses two banks and all manner of new shops where you can buy a wide range of goods, including ice. Maun has 24-hour fuelling points, garages, mechanics, spares and tyres. There are two new pharmacies, a hospital, and private doctors.

Despite the high number of tourists visiting it, Maun does not cater for visitors in terms of places of interest; most travellers use the town only as a springboard into the wildlife areas surrounding it. However, there are several

ABOVE: *Matlapaneng Bridge is now protected as a national monument.*
RIGHT: *The oldest building in Maun was once part of the town's commercial centre.*

attractions in the vicinity of Maun which are well worth a visit:

Crocodile Farm Twelve kilometres out of Maun, on the Toteng road, is the signposted turn-off to the crocodile farm belonging to John and Urusla Seaman. Visitors are welcome to view the breeding pens. The crocodiles live in pleasant surroundings in near-natural conditions. On arrival you may request a guided tour any time between 08h00 and 17h00. Entrance fees are reasonable.

The main commercial growing tanks are not open to the public, as young crocodiles are very susceptible to stress. These tanks constitute state-of-the-art technology, much of which is being developed by the Seamans on their farm.

Maun Game Reserve This small reserve, less than eight square kilometres in area, is on the Thamalakane River opposite Riley's Hotel. The 'place of the reeds' is still visible and forms part of the reserve. It is open to visitors on foot during the daylight hours and entrance is free of charge. As there are no dangerous animals in the reserve, you are permitted to enter without a guide, and can expect to see a variety of antelope. An educational centre is being erected near the main gate where light refreshments will be available.

Matlapaneng Bridge The narrow, chalky-white, ramshackle bridge at Matlapaneng has, for many years, been the gateway to the country's northern wilderness, with lion, cheetah and hippo seen crossing it until fairly recently. It was finally declared a monument and a new bridge was built alongside it in 1992. The old mopane pole and calcrete structure has a long history and many stories to tell. It has witnessed many a driver trying to make his/her way back from the lodges after a typical

ABOVE LEFT: *Smiling pupils at the government-run Moremi III school, Maun.*
ABOVE TOP: *Aerial view of the road to Maun.*
ABOVE: *Several modes of transport are necessary to reach some of the Delta's more remote lodges.*
LEFT: *A typical sandy road reveals both human and animal tracks.*

night of hard drinking and then not being able to round the corner before the bridge, landing up in the water below. Local folklore has it that the depths of the waterhole at the bridge (never known to have dried up yet) will yield a wealth of interesting items, such as unlicensed guns disposed of in a hurry!

Historical buildings The oldest house in Maun is situated near the turn-off to the *kgotla* at Paws Supermarket. This old corrugated iron structure was an R.A. Baileys shop in Tsau and was moved to Maun around 1920. It housed an assortment of early traders, but has now fallen into disuse.

The Duck Inn Situated near the airport, this restaurant has become something of a tourist attraction. It is the meeting place of the hunters, game guides, travellers and tourists. Bush yarns tend to get louder and more fantastic as afternoon rolls into evening.

GETTING THERE
By air
All the lodges in this area have their own airstrips. Be sure not to exceed your baggage allowance of 10 kilograms, as the pilot, at his sole discretion, has the right to insist that you leave any excess baggage behind.

By road
The southern Delta is essentially closed to traffic and the main access is by air or water. Obtain permission and directions from the lodges if you do wish to drive.

One of the few areas which is open to vehicles, Ditshipi – an area south-east of Chief's Island on the Santantadibe River – has been ruthlessly exploited by shoddy tour operators, car hire companies and backpackers over the last few years. Previously, the area had been particularly attractive because no park entry fees were payable and mokoro polers could be independently contracted. As a result, local villages have swelled, the surrounding area is constantly ravaged by veld fires and the islands are littered with rubbish, leaving the whole area rather unsavoury for visitors. Unfortunately, the uncontrolled stream of traffic has contributed immensely to the deterioration of the area.

By boat

Gunn's Camp, Delta Camp and Xaxaba all lie on the Boro River and, as such, are accessible from Maun. Only Gunn's Camp offers the option to boat into the lodge, while Delta Camp has stopped using boats because of noise pollution and the environmental damage that they cause; Xaxaba flies all visitors in to their camp. A popular option at Gunn's Camp is to boat one way and fly the other, to gain two different perspectives of the Delta.

WHAT TO SEE AND DO

All the lodges offer conducted walks on nearby islands, as well as on Chief's Island, water levels permitting.

Game-viewing flights are well worth doing, particularly between May and June when the floodplains are at their best – this part of the Delta is spectacular then and the game prolific. It is also interesting to get a bird's eye view of the area with its complex system of waterways and floodplains.

With the exception of Pom-Pom and Abu's Camp, none of the camps offer game drives. Activities revolve around the water and walks on the islands.

As the water level in the Boro River drops during the summer months, it exposes beautiful white sandbanks on which crocodiles regularly sun themselves.

CHIEF'S ISLAND

Chief's Island, a vast tongue of sand comprising nearly 1 000 square kilometres, is the largest land mass in the Delta, stretching from the southern Okavango to the permanent waters near Mombo. It is an extention of the mainland and, because it is slightly higher than the general level of the Delta, it never floods. The Boro River, which runs south-east through the centre of the Delta, skirts the western boundary of Moremi Wildlife Reserve. It is called Chief's Island as this used to be the traditional hunting ground of Chief Moremi, but is now incorporated into the reserve and no hunting is allowed. It is home to a vast number of animals who benefit from the Kalahari sandveld habitat with its close proximity to water. The arid interior of the island is covered by mopane (*Colophospermum mopane*) woodlands and acacia thornscrub interspersed with clay pans. This is where the large resident buffalo herds of the Okavango are often to be found as they prefer to drink from the rain-filled pans and give preference to the sparsely growing but sweeter grasses of the sandy areas rather than the coarser grasses with lower protein yield of the floodplains.

Each of the lodges in the area has its own look-out point, providing ideal spots for quiet sundowners and superb sunset photographs.

Fishing

The lower Delta is not renowned for fishing, although it can be quite rewarding in the summer months when the floodplains are dry and the fish are forced into the permanent channels. Tigerfish seldom venture this far south but pike ensure good sport-fishing, and bream and barbel also occur in the region. Fishing is generally better in the main rivers after the floodplains have receded.

Seafood lovers may like to try the river mussels that dig themselves into the white sands, a favourite with the openbilled stork.

Wildlife

Chief's Island possesses extensive open grass-land areas which provide an excellent habitat for the plain's game. Buffalo, tsessebe, giraffe, wildebeest and zebra are commonly sighted. Lechwe, waterbuck, reedbuck and other water-related animals, as well as hippo and all the major predators, are also found there.

The hunting of elephants caused them to move out of the Okavango, to the extent that it became rare to see one of these beasts even as recently as the early 1970s. In 1983, a moratorium was placed on elephant hunting, allowing them to return; today, it would be disappointing not to see elephant while on a safari to southern Okavango. The first elephant-back rides in Africa are available at Abu's Camp near Pom-Pom offering a unique and exciting, if somewhat expensive, experience (see *Special Interest Safaris*, page 38).

Bird-watching

A visit to the southern section of the Delta complements one to the northern part, as this

In other areas of southern Africa the wattled crane is rarely found, but it thrives in the Okavango in great numbers.

region hosts different vegetation and a correspondingly different population of birds. Lily-covered lagoons may hold pygmy geese, whitefaced, fulvous and whitebacked ducks, African and lesser jacanas, black crakes and purple gallinules.

Birds to be found in the riparian forest on the fringes of the water include the coppery-tailed coucal, whiterumped babbler, brown firefinch and chirping cisticola.

The wattled crane faces extinction in South Africa, as farming activities encroach ever more onto wetlands. The Okavango, home to the largest flocks in southern Africa, however, boasts a population estimated to number up to 5 000 birds. They are usually seen on open floodplains in pairs or family groups.

The saddlebilled stork, a large bird with a beautifully coloured bill, is also on the endangered list in South Africa, but there are close to 2 500 birds in the Okavango Delta – a superb bird to photograph.

Vegetation

In the lower reaches of the Okavango, vegetable ivory palms replace the wild date palms of the permanently flooded zones. As a result of the earlier absence of elephants who would

RIGHT: *Tented accommodation at Gunn's Camp.*

RIGHT: *Tented accommodation at Gunn's Camp.*

have thinned their numbers, they occur in unusually large stands. However, elephant are now again pushing over great numbers of palm trees around Xaxaba and Delta Camp.

The mangosteen and ebony trees not only provide wonderful, thick shade on the islands, but also bear succulent, sweet fruits that are favourites with man and beast alike.

A mokoro trip will reveal an astounding array of water plants commonly seen here. Water lilies are prevalent, and where these occur you will find jacana hopping around the big leaves in search of insects, or pygmy geese feeding off the seeds. You will also come across the free-floating water chestnut (*Brasenia schreberi*), with its rosette-like, triangular leaves and massive two-pronged seed-pod.

Aquatic ferns and sedges, as well as phragmites reeds with their woolly heads line the river banks, replacing the papyrus of the north. The reeds which grow up to 4 metres high, are used for building the walls of local houses.

The People

There are few villages around the lower section of the Okavango west of Moremi. Primarily they provide the lodges with labour and mokoro polers. Ditshipi is dotted with villages where you may see traditional rural life, which is largely centred on fishing and hunting.

ACCOMMODATION

Abu's Camp

Run by Ker and Downey, this is the camp from which elephant safaris are operated.

Features:
• Accommodation in Meru tents
• Rudimentary private facilities (bucket showers and pit latrines • Elephant safaris
• Bush walks • Mokoro rides and boat excursions • Fishing

Delta Camp

Built with charm and originality, the camp's informal atmosphere lends itself to relaxation. Owner Peter Sandenburgh was the first to take

a stand against the insidious noise pollution encroaching onto the Delta, thus powerboats are banned from the area. Located on Noga Island to the west of Moremi, this camp's attractions include extended mokoro trips lasting several days, in addition to a range of other activities.

Features:
• Accommodation in rustic reed, thatch and timber chalets • *En suite* facilities
• Fishing and birding • Mokoro trails
• Bush walks • No motor boats allowed

Gunn's Camp

This small camp is renowned for the big welcome you'll receive from owners Mike and Lindy Gunn. Based on Ntswi Island, the camp boasts an elevated bar/restaurant on the edge of the Boro River. A small adjacent island is home to the campsite.

Features:
• Accommodation in Meru tents • Private shower and toilet facilities • Game walks
• Boats and mokoro trails • Fishing and birding • Access by aeroplane or boat

Pom Pom Camp

Situated in the lower stretches of the Okavango River and close to Moremi, this small tented camp offers guests a range of outdoor activities including excellent bird-watching, fishing, mokoro trips and game viewing.

Features:
• Accommodation in Meru tents
• Restaurant • Game drives and walks, depending on flood levels • Fishing and birding • Mokoro trails

ABOVE: *The Fish Eagle Bar in an idyllic setting at Xaxaba camp.*
ABOVE TOP RIGHT: *Crossing the mopane pole bridge into Moremi Game Reserve.*
ABOVE RIGHT: *The Buchebuche Cafe in Khwai village.*

Xaxaba

One of the oldest camps in the Delta, Xaxaba is situated on an extremely beautiful island overlooking a tranquil lagoon. Guests are treated to gourmet cuisine and excellent service. Superb bird-watching, powerboat and mokoro rides and pontoon cruises are some of the activities on offer. This is another of the Okavango's camps that is now part of the Orient Express Hotels portfolio.

Features:
- Accommodation in chalets
- *En suite* facilities • An elevated bar offers good sunset views • Swimming pool
- Curio shop • Walking and mokoro trails • Boats and pontoon cruises
- Fishing and bird-watching

Public campsites
Gunn's Camp

This campsite, owned by Mike and Lindy Gunn, is picturesquely situated on one of a cluster of three islands.
Features:
- Access by plane or boat • Hot and cold showers • Bar • Meals • Kitchen
- Mokoro trails • Game walks on Chief's Island • Power boats

Oddball's Palm Island Camping Lodge

This campsite owned by Peter Sandenburgh exhibits the same original style as its sister lodge, Delta Camp, but is not as luxurious and caters for guests who want to look after themselves. A feature of the camp is its tree house, built some five metres above the ground.
Features:
- Camping equipment for hire
- Well-stocked bar and a shop
- Mokoro trails to Chief's Island • Rustic restaurant/bar Hot and cold showers
- Access by plane

MOREMI GAME RESERVE

The eastern section of the Okavango has been preserved by the Batswana tribe as the Moremi Game Reserve. Much of the reserve is not accessible by vehicle due to the waters of the Okavango and because Chief's Island, in the west, is closed to vehicles. This section deals only with the eastern portion of Moremi, where you can drive. (For Chief's Island, see *Southern Okavango*, page 71).

Moremi falls within the tribal land of the Batswana, who are headquartered in Maun. In the early 1960s the tribe was under the regency of Mrs Moremi, whose husband Chief Moremi III, had died and whose son Matiba, was still too young to assume his inherited position. With the encouragement of early conservationists (especially Robert and June Kays) the tribe realised that game in traditional hunting areas was fast disappearing. They proposed that part of the Okavango be protected and on 15 March 1963, the Moremi Game Reserve was proclaimed and the people who lived in the

Lechwe are very much at home in the water and venture onto land to rest and calve.

new reserve agreed to move. It was named after the late Chief Moremi III.

Moremi rates as one of the leading wildlife areas in southern Africa and must certainly be one of the most beautiful. Where land and Delta meet, a mosaic of pans, grasslands, rolling parklands, forests, lagoons and floodplains combine to provide a richly diverse habitat in which wildlife can flourish.

The reserve comprises an area of 3 900 square kilometres which includes the areas Maqwee (South Gate), San Ta Wani, Khwai (North Gate), Third Bridge, Mboma Island, Chief's Island and Xakanaxa, and is dominated by a mopane tongue that penetrates deep into the eastern section. As you get closer to water, the mopane give way to floodplains and riverine forests, and it is here that game is most visibly abundant. Permanent structures are not legally permitted in the reserve and none of the camps are fenced. The roads are sandy in the dry season and muddy during the rains, a legacy of Government policy to keep the parks as natural as possible. All large African mammals except the black and white rhinos are found there.

The River San, or Banoka, are descendants of the Khoi and were the earliest settlers of the

ABOVE: *Cheetah enjoy their kill in the Reserve.*
LEFT: *Having eaten her fill a young lioness basks in the afternoon sun.*

Okavango. Many of the place names in Moremi come from their language. The X and Q sounds represent clicks formed on different parts of the palate. The San hunted using poison arrows and pits dug along the river banks, and built make-shift shelters whenever they stayed in Moremi for a time. Today, they are still to be found in surrounding villages such as Khwai, Zankuyo and Kudumane.

GETTING THERE
By air
Three airstrips serve Moremi: Khwai, Xakanaxa and San Ta Wani. Twin-engined aircraft are not permitted to use Xakanaxa airstrip.

By road
Note that a four-wheel drive vehicle is required for Moremi. You can reach the reserve from either Maun or Savuti. From Maun, follow the tarred road east, across the bridge over the Thamalakane River to Shorobe. Then continue along the sand road. Ignore any turn-offs to left and right until you reach the gate at the buffalo fence. Once past the gate, the road forks. Take the left hand fork (the right goes to Savuti) and continue along this road until you reach South Gate. The total distance from Maun is 95 kilometres, and should take just under three hours to complete.

From Savuti, take the Mababe road in winter (to avoid the sand) and the Sand Ridge road in summer (to avoid the wet black cotton soil). The Mababe road is reached from the road on the western side of the marsh and is signposted. To take the Sand Ridge road from the campsite, go past Leopard Rock and continue on this road until it meets the Mababe road, about 15 kilometres before the Mababe Gate. The distance from Savuti to Mababe Gate is 58 kilometres. Fifteen kilometres beyond the Mababe Gate, the road forks and may easily be missed as it is not signposted. Take the right-hand fork to Moremi (the left goes to Maun and by-passes Moremi via Kudumane and Zan-kuyo villages). Follow this road for 38 kilo-metres over the Magwikwe sandridge and along the Khwai River, until you get to Khwai village and North Gate. Many turn-offs along this road are used by hunting companies, so follow the most frequently used road.

By boat
Access to Xakanaxa by boat from Maun or Shakawe is possible, however it is a safari in itself and you are advised to contact an oper-ator specialising in this type of excursion.

For access to Chief's Island, see *Southern Okavango*, page 71.

BELOW: *Wattled crane take flight along a typical bush road.*
RIGHT: *Enormous edible mushrooms sprout on termite mounds after the first rains.*

SOUTH GATE (MAQWEE GATE) AND SAN TA WANI

The south-eastern part of Moremi around South Gate is known as Maqwee, with San Ta Wani being part of the are that flanks the cut line of the reserve and the Mogogelo River immediately south.

GETTING THERE

By air

The closest airstrip is at San Ta Wani Lodge, about 15 kilometres south of Maqwee Gate.

By road

See *How to get to Moremi by road*, page 76 for details on road access from Maun.

From Khwai, continue south for 30 kilometres on the road that crosses the Mogogelo River. The road does have some very sandy patches where you should take detours off to the side. Allow an hour for this journey.

The drive from Maun takes you past Shorobe and onto the sand track, where you will cross a series of low sandy ridges with a layer of calcrete along the crest. These are, in fact, ancient sand dunes from a more arid period 2 million years ago or more, and are regarded by some scientists as being older than the Okavango itself.

An elephant family strolls through the lush green undergrowth of Moremi Game Reserve.

WHAT TO SEE AND DO

Wildlife

South Gate is the only campsite in Moremi situated in mopane forest. However, it is also right on the edge of the floodplains and driving back out the gate toward Maun, or along the Third Bridge road, offers a good diversity of habitat and game. In the mopane you stand to see elephant, impala, kudu, sable, roan antelope and baboon, while the floodplains hold almost the full spectrum of game to be found in the Okavango.

The Khwai and Xakanaxa roads take you through seemingly endless mopane forests where game is quite difficult to spot. Water is pumped into a pan near South Gate (first track to your right past the gate if you are travelling north) and although fairly inactive while the natural pans in the vicinity still hold water, it does attract baboons, impala, warthog, zebra, elephant and even wild dog and leopard on occasion. It is, however, too enclosed by mopane and too close to the game scouts' living quarters to be a prime viewing spot.

During the rainy season, an interesting phenomenon may be observed at all the water-filled pans along the way. Masses of white, meringue-like froth, the size of ostrich eggs or even bigger, may be seen dangling from the trees overhanging water-filled pans. Foam nest frogs, or grey tree frogs (*Chiromantia xeramperlina*) as they are also known, froth up their nests with their back legs during the night. When the tadpoles are old enough, they simply drop out of the bottom of the nest into the water below.

Bird-watching

This is an excellent area for bird-watching, as relatively easy vehicle access to the permanent water pools together with a good diversity of habitat allows for close up sightings of many differentand interesting species. Saddlebilled storks, wattled cranes and a host of other water birds are found around the plentiful, permanent water sources. Arnot's chats, barbets, whitehelmet shrikes and woodhoopoes favour the mopane. It is also a good area for ground hornbills, who nest in large holes in the thicker tree trunks.

Vegetation

Mopane, identified by its butterfly-shaped leaves, dominates the scenery. Every now and then you will come across a stretch of mopane that is stunted and bush-like, instead of the normal tall multi-stemmed forests. This is due to restricted root development caused by a layer of calcrete near the surface.

Rain trees (*Lonchocarpus capassa*) can be recognised by the sweet-smelling violet-blue sprays of flowers, regularly seen between September and November. The name rain tree comes from the little spittle bug or froghopper (*Ptyelus grossus*), a leaf-cutting insect that creates a fine mist under the tree while it feeds off the leaves. The insects produce a froth by blowing air through the honeydew, a waxy substance they excrete in order to protect themselves from predators and the sun. Excess foam drops onto the ground and can saturate the soil underneath the tree.

ACCOMMODATION
San Ta Wani Gametracker's Lodge

Situated near South Gate, this is the only lodge in the area and boasts exceptionally beautiful gardens. Mokoro trails used to be run from here but due to geological changes, the water from the Okavango has not reached this far in the last eight years. Game viewing in the area is superb, as is the bird-watching. This is another of the establishments that has been added to the Orient Express Hotels portfolio.
Features:
- Accommodation in thatched chalets
- *En suite* facilities • Outstanding game viewing outside the park in late winter
- Game drives

Public campsites

The public campsite at South Gate near San Ta Wani is the one least used in Moremi. This may be an advantage for those visitors in search of the true wilderness experience.
Features:
- A well-kept ablution block and tap stand
- Concrete tables and benches • Flat hard surface and reasonable shade for camping

NORTH GATE AND KHWAI

North Gate is the exit point on the north-eastern side of Moremi. The area around North Gate is referred to as Khwai, which has earned itself the reputation of being one of the best game areas in Botswana. The Khwai River, which is the easternmost branch of the Okavango Delta, brings water to an otherwise arid area and attracts a spectacular array of animals in winter.

Khwai village was originally a small San settlement, but in recent years it has grown into a fair-sized community, situated directly outside North Gate. There are a number of small stalls selling basic foodstuffs and drinks. Cattle are not permitted north of the buffalo fence or into Moremi, but as donkeys are regarded as beasts of burden, they are allowed at Khwai village. Campers may find themselves waking up to braying donkeys, barking dogs and crowing cocks.

Dense riverine forest fringes the expansive, grassy floodplain at Khwai.

Home to one of the first non-hunting lodges in Botswana, Khwai can lay claim to being among the first areas in the country where photographic safaris were offered. However, only with the final eradication of tsetse fly in the early 1980s, did it become a popular destination among tourists.

In the 1950s and 1960s when the waters from the Okavango pushed as far east as Mababe and Savuti, the area around Khwai used to be a favourite crocodile hunting spot. This is also where June Vendall Clark and her husband, Robert Kays, found two orphaned lion cubs and raised them by hand, as she recounts in her autobiography *Starlings Laughing*.

GETTING THERE
By air
The airstrip near Khwai River Lodge services the area.

By road
See *How to get to Moremi by road*, page 76 for details on how to get to North Gate from Savuti. Four-wheel drive is required.

From South Gate, continue north for 30 kilometres along the same road by which you entered the reserve.

By boat
The Khwai River is not navigable by boat.

WHAT TO SEE AND DO
The Khwai area is remarkably picturesque with riverine forests of tall shady trees lining yellow, grassy floodplains. Termite mounds of all shapes and sizes break the uniformity of the grass, as does the green ribbon of the narrow Khwai River with its water lilies and sedges. The Khwai valley cuts through tree savanna and forms large open grassland areas that the game must cross to get to water, making this an excellent game-viewing area.

Wildlife
The Khwai floodplain offers outstanding game drives in both directions. To the east downstream along Khwai Loop, you have several options. You can follow the road along the Khwai Lop road along the riverfront (normally better in the afternoon), or the Makgapha road, which leads further inland through mopane forest.

TOP RIGHT: *Khwai River Lodge.*
BELOW: *An elephant visits Khwai campsite.*

You will see Khwai River Lodge on the opposite river bank, near the airstrip. Courtesy dictates that you do not drive or park directly in front of the lodge – use the short loop that shields you from sight. Beyond the lodge is a widening in the river where hippo are commonly found and elephants come down to drink. This is a favourite place for sunset photography. The tented camp beyond Khwai River Lodge is Machaba. If you select this route for an early morning drive, be prepared to have the sun in your eyes.

You can get to the western floodplain (upstream) by taking the first turn-off to the right after crossing the bridge. The roads along the floodplain have been created more by random off-road driving than by design. You may take any of these roads without fear of getting lost, as you are always between the Khwai River and the main road to Xakanaxa, which runs parallel to the river through the mopane forest.

If you select to drive along the water's edge, you will see Tsaro Lodge set back under the trees on the far bank. Some 15 kilometres upstream, you will come to two attractive large open lagoons, known as the Dombo hippo pools. Apart from hippo which you may find near the road, these lagoons are also home to red lechwe and waterbuck. The area also forms part of the territory of a family of rhino so keep your eyes peeled, as you are unlikely to see rhino elsewhere in Moremi.

Lion, leopard, cheetah, wild dog and hyaena commonly sighted at Khwai. Elephant, sable and a host of other animals come to drink along the river. Other species you may see are kudu, tsessebe, warthog, vervet monkeys, crocodile, water monitor, zebra and wildebeest. If you can endure the heat, September and October are the best time to visit.

Tsaro, Machaba and Khwai River Lodge all have hides overlooking the water. There are no water activities available in this part of the park as the river is too narrow and shallow, and the hippos too numerous.

Bird-watching

Prolific bird life adds to the appeal of Khwai. Wattled crane, saddlebilled storks and an amazing collection of raptors are found along the banks of the river. Once again, this abundance of birds is due to the diversity of habitat. Exploration of the northern part of the reserve and around the thickly wooded islands may reveal Senegal and black coucal, Cape glossy and Burchell's starlings, whitebellied sunbirds and a host of other species. Eight owl species occur in the reserve and are commonly seen even in broad daylight. Often spotted in the larger trees along the Khwai River are giant eagle owls, identified by their large size and pink eyelids, and the spotted eagle owls which will drop their eyelids halfmast and raise their eartufts when disturbed.

Vegetation

The floodplains of open grassland are dotted with islands of riverine forest. Pure stands of leadwood (*Combretum imberbe*), identified by its silvery-green crinkly leaves and evenly sectioned grey bark, occur along the floodplains. Khwai campsite has beautiful specimens of the

ABOVE: *Scat-Spoor Museum and Shop, located at Machaba Camp.*
LEFT: *Scenic hippo pool near Xakanaxa.*

sycamore fig with its thick yellow trunk and huge spreading canopy, and of the tall sickle-leaved albizia (*Albizia harveyi*). Camelthorn acacias (*Acacia erioloba*) with their large ear-shaped grey pods, knob-thorn acacias and rain trees dominate much of the riverine woodland, while mopane forests are never far away. Elephant damage to these areas is widespread.

ACCOMMODATION
Khwai River Lodge
This establishment – now operated by the Orient Express group – is one of the oldest in the area and was the first photographic lodge in the country. It is situated outside Moremi Game Reserve near North Gate and overlooks the Khwai River floodplain.Game viewing and bird-watching in this area are extremely rewarding.
Features:
• Accommodation in bungalows of brick and thatch • *En suite* bathrooms
• Swimming pool • Curio shop • Hide
• Game drives • Canoes are available, but the river is too narrow and hippo-infested to consider the use of boats or mekoro

Machaba Camp
This camp, situated on the Khwai River in a private hunting concession opposite Moremi Game Reserve, offers spectacular game-viewing and photographic opportunities. Both day and night game drives are offered, and bird-watching is also excellent.
Features:
• Accommodation in Meru tents
• Private bathrooms • Curio shop • Hide

Tsaro Safari Lodge
Sister camp to Xugana, this luxury lodge is overlooks the Khwai River and is just outside the game reserve. Because of the area's prolific wildlife, morning and evening drives, photographic excurions and boat trips are the most popular activities.
Features:
• Accommodation in brick-and-thatch chalets, some of which are split level with sunken baths • Excellent cuisine • Pleasant swimming pool/bar area • Curio shop
• Game drives • Bush walks • Hide

Public campsite
Situated near the wooden bridge that crosses the Khwai River, this is a pleasant campsite when not overcrowded; however, the ablution blocks are hopelessly inadequate during the

ABOVE: *A leopard descends a termite hill.*
RIGHT: *Saddlebilled stork casts an elegant reflection in the still waters of Xakanaxa lagoon.*

peak safari months. Showers can be heated. Monkeys and baboons are a nuisance during the day and any foodstuffs left unguarded will be stolen. Do not leave your vehicle windows open, as you will attract unwelcome visitors.

Features:
* Two ablution blocks • Concrete tables and benches • Plenty of shade
* River view

Game Scouts' Camp

This is located at the entrance gate. Safari companies registered with *Hatab* may pre-book one of the private *Hatab* campsites slightly downstream from Khwai campsite.

XAKANAXA

Xakanaxa is the only developed area within Moremi Game Reserve, with four lodges and a campsite. Its name is derived from the crescent-shaped lagoon overlooked by Camp Moremi and utilised by all the camps. Offering a combination of game viewing and water activities, it is generally regarded as an ideal tourist destination.

GETTING THERE

By air

Because of tall trees on either end of the airstrip and the need for the airplane to gain height rapidly, pilots are particularly strict regarding the baggage limit of 10 kilograms, so do not exceed it.

By road

Three roads lead to Xakanaxa: one each from Khwai, South Gate and Third Bridge.

Xakanaxa is 43 kilometres from Khwai on a signposted road. When the road is dry, allow two hours for the trip on a reasonable surface. If the road is wet, driving may be very tricky, so enquire about the condition of the road before going this way.

The direct road from South Gate traverses the mopane tongue. There are sandy patches as well as some awkward spots during wet weather. Under normal conditions, this 42-kilometre trip should take under two hours.

Xakanaxa is only 16 kilometres from Third Bridge, which is close enough to be incorporated into a game drive. The road is extremely sandy in places, particularly just before the Magwegqana Pools; if you are towing a trailer, engage a low gear before entering the very soft spots. The shortest route to Xakanaxa is via Fourth Bridge and through the mopane. During the rainy season when the river is in flood, Third Bridge may be impassable.

TOP LEFT: *It is not advisable to wear brightly coloured garments on a game drive.*
BELOW: *A family of warthogs forage in Moremi.*

Moremi Safaris established the first camp in Moremi. It was built and run by Dougie Skinner and Tony Graham from Maun. For many years, Skinner lived on his own in this wilderness paradise. He was also responsible for creating most of the game drive roads in the area, as well as for spotting the pools at Nyandam Besha from the air, and then locating them on the ground. He jealously protected this as a secret by never leaving a visible track to his special hide-away. He claimed that he was followed by one of his competitors who let his secret out, and today, instead of a tiny track, there is a large graded road. These pools have been named Dougie's Pools in honour of the man who found and then protected them for so many years.

All the lodges make good use of the Xakanaxa lagoon and beyond. Fishing, swimming, visits to the heronries (see *Bird-watching*, page 85), walks on islands and sunset cruises form part of what is on offer by boat. Okuti Safaris hire boats to private groups.

By boat
See *How to get to Moremi by boat,* page 77.

WHAT TO SEE AND DO
Situated in one of the most beautiful parts of the Okavango, Xakanaxa is a place of secret pools, tall forests, open grasslands and lagoons. Virtually every corner reveals a scene of exquisite beauty. Many of the pools and lagoons offer excellent look-out points with sufficient space for you to find your own exclusive sunset spot. Favourites are at Nyandam Besha (Dougie's Pools), Hippo Pools, Dead Tree Pan and Magwegqana Pools. If you wish to take sunset shots, ensure you are close enough to the camp to get back before regulation closing time (see *Advisory*, page 91. These times should be strictly adhered to, not only to avoid being fined for driving after hours, but also because it is easy to become hopelessly lost).

Wildlife
Game viewing in Xakanaxa can be a frustrating experience. There are times when it is absolutely unbeatable and then, from one day to the next, many of the animals move off to greener pastures and you are left searching empty bush. At its best, Xakanaxa has all the major predators as well as elephant, buffalo, sable, roan antelope, zebra, hippo, giraffe, wildebeest, kudu and the ever-present tree squirrels dashing for cover in front of approaching vehicles. Game viewing and close-up photography are extremely rewarding because the animals are very relaxed – there is no hunting pressure on them, as they are separated from the adjacent wildlife management areas by deep water.

Constant game movement typifies the area and game drives should be kept flexible enough to accommodate this. Take the road towards Khwai to visit Dougie's Pools at Nyandam Besha or alternatively set off in the direction of Third Bridge.

To get to Dougie's Pools, home to some rather inquisitive hippos, drive past the airstrip on the Khwai road. Five kilometres from the camp, there is a turn-off to your left. A loop will bring you back onto the Khwai road, a few hundred metres further on.

Towards Third Bridge, an intricate system of tracks on the floodplain offer a wide choice of routes. If you continue past Xakanaxa Hippo Pool and keep bearing right, you will come to a short wooden bridge that will take you to Dead Tree Pan where a large number of dead acacia and leadwood trees are visible.

A visit to the crocodile-infested Magwegqana Pools *en route* to Third Bridge is a must if you want a good look at these reptiles. Although there is no river filling them, these pools are permanently full as a result of underground seepage. They are ideally suited to barbel and the high population of these catfish supports an extraordinarily high number of

Yellowbilled storks nest in large numbers at Gedikwe heronry.

crocodiles; it is common to see 30 or more basking in the sun at any given time.

Hippo, lechwe and an array of water birds can normally be seen here as well. A picnic at Third Bridge makes for a pleasant day-long excursion. An extensive game drive to South Gate is seldom productive, but a short drive may be worthwhile, as this route is used by many animals that come to drink at Xakanaxa.

Bird-watching

Bird-watching in the area is excellent. In the north of the reserve, many breeding colonies of heron, ibis and stork may be found on lagoons and along some of the channels in water figs. You can boat to the heronries at Xakanaxa and Gedikwe lagoons, where large colonies of stork, heron, and reed cormorant nest. Because this provides such a spectacular sight, it is a great temptation to get as close as possible, but this has caused disturbance to the breeding birds so you are urged to maintain a respectable distance.

Along the channels, blackbacked, chirping and redfaced cisticolas in the reeds, as well as the greater swamp warbler in the papyrus, may easily be identified by their calls. Longtoed

ABOVE: *Elephants have caused considerable damage to the trunk of this baobab tree.*
ABOVE RIGHT: *Marabou storks congregate at a rain-filled pan in Moremi.*

plovers, slaty egrets, malachite kingfishers, little bee-eaters and black crakes may be seen on the edges of the waterways. Game drives through the woodlands may reveal a wealth of birdlife including Arnot's chat, redcrested korhaan, Burchell's sandgrouse and redbilled woodhoopoes.

Vegetation

The vegetation is typical of the southern Okavango Delta: mopane forest leads into mixed riverine forest, with open floodplains and aquatic vegetation in the wetter areas. The mopane trees around the airstrip are particularly massive, reaching heights of up to 30 metres. A large baobab past the Hippo Pool has been eaten into by elephants and is worth stopping to have a look at.

ACCOMMODATION

Camp Moremi

This luxury camp is sister to Camp Okavango, and shares the same enviable reputation for superb service and fine cuisine. While Camp Okavango's activities are focused on the water, attractions at this camp are centred on the area's outstanding wildlife populations. Game drives and bird-watching (to spot some of the region's 400 recorded species) dominate. Transfers to Camp Okavango by boat are avail-

able, and many guests like to spend time at each camp.

Features:

• Accommodation in Meru tents • Private facilities • A large, elevated restaurant/bar made of wood affords an excellent view over Xakanaxa Lagoon • Outdoor boma and fireplace • Boats

Camp Okuti

The newest of the Xakanaxa camps, Camp Okuti is owned and run by Rolf and Helma Schleifer. The lodge is very pleasantly nestled in the shade of large trees at the edge of Xakanaxa Lagoon. On offer are game-viewing drives, walks on some of the area's many islands, boating and fishing.

Features:

• Accommodation in thatched chalets
• *En suite* toilets and basins with outside showers • Superb cuisine

Safaris Unlimited

This camp is owned by Willie Zing and caters largely for groups booked through Switzerland.

Features:

• Accommodation in tents
• Communal ablutions

Xakanaxa Camp

The original camp in the Xakanaxa area is still reminiscent of the old-style bush camp introduced by Dougie Skinner and Tony Graham. Located inside Moremi, it offers year-round boat trips, and game-viewing drives in prime wildlife areas. Lagoons in the vicinity are breeding sites for herons and storks.

Features:
- Accommodation in Meru tents on raised, wooden platforms • *En suite* facilities
- Outdoor *boma* and fireplace

Public campsite

Situated along the Khwai River, this campsite has no facilities apart from a few pit latrines, and you will have to bring your own shower. Animals have not yet become the pests that they are in other campsites, but be careful when walking in the dark, as there are regular nocturnal visits from the resident hippos. Xakanaxa was the scene of two tragic events when tourists did not heed the fact that this is a wilderness area where numerous dangerous animals abound.

Features:
- Secluded campsites • Good shade
- Views over the river and lagoon
- Registered *Hatab* members may pre-book the private campsite.

THIRD BRIDGE AND MBOMA ISLAND

Third Bridge, situated 15 kilometres south-west of Xakanaxa, is a very popular campsite with self-drivers and is possibly the only camp-site in Moremi still to retain the flavour of a true wilderness experience. It gets its name from the wooden bridge straddling the Sekiri River which bisects the campsite. During the heat of the day the pole bridge doubles as a sun-bathing platform and springboard for campers to cool off in the tempting waters. This practice is not without danger; a crocodile attack on a woman left her with part of her buttocks removed! If you choose to swim, then paddle in the shallow waters and be out of the water at dawn and dusk. Note that crocodiles are at their most dangerous after the long winter fast, during which their metabolism

slows down and they eat less frequently. Once it starts to warm up in September and October, they are ravenous. Hippos tend to remain in the quieter reeded parts of the river and are seldom seen during the day at the bridge. As there are no human settlements upstream from Third Bridge, it is unlikely that you will catch bilharzia (see *Visitor's Digest*, page 185).

To the west of Third Bridge lies Mboma Island. Comprising nearly 100 square kilometres, it is cut off from the mainland by the Sekiri River which Third Bridge crosses. One of the larger islands in the Okavango although much smaller than Chief's Island, it is split neatly in two by a road that cuts across the middle of the island.

GETTING THERE

By air
There is no airstrip at Third Bridge. The closest is 13 kilometres away at Xakanaxa.

By road
Third Bridge is accessible from Xakanaxa and South Gate. From Xakanaxa, take the road past

ABOVE RIGHT: *Lofty lodge at Camp Moremi.*
RIGHT: *A rather unusual bar built around an ebony tree at Camp Okuti.*

Hippo Pool in a southerly direction through the mopane forest until you reach Fourth Bridge. Cross this and continue until you arrive at Third Bridge 16 kilometres from Xakanaxa. The road is very sandy in places (see *Xakanaxa*, page 83).

There are two routes from South Gate. Take the first road left, past the entrance gate and travel through a mixture of mopane forest and open grassland for 24 kilometres. Take the signposted turn-off to the right. This shorter and more popular route takes you over First and Second bridges. At the T-junction, continue on for 17 kilometres (this road has a number of thick sandy patches). Allow two-and-a-half hours to complete the journey from South Gate to Third Bridge.

The alternative route is a turn-off to the right that takes you past Bodumatau Bridge, and on to join the Xakanaxa/Third Bridge road at the Magwegqana Pools after 14 kilometres. This is a picturesque but little-used track and you must be prepared to drive through long stretches of water if the floods or the rains have been good. Once you reach the Third Bridge road (the first you will come too), turn left. You will travel along 6 kilometres of thick sand before getting to Third Bridge, a route that will take you an hour longer than the direct road.

By boat

It is not possible to get to Third Bridge by boat. Although Mboma can be reached from Xakanaxa, this is not standard practice so enquire at the lodges if you are interested.

WHAT TO SEE AND DO

A game drive to the east on the Xakanaxa road will take you to the Maqwegqana Pools located between Xakanaxa and Third Bridge, which are an outstanding feature of the area. If you plan to make a day trip, you can take either the Bodumatau road and do the full loop back to Third Bridge (a 50 kilometre round trip), or you can go to Xakanaxa and return the same way.

Unless you want a full day's outing, it is best to treat northern and southern Mboma Island as two separate game drives. Because the Sekiri River is shallow, game has easy access to the island, and elephant breeding herds, buffalo, giraffe, wild dog, lechwe, hyaena and warthog are commonly seen.

A drive toward South Gate can be rewarding, as this road is often used by predators. Xini Lagoon, about halfway between South Gate and Third Bridge, is an excellent area for viewing tsessebe, zebra, impala, lion, wildebeest and wild dog.

There are no mekoro in this region. If you wish to hire a boat, you may do so from Okuti Lodge at Xakanaxa – book in advance to avoid disappointment. Swimming at Third Bridge is a popular activity, but not without danger (see page 87).

Wildlife

Mboma has a resident pack of wild dogs that den annually during the winter months in the northern half of the island and a large herd of buffalo also usually winter there. The breeding herds of elephant on this island are notoriously intolerant of vehicles and it is risky to approach them too closely. Beware of getting yourself surrounded as they operate in thick bush and you may easily become cut off from your escape route.

Lions regularly use Third Bridge to cross the river. If you hear them roar around dawn in the vicinity of the camp, go down to the road as early as possible to check the direction in which their tracks lead. You may even find the lions walking down the road.

If you sit quietly in the campsite, you may be rewarded with a good look at the shy bushbuck that live in the area. Other animals you can expect to see include lechwe, waterbuck, tsessebe, reedbuck, giraffe, zebra, wildebeest, side-striped jackal, bat-eared fox, vervet monkeys, baboons and warthog.

Bird-watching

Birding around Third Bridge and Mboma is generally fair, but seasonally excellent when the migrants arrive and the flood arrives from the north. Common residents around the campsite are little bee-eaters, blackcollared

Sunset at Moremi Game Reserve.

barbets, kurrichane thrushes and a variety of starlings. African skimmers, spoonbills and yellowbilled storks, as well as a variety of duck species are often found at the Magwegqana Pools during the summer months. Watching at Third Bridge may afford you a glimpse of black crakes darting in and out of the reeds.

Vegetation

This area is one of the few places to where the mopane tongue does not extend, offering instead more open grassland and acacia woodland. Around the campsite jackalberry, African mangosteen, sausage tree and marula (*Sclerocarya birrea* subsp. *caffra*) dominate. The marula can be identified by its fruits which resemble limes in colour, size and smell, and in winter by its grey and yellow mottled bark and its bare stumpy branches. Mboma Island is very densely wooded; its riverine forest through which the western road winds is made up chiefly of the same species as in the Third Bridge campsite, while its sandy centre is dominated by silver terminalia.

ACCOMMODATION

Public campsite

There are no lodges at Third Bridge and the campsite is the only place to stay. It is the most popular in Moremi and here you will have your own spot, well away from other campers and some delightfully shady places to choose from. Note that it can be unpleasantly overcrowded during the peak safari seasons (April, August to October and December).

Features:

- An ablution block, with a solar pump
- Pit latrines near the campsites
- One water tap near the ablution block
- Warm showers, if you light a fire under the boiler

If the water tank is empty, you will have to start the pump by means of a switch under the solar panel. Ensure that it is turned off before you leave.

The campsite is unattended and the rubbish disposal system totally inadequate. To compound the situation, baboons are extremely brazen and will raid the bins, even in the presence of humans.

To avoid having your campsite completely destroyed by these animals, pack everything away in securely locked trunks or trailers and drop your empty tents. It is even better to leave someone behind to stand guard, and should be possible to enlist the services of a general camp hand from one of the villages *en route* to Moremi. Remember that anyone hired from a village will require transport home again after your safari.

ADVISORY:THE OKAVANGO DELTA

CLIMATE
The Okavango has a long dry winter with little or no rain from May to December. The heaviest rainfall months are from December to February. Even under the moderating influence of the river, early mornings can be bitterly cold while afternoons of the same day may be uncomfortably hot. Although protected, some areas of the Delta can experience unpleasantly strongwinds, especially in August and September.

BEST TIMES TO VISIT
In the Okavango Delta as in Moremi, the game viewing improves as the rain-filled pans dry up and game comes to the permanent water sources.

August to November is considered optimal, however, the later in the year you visit, the greater the chances of early rains spoiling your viewing.

November is very hot and dry, with few tourists. If rains are late, game viewing can be spectacular.

December to February arethe wet months when the game has dispersed and the roads can be impassable. Recommended as a good time for the adventurous who like to be alone. Some lodges may be closed for annual leave and renovations in the rainy season.

March to July offers good game viewing with fewer people around. There is also green vegetation at this time of year in contrast to the much drier later months. Game is attracted to water in winter.

MAIN ATTRACTIONS
The crystal clear waterways of the Delta, and the activities associated with them – mokoro excursions, boating and superb fishing. Excellent game-viewing opportunities, especially in Moremi Game Reserve. Water-adapted antelope, in particular lechwe and sitatunga, are evident on the floodplains and reed banks. Birds are plentiful with over 400 species identified; viewing is best from October to March.

TRAVEL
In general, it is best to contact a reputable safari company who will make all necessary arrangements for you. Most visitors fly into the Delta from either Maun or Kasane, and sometimes a boat trip is necessary to get from the airstrip to your camp or lodge.

If you prefer to go it alone, then a four-wheel drive is essential for travel in Moremi. The only fuel stops are in Maun and Etsha 6. Maun is the only reasonably-stocked supply station for the whole region, and the only place where ice is available.

ACCOMMODATION
Below is a brief summary that lists accommodation included in the Okavango section of this guide. For a more detailed description of each establishment, refer to page numbers indicated.

THE PANHANDLE (see pages 59 to 60)
Drotsky's Cabins On the banks of the Okavango River, 5 kilometres from Shakawe; excellent fishing and boating. Private Bag 13, Maun; Tel 660-351; Fax 660-571; Telex 2612 BD.
Nxamaseri Fishing Camp Accessible only by air and water; a fisherman's paradise. PO Box 785222, Sandton 2146, South Africa; Tel: (011) 886-1981; Fax: (011) 886-1778.
Shakawe Fishing Lodge Ten kilometres south of Shakawe; renowned for superb fishing and bird-watching. PO Box 326, Maun; Tel/fax: 660-493.
Xaro Lodge Luxury tented camp, catering especially for keen anglers. Private Bag 13, Maun; Tel: 660-351; Fax: 660-571; Telex: 2612 BD.
Campsites
Drotsky's Cabins Private Bag 13, Maun; Tel: 660-351; Fax: 660-571; Telex 2612 BD.
Shakawe Fishing Lodge PO Box 326, Maun; Tel/fax: 660-493.

CENTRAL OKAVANGO (see pages 64 to 67)
Camp Okavango Luxury tented camp. Known for its sightings of the elusive sitatunga. Desert and Delta Safaris, PO Box 2339, Randburg 2125, South Africa; Tel: (011) 789-1078; Fax: (011) 886-2349.
Guma Lagoon Accommodation in chalets and tents overlooking the limpid lagoon. Fine fishing, bird-watching and boating as well as island walks. Private Bag 13, Maun; Tel: 660-351; Fax: 660-571.
Jedibe Camp Permanent tented camp offers a water-based experience of the area. Okavango Wilderness Safaris, PO Box 651171, Benmore 2010, South Africa; Tel: (011) 884-1458; Fax: (011) 883-6255; Telex: 2612 BD.
Mombo Camp Tented Camp which focuses on land-based experiences. Excellent game viewing. Okavango Wilderness Safaris, PO Box 651171, Benmore 2010, South Africa; Tel: (011) 884-1458; Fax: (011) 883-6255; Telex: 2612 BD.
Qhaaxwa Luxurious lodge where activities are centred on the water. Excellent birding. Gametrackers, PO Box 786 432, Sandton 2146, South Africa; Tel: (011) 884-2504; Fax: (011) 884-3159.
Shindi Tented camp offering a combination of land and water activities. Fishing and birding – mokoro trips to heron breeding colonies. Ker and Downey Safaris, PO Box 40, Maun; Tel: 660-211/3; Fax: 660-379; Telex: 2485 BD.
Xugana Accommodation comprises brick, thatch and reed chalets on stilts. The owners specialise in photographic safaris. Mokoro trips, fishing and game viewing. Hartley's Safaris, PO Box 69895, Bryanston 2021, South Africa; Tel: (011) 708-1893; Fax: (011) 708-1569.
Campsites: None in this area.

Maun
Cresta Riley's River Lodge Has *en suite* bedrooms with air conditioning, telephone and TV, and a

restaurant and bar, swimming pool and curio shop. Trips into the Delta and national parks can be arranged. PO Box 29, Maun; Tel: 660-204; Fax: 660-580.

Crocodile Camp Quaint reed and thatch camp 10 kilometres east of Maun on the Thamalakane River. Safaris into the national parks are offered; Semetsi Camp in the Delta is exclusively for their clients use. PO Box 46, Maun; Tel: 660-769; Fax: 660-793.

Island Safari Lodge 12 kilometres from town on the river. Has *en suite* chalets, swimming pool, restaurant and bar. Offers economy safaris into the Delta and national parks. PO Box 116, Maun; Tel: 660-300; Fax: 660-222.

Sedie Motel 5 kilometres east of Maun. Has 24 rooms and 6 cottages, restaurant, bar and swimming pool. PO Box 29, Maun; Tel /fax: 660-177.

Sitatunga Camp On a crocodile farm, 10 kilo metres west of Maun. Offers reed chalets, cooking facilities, shop, bottle store and ice. Safaris can be arranged. Private Bag 47, Maun; Tel /fax: 660-570.

Campsites

Kubu Campsite Private Bag 39, Maun; Tel; 660-220; Fax: 660-589.

Sitatunga Camp Private Bag 47, Maun; Tel/fax: 660-570.

SOUTHERN OKAVANGO (see pages 73 to 75)

Delta Camp Bordering on Chief's Island, the camp offers mokoro excursions (no powerboats) and other water activities, as well as walking. Okavango Tours and Safaris, PO Box 52900, Saxonwold 2132, South Africa; Tel: (011) 788-5549; Fax: (011) 788-6675.

Gunn's Camp Luxury tented camp on a small island. Owners renowned for their warm hospitality. Water and dry-land activities on offer. Trans Okavango Safaris, Private Bag 33, Maun; Tel: 660-023; Fax; 660-040.

Pom Pom Camp Comfortable tented camp offering fine birding and fishing as well as game drives and walks. Ker and Downey Safaris, PO Box 40, Maun; Tel: 660-211/2; Fax: 660-379; Telex: 2485 BD.

Xaxaba De luxe tented camp on a very beautiful island. Superb bird-watching (350 species identified), mokoro and powerboat trips, river cruises, and fishing. Gametrackers, PO Box 786432, Sandton 2146; South Africa; Tel: (011) 884-2504; Fax: (011) 884-3159.

Campsites

Gunn's Camp Good facilities and a range of water and dry-land activities available. Trans Okavango Safaris, Private Bag 33, Maun; Tel: 660-023; Fax: 660-040.

Oddball's Palm Island Camping Lodge An excellent option for the budget conscious traveller. Okavango Tours and Safaris, PO Box 52900, Saxonwold 2132, South Africa; Tel: (011) 788-5549; Fax: (011) 788-6575.

MOREMI GAME RESERVE
(see pages 75 to 89)
Moremi GameReserve falls under the jurisdiction of Department of Wildlife and National Parks, PO Box

131 Gaborone; Tel (267) 371-405, or the Regional Wildlife Office in Maun. There is no overall authority that administers the Okavango region. The reserve's opening times are:
1 October to 31 March: 05h30 to 19h00
1 April to 30 September: 06h00 to 18h30
No permanent structures permitted in the reserve; all the lodges are located just outside its boundaries.

Camp Moremi First class tented camp known for its outstanding service and excellent cuisine. Large numbers of lion and buffalo in the area, as well as 400 species of birds. Desert and Delta Safaris, PO Box 2339, Randburg 2125, South Africa; Tel: (011) 789-1078; Fax: (011) 886-2349.

Camp Okuti On Xakanaxa Lagoon. Accommodation in brick and thatch chalets. Game viewing, boat trips and walks on the area's many islands. Okuti Safaris, Private Bag 49, Maun; Tel: 660-307; Fax: 660-307; Telex: 2618 BD.

Khwai River Lodge Accommodation in luxury thatched chalets. Game drives and good bird-watching. Gametrackers, PO Box 786 432, Sandton 2146, South Africa; Tel: (011) 884-2504; Fax: (011) 884-3159.

Machaba Camp Small luxury tented camp on the Khwai River. Outstanding game viewing and photographic opportunities. Ker and Downey Safaris, PO Box 40, Maun; Tel: 660-211/3; Fax: 660-379; Telex: 2485 BD.

San Ta Wani Luxury brick and thatch chalets in beautiful grounds, just outside Moremi. Superb game-viewing and bird-watching. Gametrackers, PO Box 786 432, Sandton 2146, South Africa; Tel: (011) 884-2504; Fax: (011) 884-3159.

Tsaro Safari Lodge A de luxe camp of brick and thatch chalets. Activities centre on the area's spectacular game populations. Hartley's Safaris, PO Box 69895, Bryanston 2021, South Africa; Tel: (011) 708-1893; Fax: (011) 708-1569.

Xakanaxa Camp Tented camp offering year-round boat trips. Excellent game viewing and bird-watching (close to spring breeding grounds of storks and herons). Moremi Safaris, Private Bag 26, Maun; Tel: 660-222; Fax: 660-205; Telex: 2482 BD.

Campsites
All campsites in the reserve are administered by the Department of Wildlife and National Parks, PO Box 131, Gaborone; Tel (267) 371-405.

HEALTH HAZARDS
Beware of malaria, particlularly in the summer months; sleeping sickness (tsetse fly), ticks; bilharzia occurs along the western and southern fringes of the Delta; crocodiles, hippos and other potentially dangerous animals.

ANNUAL EVENTS
The annual floodwaters reach Shakawe in February; the Barbel Run (see page 56) takes place in the Panhandle between September and December.

CHOBE NATIONAL PARK

Situated in the north-eastern corner of Botswana, this national park takes its name from the Chobe River which acts as its northern boundary. This watercourse changes name four times after it enters Botswana; first from Kwando to Linyanti, and then to Itenge, before it finally becomes the Chobe. The park constitutes a total of some 11 000 square kilometres, making it the country's third largest wildlife area. It harbours a great diversity of habitats, ranging from the riverine areas of Linyanti and the Chobe, to the mixed deciduous and mopane forests of Nogatsaa and the open grasslands and rocky outcrops of Savuti.

Home to an exciting array of large mammals and over 450 species of birds, Chobe is most famous for its large populations of elephant and buffalo. The breeding groups of up to 300 beasts are an impressive sight and make Chobe a must for tourists. Savuti is renowned for its lions, who have featured in a number of documentary films.

Chobe's proximity to Zimbabwe also makes it an ideal base for visiting one of Africa's most awesome spectacles, the Victoria Falls. Situated on the border between Zambia and Zimbabwe, the falls are an hour's easy drive away from the northernmost section of the park.

SAVUTI

Long regarded as a must during any visit to Botswana, Savuti offers exciting wildlife and some of the most diverse landscapes in the country reminiscent of the Serengeti plains in Tanzania. Savuti, an area of roughly 5 000 square kilometres, lies within Chobe National Park near its western boundary and includes the Mababe Depression and the Savuti Marsh and Channel. In addition to its lion population, it is also known for its high concentration

Baobabs straddle the road through Kavimba.

of hyaena and the annual zebra migrations (see page 97).

Whether arriving by air or by road, the Gubatsa Hills that dominate Savuti are a striking feature in an otherwise extraordinarily flat landscape. These hills are a series of dolomitic outcrops or *Inselbergs* formed some 980 million years ago.

Savuti was once part of the giant Lake Makgadikgadi and, in those days connected to both the Okavango and Zambezi rivers. When Lake Makgadikgadi started drying up some 30 000 years ago, Lake Mababe was left behind as a giant pool which also dried eventually, leaving behind the Mababe Depression. A garden paradise in the time of Livingstone, it has now become a flat, dry scrubland where fine, powdery, black dust billows high behind vehicles. The Magwikwe sandridge, 100 kilometres long, 20 metres high and 180 metres wide which has tormented so many travellers in the past, encircles the western edges of Savuti and was the shoreline of this internal lake. The smooth pebbles found around the base of the hills indicate the old shoreline.

The dry Savuti Channel, on the banks of which all the camps are built, winds its way through the Savuti area. This channel last flowed in 1979; when it does flow, it empties into the marsh – the vast open grassland south of Savuti – but this happens irregularly as evidenced by the large dead camelthorn trees in the channel bed. The cause of its drying up is not absolutely clear, but seems to be linked to a papyrus blockage on the Kwando River which feeds into the channel, or to tectonic movements, which may have lifted the upper area of the channel sufficiently to have affected the flow. It is likely that the channel will flow again, but when this will happen is uncertain – perhaps not within any of our lifetimes. Without the underground water supply constantly being replenished by the channel, Savuti is becoming progressively more arid, causing an alteration in both vegetation and game patterns.

Another striking element of the Savuti region is the large number of pans that hold

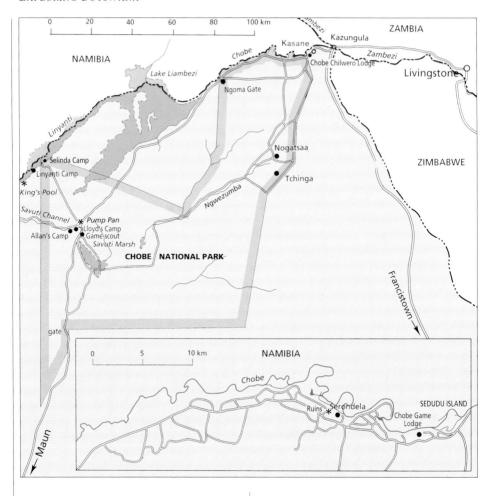

water for months after the rains. These allow game to remain in the region long past the wet season. During the dry season (May to October), the pans dry up and the animals are attracted to the three artificial waterholes in the area. Expect to see these being dominated by elephants, with other game waiting their turn for a drink. September and October in Savuti can be stiflingly hot and depressingly arid but game viewing is rewarding, as predators are concentrated around the waterholes. When the rains fall (from November to April) the animals move off to pristine pastures. Among the most notable are the elephant herds moving away, leaving only a few old bulls behind.

GETTING THERE

By air

An airstrip at Savuti that can be used by single- and twin-engined planes serves the area. It is a long strip, with good approaches from both sides and can take an aircraft as large as a DC3. If you are on a private charter and are booked in at one of the camps, ask your pilot to buzz the camp you are visiting before landing, as the airstrip is some distance from the camps. Do not allow your pilot to abandon you on the airstrip if the camp vehicle does not arrive, as this is a favourite area for lions. Aircraft left at the strip must be protected from hyaenas who will chew the tyres. This is best done by placing thorny branches around the wheels.

ABOVE RIGHT: *The entrance to Chobe National Park, Kasane.*
BELOW: *Camelthorn trees alongside the road to Savuti.*

By road

Savuti is accessible by road from Maun (directly or via Moremi), Kasane (directly or via Nogatsaa) and Linyanti. All roads are sandy in the dry season and sticky in the wet season. They definitely require four-wheel drive vehicles.

From Maun, take the tarred road to Shorobe and continue along the main dirt road until you pass through the gate at the buffalo fence. One kilometre past the fence you will see a fork. The right-hand fork takes you directly to Savuti, while the left one goes to Moremi. The distance from Maun to Savuti is 170 kilometres. Allow seven to eight hours travelling time. The Moremi road is about 30 kilometres longer, which will take about an hour longer, and park entrance fees for Moremi must be paid. Five kilometres past the Chobe National Park gate, there is a fork in the road. Take the left branch if you are travelling in the wet season, as the cotton soil along the right road becomes impassable during the rains. In the dry season, the right-hand fork is preferable, as the left one is very sandy.

From Kasane, the main road leads you through the park toward Ngoma. Immediately after exiting the park gate, turn left towards Kachikau. The road leaves the park and passes for 66 kilometres through the Chobe Enclave, an area excluded from the park in 1968 when Chobe was proclaimed a national park because it was well populated. The distance to Savuti via Kavimba and Kachikau is 150 kilometres and takes four to five hours to complete. The section from Kasane to Kachikau is on graded gravel roads (sometimes badly corrugated between Ngoma and Kachikau) and good time can be made, even in a two-wheel drive vehicle. There are reasonably well-stocked shops and liquor stores in both villages, but vehicle spares and petrol are not available.

Beyond Kavimba, the road follows the southern edge of the floodplains of Lake Liambezi which, like Lake Ngami, has been dry for some years. It cuts through very scenic parts of Chobe Forest Reserve where you cross linear dunes – the sand is thick and four-wheel drive is essential. If you are do not have experience of driving on sand, and particularly if you are towing a trailer, prepare for some digging and pushing. You will re-enter the park at the north-west cut-line to Linyanti, near Goha Hills, 35 kilometres before Savuti. Do not expect to see very much game between Kasane and Savuti, although you will be travelling through game management areas and forest reserves adjacent to the park. The only place where you could expect to find a concentration of game is around Goha Hills, once you have re-entered the park.

The route via Nogatsaa is longer, both in distance and in time, but you do remain within the national park the whole way. Drive to Nogatsaa and then to Ngwezumba Dam. Continue straight ahead, with the Ngwezumba Dam on your left, onto a small ungraded track. This track does not have any turn-offs and once on it, continue for 120 kilometres until you arrive at Quarry Hill, or Big Kanku Koppie as it is also known, at Savuti. This is an attractive drive that follows the Ngwezumba riverbed for much of the way. Count on nine to ten hours for this journey, but do not forget you may break up the trip with an overnight stop at Nogatsaa.

WHAT TO SEE AND DO

All activities revolve around daily game drives only, whether you are staying in one of the lodges, have embarked on a mobile safari or are travelling privately. Neither game walks nor night drives are permitted.

The Seven Hills of Savuti, collectively known as the Gubatsa Hills which means 'place where water can be dug in river sand', are no higher than 90 metres but given the flatness of the surrounding landscape are quite spectacular. They are of volcanic origin and are some 980 million years old. During the time of Lake Mababe, they were islands in the vast lake. Today, pebbled beaches created by the lake can still be seen at the base of the hills.

The dry Savuti Channel winds through the region and is often encountered on a game drive. With its steep sides and deep sand, it can present quite a challenge to vehicles which cross it. If you are not confident of your driving skills in the sand, or if your vehicle is not suited to sand, it is wiser to reverse and try an alternative route.

Situated south of the camps on the road to Maun is the Savuti Marsh, a vast open grassland and an area well worth including in a game drive. The plain's game utilise this area to graze at night and during the cool hours of the day, while they take refuge under the giant acacias during the heat of the day. Lions are commonly sighted on the marsh or in the adjacent scrub, while cheetah are also seen frequently.

The marsh, now a misnomer, was formed during times when the channel still flowed. Dead camelthorns, which grew during a long period when the channel was dry, lend a rather eerie appearance to its northern section. They were subsequently drowned when the channel flooded the marsh between 1958 and 1979.

Careful observation will reveal new tree growth over most of the marsh, indicating that this open area is likely to change character again as these trees mature.

Overlooking the channel not far from where it enters the marsh, you will notice two square concrete slabs that were the floors of an old research station. The late President Sir Seretse Khama wistfully referred to this spot as 'the ideal bush retreat', although contrary to common belief and the name 'President's Camp', he never stayed there.

There are no hides at Savuti other than the one at Lloyd's Camp, which is solely for their own clients use; however Bushman Hill provides some good lookout points.

Generally you are required to remain in your vehicle except in the official camp grounds but you are, however, permitted to leave your vehicle to clamber up Bushman Hill (also known as Gobabis) to view the rock paintings on the eastern face. The rocks are slippery and suitable shoes are advisable. The paintings, not carbon dated, are thought to be between 3 000 to 4 000 years old. They depict various animals of present and past Savuti vintage. Eland, elephant, sable, giraffe, a puffadder and a hippo from wetter times feature on the same panel. A mixture of plant juices, and animal fat coloured with the rusty ironoxide from the rocks, was used to create this incredibly durable paint, but its exact composition is unknown. There are 22 known sites of paintings around Savuti, most being very faint due to exposure to the elements.

Wildlife

Savuti is famous for its high percentage of lions and hyaenas due to the high prey population, but other large predators such as leopard, wild dogs and cheetah are also found. They are most active in the cool hours of the day and an early start to your game drives should prove very rewarding.

During the dry season, there is a large concentration of bull elephants around the waterholes. On the marsh herds of tsessebe, wildebeest and the ubiquitous impala, as well as giraffe, warthog and black-backed jackal may be seen. The wooded areas yield sightings of kudu, while roan, sable and buffalo are also seen, if infrequently. White (square-lipped) rhinos are rare visitors. During the wet season, hippo may be encountered on their way to or from a rain-filled pan.

A number of rain-filled pans in the area hold water late into the dry season. As the smaller holes are drying up, these attract game on an increasing scale. The larger pans in the Savuti area may be found at Harvey's Pans on the way to the airstrip, and in the mopane to the west of the marsh. In addition, a number of pans are artificially filled. Pump Pan is not far from the public campsite on the road to Kasane, and there are two new sites near the marsh – one at Marabou Pan and the other at Rhino Vlei. Enquire from the game scouts as to the condition of these pans as some of them may not be operational. To see a good variety of habitats, a suggested game-viewing route would encompass Pump Pan, Harvey's Pans and the Savuti Marsh.

RIGHT: *Elephants and lions abound in the Savuti region of the Chobe National Park.*
BELOW: *Kudu and impala quench their thirst in elegant unison.*

Tsessebe Road at the bottom end of the marsh has become heavily overgrown and littered with potholes dug by elephants, and you are advised not to consider this as an alternative game-viewing route.

Zebra migration

Zebra migration during summer is spectacular – thousands of zebra on the move is a never-to-be-forgotten sight. Herds of up to 25 000 animals pass through Savuti twice during their migration, spending their winters near the Linyanti River in the north and then moving south to the Mababe Depression for the wet period. The timing of the migration is determined by the rains, but it usually occurs between November and December for the

ABOVE: *The breathtaking spectacle of the annual zebra migration.*
LEFT: *A lone wildebeest on Savuti Marsh.*

during late summer, peaking around April when columns of nearly 5 kilometres long may be seen rising and falling in the sky.

Vegetation

Savuti Marsh is a wide expanse of open grassland with a variety of nutritional grasses, the dominant one being couch grass (*Cynodon dactylon*), which attracts herbivores. Scattered throughout the marsh are small islands of bushes and shrubs clumped together, such as Motsebe Island which consists of the large fever-berry trees (*Croton megalobotrys*) with their apricot-like fruits and bright green heart-shaped leaves.

Huge camelthorn trees line the road alongside the marsh – an invaluable source of shade for game. Two large baobabs in the Savuti region are worth a visit; one is situated behind Quarry Hill and the other is visible from the main road near Bushman Hill.

A characteristic smell pervades Savuti. This is caused by the bluish-green sage bush, also called the bitter bush (*Pechuelloeschea leubnitziae*) that grows in the sandy soils of the region. If you crush a fresh leaf from this herb, it will release a powerful smell of sage. This plant is not eaten by any game species because of its strong bitter taste.

southward journey, while their return to the Linyanti generally takes place during February to April.

Bird-watching

Savuti boasts close on 300 bird species and is generally included as the dry land region on bird-watching safaris. Kori bustards and secretary birds are two of the larger birds seen on the marsh. Your morning wake-up call will be provided by the raucous cries of the redbilled francolin. The ubiquitous but exquisitely coloured lilacbreasted roller will provide ample opportunity to test your photographic skills as it hawks from branches near the road.

During summer a great number of migrants and water birds are attracted to the region. Among these are the Abdim's stork, carmine bee-eaters, waders fresh from their breeding grounds in northern Europe and even fish eagles. Quelea, a small finch, group in their thousands along the Mababe Depression

ACCOMMODATION

There are three permanent camps in the Savuti area. Although they accept drive-in custom, it is advisable not to arrive without a booking, as they are frequently full and it is a long way to the nearest alternative accommodation.

All of Savuti's camps, being unfenced, regularly receive visits from both diurnal and nocturnal creatures.

Allan's Camp

Overlooking the Savuti Channel, this attractive camp is another of the Gametrackers operations that has recently been taken over by the Orient Express group. Game viewing and birdwatching excursions are offered – the former being more rewarding during the later months of the year when animals gather around waterholes south of the camp.

Features:
• Reed and wooden chalets (plans are afoot to upgrade to luxury tents as in Savuti South) • *En suite* facilities • Game drives, traditionally taken after breakfast

Lloyd's Camp

This camp is owned and operated by Lloyd and June Wilmot, who place a strong emphasis on providing guests with a wilderness experience. A hide overlooking the camp's waterhole offers guests the opportunity for some excellent game viewing.

Features:
• Large, comfortable Meru tents, with shared external facilities • Good food, friendly staff and an informal atmosphere
• Reputation for very early and enthusiastic (if sometimes bitterly cold) game drives

Savuti South

Another Gametrackers establishment on the Savuti Channel, this is a sister to Allan's Camp, and its facilities have recently been upgraded.

ABOVE RIGHT: *A lilacbreasted roller adds a vibrant splash of colour to the Chobe landscape.* BELOW: *A trip along the Chobe River provides a close-up view of one of the 'big five'.*

Game viewing and birding are superb, especially when the channel floods (although this has not occurred since 1979).

Features:
• Luxurious Meru-type tents
• *En suite* facilities • Operates on a similar schedule to Allan's Camp

Public campsite

Savuti is undoubtedly the most controversial of Botswana's public campsites, but it has also provided the most exciting experiences for its campers. You will sink up to your ankles into the thick, dirty-grey sand, and a flat, pleasant camping spot is difficult to find. Rubbish is often scattered around the campsite by baboons. Water is pumped to a pan not far from

Elephants often venture into camp.

the campsite and if this supply is not consistent, the elephants regularly come into the campsite and destroy the ablution and shower facilities. Water can therefore be unavailable and it is important to carry your own emergency supplies for drinking. Before you leave for Savuti, enquire as to the water situation and the state of the ablution facilities. This area can be oppressive if you do not have sufficient water, and you may wish to shorten your stay as a result. The most destructive of the campsite visitors are elephants and hyaena. An electric fence has been erected around the camp in an attempt to prevent elephant damage, but this has proved to be neither aesthetically pleasing nor successful in keeping animals from the campsite.

Features:

• Three ablution blocks • Water taps at most camping spots

Other camps

The private research station and game scout's camps offer no accommodation, while the *Hatab* campsite is available only to tour operators who are *Hatab* members, and who have booked and paid in advance.

LINYANTI

North of Savuti is Linyanti, a forgotten corner of the Chobe National Park. With its mature woodland and beautiful river frontage on the Linyanti Swamp, it is one of the most attractive areas in the park. It boasts a great diversity of game and a restful atmosphere. The major drawback is that there is only a narrow seven-kilometre strip of river frontage within the national park; hunting concession areas to both sides restrict you to the park, unless you are travelling with Photo Africa or a *bona fide* Botswana-registered safari company which has booked one of the camps in advance. Due to increased poaching, especially of elephant, the Botswana Defence Force has been based in the area and do constant anti-poaching patrols.

GETTING THERE

By air

An airstrip situated within the hunting concession serves the Photo Africa Lodge at Linyanti and hunting camps further along the river. Their permission must be obtained to use this airstrip. Otherwise you must use the airstrip at Savuti, two hours' drive away.

By road

Linyanti is accessible from three directions: Kasane, Savuti and Moremi. From Kasane, take the Kavimba road to Savuti (see page 95) and turn right at the cut-line, where the sign for Chobe National Park is positioned. You will arrive at the river after a 40-kilometre drive. Turn left towards the game scout's camp and park gate, then follow the river for about five kilometres until you reach the campsite. The road is sandy in parts and a four-wheel drive is essential. Allow six hours for this journey.

From Savuti, cross the sandridge beyond Linyanti Plain and take the only road to your right. This will take you to the campsite, some 40 kilometres away. The ridge is very sandy and it is not advisable to tow a trailer on this road. Two hours should be sufficient to cover the trip and a four-wheel drive is essential.

From Moremi, it is possible to take the cut-line from the Khwai River to Linyanti. Take the Savuti road, following the river for some 15 kilometres, then turn left at the Chobe National Park sign. The road is little used and the first section is seriously overgrown. Do not take this route unless you are

Riverine forest is reflected in the limpid waters of the Linyanti River.

with a professional guide, or unless you are confident of your navigating abilities; it is very easy to lose your way. Once you turn off the Savuti road, continue straight ahead for 90 kilometres, crossing the Savuti Channel. Ignore all tracks to the left and right until you reach the Linyanti River, then take the right-hand turn which will lead you to the campsite.

WHAT TO SEE AND DO

The Linyanti River is strongly reminiscent of the Okavango Delta with its papyrus-lined waterways, extensive reed banks and towering riverine forest. The river forms a swamp area, very much like that found in the Okavango, although it is not more than 900 square kilometres in extent, as opposed to the much larger Okavango Delta.

The Savuti Channel flows out of the Linyanti and, although no longer strong enough to reach the Savuti Marsh, it has water in the top section. Depending on the annual flood, it can push south of Zibadianja Lagoon.

David Livingstone crossed the Linyanti River east from the cut-line on his journey to discover the Victoria Falls in 1855. This was also the major route that traders and missionaries followed to get to Linyanti village on the Namibian side of the swamp.

There are no man-made hides in the region, but there are endless natural ones where you can park and overlook the river. If you are a keen photographer, this is an excellent spot for taking spectacular sunset pictures.

There are no boats or mekoro available for hire from the campsite; however guests at Linyanti Camp have the option of using powerboats or a barge to explore the swamps.

A day trip to Savuti is feasible, but take a picnic lunch along. For those staying at a Photo Africa Lodge, a trip to the Savuti Channel will give you the opportunity to see large numbers of hippo.

If you are staying at the public campsite, your choices for game drives are limited to the riverfront and the access roads. As the dry season lengthens and other water sources to the south dry up, it is not necessary to travel long distances to see dense concentrations of game; therefore, the winter months offer the best game viewing. Breeding herds of elephant, as well as zebra herds are probably the most well-known, but a wide selection of species are to be found here, including lion, leopard, hyaena, roan antelope, sable, waterbuck, lechwe, sitatunga, giraffe, hippo, wildebeest, steenbok, warthog and wild dog.

Wildlife

Zebra migrating through Savuti to the Mababe Depression in summer return to Linyanti for the winter, so the whole length of the Linyanti, as well as the forests and savanna to the south, contain large numbers of these animals.

The game is generally more skittish in this area than in other parts of the park, due to the close proximity of the hunting areas and poaching, which is perpetrated from across the border. The whole region is patrolled by the Botswana Defence Force, who assist with anti-poaching work.

Bird-watching

Linyanti affords fair birding opportunities. Many waders and water birds may be found here and Pel's fishing owl is often heard calling from the densely foliaged trees. This is one of the few places in the country where the stunningly beautiful Narina trogon could occur.

ABOVE LEFT: *Carmine bee-eaters nesting on the banks of the Chobe River.*
BELOW LEFT: *Kachikau village is set high on a ridge overlooking the Chobe floodplain.*
BELOW: *Hippo and fish eagle in Savuti.*

ABOVE: *Wattled plover.*
RIGHT: *Elephant bathing on the banks of the Linyanti River.*

Carmine bee-eaters, redbilled woodhoopoes, crested barbets, emeraldspotted doves, darters and fish eagles are a few of the colourful birds of the region found along the waterfront.

Vegetation

As you approach Linyanti, you will notice the large, mature acacias, leadwood, marula, mangosteen and ebony trees, their size and green canopies indicating that you are not far from the river. Unlike the Serondela region, Linyanti has huge trees that seem impervious to elephant damage, possibly because the elephant have been kept away by hunting and poaching in the past. Other trees that commonly occur include Kalahari apple-leaf, rain tree and mopane. During the winter months when only the bare trunks are visible the area takes on a strange grey hue because of the density of mopane forest.

ACCOMMODATION

James' Camp

This is a hunting camp during the winter months and operates as a photographic camp during the off-season. Being far removed from other tourist activities, it offers guests a real wilderness experience.
Features:
• Accommodation in Meru tents
• Private facilities • A double-decker barge operates on the Kwando River
• Game drives and walks

King's Pool

Another hunting camp available for hire through Photo Africa, during the off-season, King's Pool overlooks a picturesque pool, 11 kilometres upstream from Linyanti Camp. As there is no permanent guide available, you are advised to hire a guide beforehand or be prepared to conduct your own game drives.
Features:
• Accommodation in Meru tents
• *En suite* facilities • Boats available

Linyanti Camp

Operated by Photo Africa, this camp has a superb setting under shady knobthorn trees on the river's edge. Fishing and bird-watching are some of the activities on offer.
Features:
• Accommodation in Meru tents • Shared facilities • Game drives • A barge or power boats available for cruises on the Linyanti River • Guided walks

Selinda Bush Camp

This small camp, comprising only four tents, is operated by Photo Africa and is a sister to

Linyanti Camp – bar and typical Meru tent.

Linyanti Camp. It offers very personalised service in a remote, secluded area and, because of its size, is ideal for small groups. Bird-watching and game viewing are excellent.
Features:
• Accommodation in Meru tents • Private facilities • Night drives • Game walks

Public campsites
The campsite at Linyanti is the most attractive in Chobe as it is situated under beautiful shady trees. Quiet and peaceful, it affords a true wilderness experience. The game scout's camp, where park fees must be paid, is nearby.
Features:
• Well-maintained ablutions • Trees provide ample shade • A water tap

Other camps
The Botswana Defence Force has a camp upstream from the public campsite, from where anti-poaching patrols are operated.

KASANE
This small and attractive border town in the extreme north-western corner of Botswana is strategically situated between the Chobe National Park and the Victoria Falls. For this reason it is very popular with travellers. The name Kasane is derived from the Subiya word 'Masane' for the waterberry tree, (*Syzygium guineense,*) which grows here.

Kasane's two main attractions are its excellent fishing and Chobe National Park (it is very close to Serondela, a popular part of the park). The entrance to the park is in the village but as there are no fences, animals – especially elephants, baboon, monkeys, warthog, banded mongoose, Nile monitor and hippo – can be seen in the village and campsites on a regular basis. Daily game drives to Serondela are on offer from all the lodges. Do not try walking into the park from Kasane, as this is strictly forbidden. *En route* to the airport is an old quarry that permanently holds water which attracts game all year round. Another rewarding game-viewing spot is Sedudu Island opposite Chobe Safari Lodge.

Bream is plentiful in the Chobe, while the Zambezi is better for tigerfish. Fishing is allowed anywhere along the river, but permits must be obtained. Boats with drivers are available for hire from Chobe Safari Lodge and Cresta Mowana Lodge.

There are no mokoro trips for tourists available at Kasane, although the local fishermen and islanders do use this mode of transport. The river teems with hippo and crocodiles and mokoro rides are not recommended. Three-hour barge trips depart from Chobe Safari Lodge and Cresta Mowana Lodge and offer superb bird-watching and game viewing.

Accommodation is available in and around Kasane, and also the national park (see *Advisory* page 117).

Only the most basic supplies can be obtained in Kasane. There are curio shops at all the lodges which are also the best places to get film, postcards and the like. The town boasts a butcher, a number of small general stores, a book store and an electrical shop that stocks a wide range of household goods. Fresh supplies are available from Chobe farms. Petrol is available in Kasane and Kazungula; spares and tyres can be obtained from the petrol station and Chobe Engineering, although not in good supply. Vehicle repairs are undertaken at Chobe Engineering. There is a bank and a hospital, but no pharmacy or vet.

Interesting places to visit include:

The Kasane rapids and Commissioner's Kop, an isolated hill next to Cresta Mowana Lodge are worth a visit and are pleasant picnic spots. Here, for a few kilometres, the Chobe River winds its way picturesquely around small islands as it bubbles over the boulders that attempt to block its path. A wealth of bird life inhabits this area (see *Serondela*, page 107). The

Botswana Defence Force currently patrol this region because the rapids provide easy access to and from Namibia.

The Seep is the local name for some hot springs near Kazungula. It was purportedly tested and found to be rich in mineral properties, but the area has never been developed.

The Chobe Reptile Park, which offers guided tours at 09h00, 11h00, 14h00 and 16h00 is situated at Kazungula next to Kubu Lodge and is signposted. The park is owned and run by Mike Slogrove who claims to have the largest captive crocodile in the world, called Nelson. There is a look-out over one of the ponds and breeding pens. Booking is not necessary and an entrance fee is charged.

An old hollow baobab at the women's prison in the centre of town was used as that institution's kitchen until a few years ago. The heat from the fires have all but destroyed the plant. Behind this tree is another baobab of equal size which was used, until recently, to detain prisoners – usually not more that two at a time were accommodated under its leafy boughs. No photographs are allowed here.

BELOW: *Nelson, considered the largest crocodile in captivity in the world.*
ABOVE RIGHT: *Shops outside Chobe Safari Lodge.*
BELOW RIGHT: *Chobe game scouts camp.*

A 20-minute scenic flight (by single-engined aircraft or helicopter) over the system of floodplains and channels of the Chobe River is an excellent way to get a bird's eye view of the area. The flight includes game viewing over Sedudu Island and valley, then follows the river east towards Zimbabwe, past the Kasane rapids and Commissioner's Kop to the confluence with the Zambezi where the Caprivi Strip (by way of Mpalila Island) protrudes into the wide current. After a glance at the 4-country border post (not physically discernible) and the Kazungula ferry the flight turns around at the Katambora rapids on the Zambezi river, follows the ridge with its teak forests and baobabs back to Kasane airport. Longer trips or transfers that encompass the Zambezi River, a 'Flight of the Angels' over Victoria Falls and landing at either Livingstone or Victoria Falls airport may also be arranged.

Because it borders on Zimbabwe, Zambia and the Caprivi Strip in Namibia, Kasane is a popular base for short excursions into these areas. There are daily UTC (United Touring Company, based in Victoria Falls, Zimbabwe) and Hertz transfers between Kasane and Victoria Falls. Hertz and Avis Car Hire are very conveniently situated in Kasane for those who prefer to drive themselves. Air transfers by plane or helicopter can also be arranged.

Victoria Falls, Zimbabwe Victoria Falls is only 80 kilometres from Kasane. Guided and unguided tours of the falls and the rain forest, 'Flight of the Angels' (a short flight over the falls), tribal dancing, white-water rafting, canoeing, horse-riding, cycling along the Zambezi River, gambling sunset cruises on the Zambezi, game viewing and bird-watching, fishing, golf, squash and tennis are some of the activities available. Places of interest to visit include Livingstone's statue, the big baobab, the crocodile farm, the snake park and the Zambezi National Park. The small town at the falls is a shopper's delight, offering hours of browsing at the curio market and the many curio shops. There are seven hotels and two campsites (with chalets) in town, as well as campsites and chalets in the park. A tourist information centre is located in town. For further details, write to the Zimbabwe Tourism Development Corporation, Box 103, Victoria Falls; Tel/fax: (263) 134-376380.

Livingstone and Victoria Falls, Zambia Cross the Zambezi at Kazungula border by ferry. Livingstone is only 60 kilometres away and offers a different perspective of Victoria Falls. On offer are white-water rafting, sundowner cruises on the Zambezi, canoeing, unguided tours of the falls and the Knife-edge footbridge, cultural dances at the traditional village, game viewing and bird-watching, golf and fishing. Places of interest to visit include the railway museum, the Livingstone museum, the cemetery of early European settlers, the Mosi-oa-tunya zoological park as well as curio shops and markets. There are seven hotels (of widely varying quality) and two campsites. For details, contact the Zambian National Tourist Board Box 60342 Livingstone; Tel: (260) 33-321404.

Eastern Caprivi and Katima Mulilo, Namibia Cross the border at Ngoma Bridge and travel for 60 kilometres to Katima Mulilo, the main town of the area. In stark contrast to the rest of Namibia, Eastern Caprivi is an area of rivers, forests, swamps and waterways. It is a new destination for travellers as it was considered unsafe during the guerilla war which culminated in independence for Namibia in 1990. The Zambezi River is an angler's paradise, with the ferocious tigerfish being the main attraction. On offer are game viewing and bird-watching, walking, canoeing, boating and cruises. There are three lodges in the Eastern Caprivi and the exquisite Zambezi Queen Luxury Boat is moored on the Chobe River opposite Kasane. A new fishing camp, Ichingo, is situated at the Kasane rapids on Mpalila Island. Two lodges, chalets and campsites are available. Campsites and chalets are available at Katima Mulilo.

Other attractions include the Caprivi Art Centre and a floating bar. For further information, contact The Directorate of Nature Conservation, Private Bag 13267, Windhoek, Namibia; Tel: (61) 3-6975.

Visitors enjoy a spectcular sunset from the Mosi-oa-tunya barge.
RIGHT: *The awe-inspiring Victoria Falls.*

SERONDELA

Serondela is the northernmost part of Chobe National Park, wedged between the Chobe River (which joins the Zambezi at Kazungula) and the east-west road that runs between Ngoma entrance gate and Kazungula, and only 15 kilometres from Kasane. As part of the traditional safari route from Maun to Victoria Falls, Serondela is extremely popular because of its beauty and vast concentrations of game that come down to drink at the Chobe River during the dry season. Northern Chobe is well known for its huge herds of elephant and buffalo, making it one of the prime game areas in Africa. It is also regarded as one of the best birding sites in the country.

GETTING THERE

By air
Situated outside the park, nearby Kasane has an airport capable of accommodating international flights. At present it is serviced by Air Botswana, which provides connecting flights from Johannesburg, Gaborone, Victoria Falls and Windhoek, all via Maun. Charter flights to tourist destinations in the Okavango, Savuti, Maun and Linyanti also depart from Kasane. Courtesy transport to the park or lodges must be pre-arranged, as there are no public transport facilities to the airport and Kasane itself is some 4 kilometres away.

By road
Kasane is accessible by tarred road from South Africa via Francistown; from Zimbabwe via Francistown or Victoria Falls, from Zambia via Livingstone and from Namibia via Ngoma Gate and the Caprivi Strip. A graded gravel road from Katima Mulilo in Namibia is suitable for two-wheel drive vehicles. Daily bus transfer services are operated by the United Touring Company and Gametrackers Zimbabwe between Victoria Falls and Kasane.

The Kazungula ferry transports vehicles between Zambia and Botswana.

The Kazungula border post is situated on the convergence of four countries, namely Botswana, Zimbabwe, Zambia and Namibia (which is not accessible from this border post), and at the confluence of the Chobe River with the Zambezi (see page 178 for opening hours). A 40-tonne ferry carts vehicles and trucks between Botswana and Zambia – one at a time. Delays are frequent, but this is worth seeing as plans are in the pipeline to build a bridge which will replace this antiquated system. You are required to pay the ferry fees in Botswana Pula, South African Rands or US Dollars. Visas are obtainable from Zambian Immigration.

Kasane is also accessible from Maun via Nata on a 600-kilometre stretch of tarred road that crosses the Makgadikgadi and Nxai Pans National Park and cuts through the agricultural fields of Pandamatenga and the beautiful thickly-wooded Sibuyu, Kazuma and Kasane forest reserves where elephants are often spotted. It can also be reached via Savuti on a dirt road that definitely requires four-wheel drive and the distance takes between ten and twelve hours to cover, depending on road conditions. The park boundary is right on the edge of Kasane, but the entrance gate is situated some two kilometres further upstream.

WHAT TO SEE AND DO

The ruins at the eastern side (downstream) of the Serondela campsite are the remains of a village that grew around a veterinary control camp during the 1930s. It increased in size as a result of a timber mill and rice paddy being established in the early 1950s. Both these projects had failed by the late 1950s and everyone moved away, except for Pop Lamont (an early game ranger who had come to work on the timber mill), who remained as caretaker in the hope that the mill would be resurrected. When Chobe was proclaimed a national park in 1968, Pop Lamont refused, at gun point, to be moved. He was permitted to see out his last days in his house on the Chobe, the remains

of which are still visible near the campsite. He is buried at the Kolwezi look-out point.

The ridge towering over the southern riverbank once formed the shore of a mightier river and now offers a spectacular view across the Chobe and Zambezi flood plains.

Sedudu Island on the extreme north-east end of the park between the main entrance gate and Kasane, plays an important role in the ecology of the area. During the winter months, when there is precious little grazing for the enormous mass of animals using this strip of water, buffalo rely on the bountiful grasses of this island. At present, a dispute is being waged with Namibia over ownership of the island. Conservationists are concerned that if Namibia takes ownership, the buffalo will be driven from the island to make way for cattle.

Game viewing involves either driving along the river, or turning south towards the ridge onto one of the game-drive loops created by the Department of Wildlife. Drives along the river are generally at their best during the afternoon when the animals come down to drink, but it may well be worthwhile venturing into the hills if you find the river area quiet in the early mornings. These hills offer particularly attractive drives through the teak forests which, alone, make it a trip worth taking.

If you are prepared to put up with some discomfort from the heat, follow the river road all the way to Ngoma at midday, when many animal species such as sable, roan, kudu and zebra who normally drink in the heat of the day, may be seen. You may miss the spectacle by sticking to the normal safari routine of an afternoon siesta. Game viewing during the dry

View of the Chobe River system.

winter months can be rewarding along the river road towards Ngoma Gate.

At dawn, lions are often active on Watercart Drive, along Bushbuck or Moselesele Drive, or the main road from Chobe Game Lodge to Serondela campsite and on the old airstrip, so an early game drive is needed to find them on the move. Buffalo may often be seen early in the morning or late in the afternoon along the same section, and also on the floodplains beyond the campsite.

The Karozike Nkanga look-out point, situated above Kolwezi Valley just before the first turn into Bushbuck Drive, allows for outstanding pictures of the setting sun over the Chobe River. Many animals, especially elephant, baboon and buffalo normally come down Kolwezi Valley to the river front to slake their thirst in the last glimmers of daylight at what is known as Elephant Beach.

Scenic and game-viewing flights may be arranged through any of the lodges who will contact the charter companies in Kasane.

Wildlife

Serondela is best known for the huge concentration of elephant breeding herds that come down to the water, especially during winter. Sometimes over 300 elephants can be seen at a time – often right in the middle of the road. These herds are generally tolerant to the presence of vehicles, but you should still be cautious not to approach them too closely, especially if you are not accompanied by an experienced guide. If you do get trapped in a herd, wait patiently and quietly for the animals to move off. If you must move, then drive slowly and without fuss.

Large herds of buffalo winter along the Chobe River and attract lions as they move up and down the riverfront. Leopard occur along the river and are not infrequently seen. Regular sightings are made of lion, cheetah, sable and roan antelope, lechwe, kudu, giraffe, waterbuck, resident hippos, baboons, vervet monkeys, warthog and banded mongoose.

The shy Chobe bushbuck (*Tragelaphus scriptus* subsp. *ornatus*) is one of the three subspecies of bushbuck that occur in Southern Africa, its habitat ranging along the Zambezi Valley to Moçambique and further north. This is the most colourful of the three, being lighter red in general appearance with more white spots on the shoulders, rump and sides, and up to eight vertical white stripes down the flank and back. The pattern of spots and stripes is unique to each individual and may be used as an identification tool. As the name implies, they live in dense bush near water, but loss of habitat has seriously affected their numbers because of the destruction of the riverine moselesele bush by the elephants. However, they seem to have adapted and as a source of concealment and food, they are now making use of the woolly caper bush (*Capparis tomentosa*) and fever-berry which have become more abundant since the destruction of other plants. The bases of these shrubs support a rich variety of grasses, herbs, new shoots, fruits and seedpods, which may otherwise not have been available to the bushbuck. They are often seen along Bushbuck Drive, between Kasane and the main gate, in the campsite and from the water along the steep ridge. They are solitary animals, and are sometimes seen in pairs.

The southern bank of the Chobe, called Puku Flats, is the only place in southern Africa where puku may be found, although they are widely distributed in the wetter areas of central Africa. They occur on the dry fringes of swampland and rivers and are never far away from water. This antelope is slightly smaller and stouter in general appearance than the impala but lacks the impala's black leg, facial markings and bushy tail, and its horns are much shorter and curved inward. Only the males have horns, which are heavily notched like those of

the lechwe. They are easily mistaken for impala or lechwe with whom they often associate. Like the lechwe, sitatunga, reedbuck and waterbuck, they have an oily, waterproof coat which also gives them a strong scent and allows them to live in an aquatic environment. They are active at sunrise and sunset, and normally spend the rest of the day lying in the shade. Calves are born in winter and soon left on their own while the females go grazing, as the mother-calf bond is not very strong.

Oribi and Sharpe's grysbok may also be found inland. These very shy animals are seldom seen and are normally confused with steenbok or duiker.

Bird-watching

For anyone interested in bird watching, Serondela is a must – approximately 450 species have been recorded to date. This is due to the diversity of habitats ranging from floodplains to broadleafed woodland as well as the proximity to Zambia and Zimbabwe. The river attracts a wide variety of water birds, including storks, ducks and geese, waders, skimmers, terns and

LEFT: *Puku prefer grassy areas close to water.*
BELOW: *Deceptively benign-looking hippos wallow playfully in the Chobe River.*

kingfishers, including the giant. Raptors include the martial eagle, marsh harriers, gymnogenes and fish eagles. Away from the water, you will find the ground hornbill and marabou storks, along with a host of the smaller riverine and dry-land birds.

Vegetation

The vegetation in the Serondela region has suffered from serious overuse. If you are visiting during the winter months, you may be excused for believing that some massive natural disaster had recently befallen the area. Away from the river, the landscape is bleak with stunted, spindly shrubs and almost no grass cover. The taller trees and mixed deciduous forests have all but disappeared under pressure from the enormous bio-mass that is dependent on the river. This habitat destruction is used as a justification for introducing elephant culling, but the high number of elephant that would have to be killed and the long time span required for the forests to regenerate themselves would render culling impractical for this purpose.

The most conspicuous trees along the river are Natal mahogany trees (*Trichilia emetica*), with huge spreading dark green crowns that provide dense shade all year round. Pod mahogany (*Afzelia quanzensis*), with its flaky, grey-brown bark and thick, woody pods and red flowers, is fairly common. Also found are baobabs, the African star-chestnut (*Sterculia africana*) with blotchy pink and yellow bark often resembling a baobab in shape, the African mangosteen, the gardenia (*Gardenia volkensii*) carrying white and older yellow flowers both on one tree and the sweet-smelling shaving-brush combretum (*Combretum mossambicense*) with its pinkish-white pincushion flowers. Black monkey orange (*Strychnos madagascariensis*) grow along the ridge and are easily identified as the tall trees with many-stemmed grey trunks. The large blue-green fruits are sought after by baboons and kudu.

Moselesele Drive, a misnomer nowadays, was named after the sickle-bush, that provided valuable cover for the bushbuck and which had encroached on what used to be overgrazed cattle country. It has since been trimmed right back by elephants so that few are left today.

Zambezi teak grows along the ridge and the Kasane-Ngoma road and has attractive, mauve flowers and brown velvety buds.

The World of Water

Game viewing from the water provides visitors with a different perspective and should definitely be considered while you are in Serondela. The three largest lodges in the region offer both powerboats and barges for this purpose. The upper deck of a barge provides a height advantage for photography, while the smaller powerboats are more exclusive and manoeuvrable, often allowing you to get quite close to the animals.

Fishing

Serondela is well known for its fishing. There are designated fishing sites within the Chobe National Park and permits must be obtained from the main gate (outside the park, permits are not required). Boats may be hired on an hourly or on a daily basis for longer excursions. For variation, you may like to trawl for tiger fish from the barge. Tigerfish are considered by anglers to offer the most exciting sport fishing, pound for pound, of any freshwater fish. A number of species of bream, which make good eating, as well as catfish may be caught along the Chobe.

ACCOMMODATION
Chobe Chilwero

Situated high on the Chobe embankment, this comfortable lodge offers a superb view of the Chobe River and its floodplains. Although the lodge is situated just outside the national park, the absence of fences allows animals to ramble freely around the grounds. Highlights include boat trips on the river, giving visitors a chance to get close-up views of game and bird life.

Features:
- Accommodation in thatched A-frames
- *En suite* facilities • Gourmet dining
- Game drives

RARE BIRDS OF CHOBE

Longtoed Plover
This shy bird can be identified by the black crown as if it is wearing a black shawl draped around its head with only its white face and neck showing. Like the jacana, it has long toes to enable it to distribute its weight evenly when walking on floating vegetation, and can be seen along the banks of the Chobe River and on Sedudu Island.

Whitecrowned Plover
Pairs of these plovers may be seen along the shoreline of the Chobe River on Watercart Drive. They are identified by the long yellow lappets that hang from the base of the bill, the broad white stripe across the forehead and the white wing stripe between the brown back and black wing. They also occur along the Zambezi, Lake Kariba and other estuaries.

African Finfoot
The only place in Botswana where these shy and easily overlooked birds occur is at the rapids in Kasane. Easily mistaken for reed cormorants, they may be seen around the quiet backwaters close to the reedbanks of around Mpalila Island where they breed, and are distinguished by their red bills and stiff fan-shaped tail.

Rock Pratincole
These small grey birds with a white collar around the back of their heads may be seen in small flocks on the boulders on the fast-flowing channels around Kasane rapids where they have been recorded to nest.

Halfcollared Kingfisher
The only known place in Botswana where these brilliant blue, but inconspicuous kingfishers occur is again at Kasane rapids along the vegetated edges of the channels, where they can be seen perched on low branches or rocks overlooking the water.

Chobe Game Lodge
This luxurious hotel in the Chobe National Park offers guests a chance to experience the natural splendours of the area without foregoing any creature comforts. Activities in the area are varied and include game drives, birdwatching and fishing.
Features:
• Forty-five luxury rooms with overhead fans • Four suites each with private swimming pool • Conference centre
• Curio shop and wildlife reference library
• Sunset cruises on the Mosi-oa-tunya barge
  There are three other lodges in Kasane just outside the national park and all are suitable bases for daily trips into the park. See *Kasane*, page 117 for details.

Public campsite
Serondela's public campsite is picturesquely situated high on the banks of the Chobe River, some 15 kilometres from the main gate at Kasane. However, the soil is black, dirty and badly littered with devil thorns. Common pests include vervet monkeys and baboons. Any food which is left unattended, even briefly, is likely to disappear into the nearest tree, with no chance of retrieval. Banded mongoose, warthog and bushbuck are resident in the campsite, but none of them are a nuisance to man; however, you should not approach any wild animal.
Features:
• Four ablution blocks • Taps (stand pipes) in many camping sites • Hot showers possible, if you stoke the boilers yourself
• Wonderful sunset views over Chobe River

Other camps
Around Pop Lamont's house are three designated and private campsites only for use by *bona fide* tour operators who are *Hatab* members. These sites must be booked and paid for in advance.

  The game scout's camp is situated at the entrance gate, and park headquarters and the anti-poaching unit is situated on the park border in Kasane.

ABOVE: *Relaxed game viewing at Nogatsaa.*
RIGHT: *The Chobe River is renowned for its excellent tigerfishing.*

NOGATSAA AND TCHINGA

Seventy kilometres south of Serondela lies one of the most under-utilised and exciting game areas in the Chobe National Park, comprising a cluster of clay-bottomed pans that hold water well into winter. They are surrounded by a mixture of open grassland, mopane forest and mixed deciduous forests which attract a variety of animal life. This area has not yet been developed, hence visitors should be prepared to camp and must be fully self-sufficient.

GETTING THERE

By air
The airstrip at Nogatsaa was built for the Botswana Defence Force anti-poaching activities. However, as there are no facilities in the area, flying to Nogatsaa is pointless unless you have arranged for a vehicle to meet you.

By road
Nogatsaa is accessible from both Kasane and Savuti. The black cotton soil in the Nogatsaa/Tchinga area, when wet, is virtually im-

passable and it is advisable not to venture there during the wet season. From Kasane, there are two routes, although the eastern route from Sedudu Valley along the cut-line is not recommended, as it is very sandy. The more preferable route is from the Serondela campsite via Nantanga Pans. This 70-kilometre trip should take under three hours to complete and is signposted. A four-wheel drive is essential.

From Savuti a track heads south-east past Quarry Hill (the last hill you get to via Harvey's Pans). Follow this road for 120 kilometres as it traverses mopane scrub, mature mopane forest and then crosses the dry Ngwezumba riverbed, following it past many interesting pans and across a sandridge to the old Ngwezumba Dam. When the track joins a wide, graded road, you will be able to see the old dam to

The malachite kingfisher is often found near lagoons and streams.

your right. The road forks 2 kilometres beyond the dam wall. Take the right-hand fork; a few hundred metres further on, the road forks again. The left-hand fork takes you to Nogatsaa, while the right hand fork goes to Tchinga.

WHAT TO SEE AND DO

The road over the old Ngwezumba Dam was the original road from Kasane to Francistown. The dam was washed away by the drought-breaking rains of 1988. The bungalows at Nogatsaa were built by the Department of Wildlife and National Parks to provide accommodation for tourists, but were never put to use. Three of the four units were severely damaged in 1992 by elephants trying to reach the water in the bathrooms.

The Ngwezumba River has its origins in this region and by the time it reaches the old dam wall, it has carved a deep gorge for itself. The river is non-perennial and flows only after exceptionally heavy rainfall. These days it holds only a few pools of rain water that gather annually in the dry riverbed and attract game.

The most profitable way of spending your game-viewing time is perhaps to take an early game drive and then to select a waterhole and stay there while quietly watching the changing scene. You may watch from the comfort of a look-out hut at Nogatsaa (one of the few in Botswana), which is ideal for this kind of viewing – unfortunately the tree-house at Kwikampa has fallen into complete disrepair. Solar power is used at Nogatsaa Pan to pump water into the pan from underground resources.

Kwikampa is a large, natural pan situated midway between Nogatsaa and Tchinga. If the

rains are good, it can hold water through most of the dry season. Tchinga has a borehole pump and provides an excellent viewing hole, if water is available. The Ngwezumba River, and many of the nearby pans are worth a visit.

Wildlife

During winter, large numbers of elephant breeding herds congregate around the waterholes before disappearing back into the forests. This region has a great diversity of game and offers some of the best possibilities to see eland. Other species include oribi, sable, roan antelope, lion, leopard, cheetah, hyaena, giraffe, buffalo and zebra, reedbuck, impala, duiker and steenbok. This was a favourite area for white rhino, but due to intense poaching pressure, the last four rhinos were moved to the Khama Rhino Sanctuary at Serowe.

Bird-watching

Not noted as a prime birding area, it nevertheless offers good birding at certain times of year. Numerous water birds visit the pans after the rains. Different species of francolin, button quail and kingfisher abound. Vultures, eagles, ostrich and ground hornbills are some of the larger birds in the region. The woodland *en route* to Nogatsaa often reveals some insectivore species such as the longbilled crombec, fantailed flycatcher, goldenbreasted bunting and cardinal woodpecker, among others.

Vegetation

The vegetation is dominated by mixed deciduous and mopane forests and the open grass plains around Nogatsaa. Commonly seen in flower in this area is the white bauhinia or coffee-bean bush (*Bauhinia petersiana*). The red cat's claws or cat's whiskers (*Clerodendrum uncinatum*) with their delicate red flowers and yellow 'whiskers' which is often the only bush to provide any colour in winter, commonly grow on the thick reddish-yellow soils. There are some baobabs in the area, including one

ABOVE TOP: *Elephant and eland at Kwikampa.*
ABOVE TOP RIGHT: *White rhino at Nogatsaa.*
ABOVE: *The distinctively marked Arnot's chat.*
ABOVE RIGHT: *The delicate white flower of the coffee bean.*

that has fallen and is slowly decomposing just south of Tchinga.

On the deep Kalahari sand you find silver terminalia and the shrubby jasmine pea (MI-*Baphia massaiensis* subsp. *obovata*), which forms a major part of the elephant's diet. It has large dull green leaves that often fold inwards, beautiful sprays of white flowers smelling like jasmine and long narrow woody pods.

ACCOMMODATION
There are no lodges in the Nogatsaa/Tchinga region, the nearest being at Kasane.

Public campsites
Camping is permitted at Nogatsaa, although there is no designated camping area. With a look-out platform and bungalows, it has the potential to become one of the finest camps in the country. However, in the past it has suffered from undisciplined, noisy game scouts, military activity, a lack of mainten-ance, elephant damage to the buildings, an unfortunate positioning of the airstrip and a BDF (Botswana Defence Force) soccer field, which spoils wildlife photographs and restricts the major approach to the pan for the animals. If promises to rectify these shortcomings are kept, Nogatsaa will once again become a worthwhile option. Check before setting out that the solar water pump is operating.
Features:
• Shower and toilet • Water tap
• Look-out over pan

Tchinga
Apart from the diesel pump supplying the pan with water, there are no facilities at Tchinga. There are also no shady trees under which to camp. Do not camp right next to the pan, as you will prevent the animals from drinking. You need to be fully self-contained to camp here.
Features:
• No facilities provided. This makes for a total wilderness experience.

ADVISORY:CHOBE NATIONAL PARK

CLIMATE

Chobe has a long, dry winter, with little or no rain from May to October. The heaviest rainfall months are from December to February.

Savuti is a place of climatic extremes. Far from the moderating influence of the Okavango, early morning game drives in winter may be bitterly cold, while the afternoons of the same day may be uncomfortably hot. The months before the rains, September to November, are generally extremely hot.

Nogatsaa and Tchinga sometimes experience unpleasantly strong and persistent winds, particularly in August and September.

BEST TIMES TO VISIT

In Chobe National Park, as in Moremi, the game viewing improves as the rain-filled pans dry up and game comes to the permanent water sources. Game is attracted to the artificial waterholes in winter.

August to October are considered optimal. However, the later in the year you visit, the greater the chances of early rains spoiling your viewing.

November is very hot and dry, and not a popular time with tourists. However, if the rains are late, game viewing around the waterholes can be superb.

December to February are the wet months, when game disperses and the roads may become impassable. Note that although the park is open all year, the Mababe Depression and Savuti Channel area may be closed during the rainy season (normally from 1 December to 31 March). Only for the adventurous who like to be alone. Some lodges may be closed for annual leave and renovations during the rainy season.

March to July offer good game with fewer people around. Vegetation is green, in contrast to the much drier, later months.

MAIN ATTRACTIONS

Chobe is renowned for its superb wildlife. During winter large herds of elephant and buffalo can be seen at Savuti, and the area is renowned for its predators, especially its lion population. The fairly rare puku and the Chobe bushbuck occur here. Thousands of zebra migrate south from the Linyanti/Chobe region to Savuti between November and December, and then return north to the Linyanti region between February and April.

Bird life is spectacular, especially around the northern wetlands – some 460 species have been identified. The birding at Chobe is at its best from October to March, when the migrants are there.

The papyrus-lined waterways of Linyanti are reminiscent of the Okavango Delta.

TRAVEL

Kasane is easily accessible by road from the southeast, from Livingstone in Zambia and from Victoria Falls in Zimbabwe. It can also be reached by air, either on a scheduled flight or by charter aircraft. There are landing strips at Linyanti and Savuti.

A four-wheel drive vehicle is recommended for touring in the park. Petrol and ice are only available in Maun and Kasane. Limited dry foodstuffs and drinks can also be bought in Kachikau and Kavimba.

Because of the park's proximity to Zimbabwe, many visitors incorporate a visit to Victoria Falls (70 kilometres due east of the park) into their itinerary.

ACCOMMODATION

Below is a brief summary that lists all accommodation included in the Chobe section of this guide. For a more detailed description of each establishment, refer to the page numbers indicated.

Savuti (see pages 99 to 100)

Allan's Camp Overlooking the Savuti Channel. Accommodation in reed and wooden chalets. Excellent birding (some 350 species have been identified) and game-viewing drives. Gametrackers, PO Box 786 432, Sandton 2146, South Africa; Tel: (011) 884-2504; Fax: (011) 884-3159.

Lloyd's Camp Luxury tented camp, known for its very early game drives which sometimes start before dawn. Superb game viewing from hide overlooking the camp's small waterhole. Lloyd Wilmot Safaris, PO Box 37, Maun; Tel: 660-351; Fax: 660-571; Telex: 2612 BD; or PO Box 645, Bedfordview 2008, South Africa; Tel: (011) 453-7649; Fax: (011) 453-7646.

Savuti South Sister to Allan's Camp – guests often stay a couple of days at each establishment. Accommodation in Meru-style tents. Excellent game viewing in the area. Gametrackers, PO Box 786432, Sandton 2146, South Africa; Tel: (011) 884-2504; Fax: (011) 884-3159.

Campsites All public campsites within Chobe National Park are under the jurisdiction of the Department of Wildlife and National Parks, PO Box 131, Gaborone; Tel: 371-405. Advance bookings cannot be made for any of these campsites nor is there any control over the number of people using them at any one time, which sometimes leads to overcrowding at peak periods.

Savuti Campsite offers three ablution blocks and water taps at most camping spots.

Linyanti (see pages 103 to 104)

James' Camp Operates as a tourist lodge from October to March each year. Because of its isolated location, this luxurious tented camp offers visitors a real wilderness experience. Activities available include barge trips on the Kwando River, game drives and walks, and fishing. PO Box 119, Maun; Tel: 660-383; Fax: 660-593.

King's Pool Overlooking a lovely, picturesque pool, this camp offers accommodation in Meru tents. No permanent guides work at the camp, so guests are advised to hire a guide or be willing to conduct their own game- viewing excursions. PO Box 11, Kasane; Tel/Fax: 605-385.

Linyanti Camp Located on the banks of the Linyanti River. Guests are accommodated in Meru tents. Activities include game drives and cruises on the camp's barge. Hunters Africa, Box 11, Kasane; Tel: 650-385; Fax: 650-383.

Selinda Camp Eight-bedded luxury tented camp on the Selinda spillway. Ideal for small groups. Night drives and game walks on offer. Hunters Africa, PO Box 11, Kasane; Tel: 650-385; Fax: 650-383.

Campsites There is a campsite at Linyanti which features well-maintained ablutions, ample shade and a water tap.

Kasane

Chobe Safari Lodge A long-established hotel situated on the border of Chobe National Park overlooking the Chobe River. An excellent tigerfishing spot in spring and early summer. Hotel is currently being modernised. Features rooms (some with *en suite* bathroom and overhead fans) and thatched rondavels, a restaurant and bar, swimming pool, curio shop, bottle store, floodlit volleyball court and courtesy transport. Boat and barge trips into the national park, game drives and fishing can be organised. PO Box 10, Kasane; Tel: 650-336; Fax: 650-437.

Cresta Mowana Lodge A new up-market lodge situated on the Chobe River, approximately 5 kilometres out of town. Offers 111 rooms each overlooking the river with *en suite* bathroom, air conditioning, telephone, overhead fan, hair-dryer and refrigerator. Has facilities for the disabled. Amenities include an à la carte restaurant and buffet, bar, swimming pool, bank and conference facilities. Game drives, car hire, helicopter flights, boating, fishing and barge trips can be arranged. Cresta Hotels, PO Box 200, Gaborone; Tel: 353-631; Fax: 351-840; Telex: 2801 BD.

Kubu Lodge Elevated Swiss-style wooden chalets at Kazungula, 12 kilometres east of Kasane. A split-level restaurant/bar overlooking the river affords wonderful sunset views. Has 11 chalets, each with *en suite* facilities, overhead fan, hair-dryer and a view of the river and Mpalila Island in Namibia, restaurant with excellent food (must be booked in advance), a bar, swimming pool, curio shop and courtesy transport. Boating, fishing (tackle provided) and game drives on offer. Border Investments, PO Box 43, Kasane; Tel: 650-312; Fax: 650-412.

Campsites

Chobe Safari Lodge Next to the Chobe National Park and within walking distance of the shops, bottle store, bank, post office and government offices. Offers ablution facilities, shaded and grassy camping spots overlooking the river, tap stands and wash basins, and electric points. Petrol is available and

fishing, boating and other activities can be organised. PO Box 10, Kasane; Tel: 650-336; Fax: 650-437.

Audi Lodge Situated at Kazungula some 12 kilometres from Kasane. Has camping spots overlooking the river (shady in summer, but trees lose their leaves in winter), budget A-frame chalets, ablution facilities, individual electric points and lights, tap stands and wash basins and laundry facilities. Fishing, boating and game drives available. Border Investments, PO Box 43, Kasane; Tel: 650-312; Fax: 650-412.

Ngoma Campsite A new campsite set on the ridge overlooking the Chobe valley, less than one kilometre from the Ngoma Gate and due to open soon. It is sign-posted. PO Box 55, Kasane; Tel: 650-430; Fax: 650-223.

Serondela (see pages 111 to 113)

Chobe Chilwero Perched on a hill overlooking the Chobe River, this luxurious lodge accommodates a maximum of 16 guests at any one time. River cruises and game drives can be enjoyed. Linyanti Explorations, PO Box 22, Kasane; Tel: 650-352; Fax: 250-352; Telex :2901 BD.

Chobe Game Lodge An exclusive resort hotel located within the national park. Excellent facilities on site, and a wide range of activities – including sunset cruises and game drives – available. PO Box 2602, Halfway House 1685, South Africa; Tel: (011) 315-1695/6/7; Fax: (011) 805-2882.

Public campsite Located some 15 kilometres from the main park gate, this campsite provides four ablution blocks, taps and hot showesrs if you are prepared to stoke the boilers yourself.

Nogatsaa and Tchinga (see pages 115)

Nogatsaa Although there is no designated camping area, a shower and toilet, a water tap and a lookout over the pan are available.

Tchinga Camping is permitted here, but there are no facilities provided so campers must be fully self-sufficient.

HEALTH HAZARDS

Take precautions against malaria. Beware of crocodiles and other potentially dangerous animals.

ANNUAL EVENTS

The zebra migration in November and December from the Linyanti/Chobe area south to Savuti, then back again between February and April.

MAKGADIKGADI AND NXAI PAN NATIONAL PARK

Three hundred kilometres south of Chobe National Park, near the eastern boundary with Zimbabwe, lies the wide expanse of the Makgadikgadi salt pans. Covering 12 000 square kilometres, it dwarfs Namibia's famed Etosha Pan which is only 4 500 square kilometres, and is the largest salt pan in the world. The Makgadikgadi consists of two major pans: Sowa (meaning 'salt' in one of the San languages) and Ntwetwe, plus a scattering of smaller pans. Nxai Pan was once part of Lake Makgadikgadi, but when the lake dried up it became one of the smaller, isolated lakes left behind. These pans used to be protected as separate entities, but in late 1993 Makgadikgadi Game Reserve and Nxai Pan National Park were amalgamated to form the new Makgadikgadi and Nxai Pan National Park, which covers an area of more than 5 500 square kilometres.

Much evidence of the changes to Botswana's water systems over the millennia are buried under the sands of the Kalahari. These pans were once a huge lake, thought to have been filled by the Zambezi, Okavango and Chobe rivers. At its largest, Lake Makgadikgadi used to cover an enormous 80 000 square kilometres with a depth of up to 30 metres. The formation of various faults diverted rivers, contributing to the drying-up process, and gradually the lake began to shrink. In addition, climatic changes have led to a drier and warmer period, and today the only body of water to remain from this once mighty lake is the Okavango Delta.

NATA

Situated on the Nata River, this little village is at the crossroads to Kasane and Maun. It is an ideal stop-over *en route* to the Okavango and the reserves in the north, Victoria Falls and

Lioness with giraffes on the semi-arid grassy plains of Nxai Pan.

Hwange National Park in Zimbabwe and even to the Caprivi and Zambia. It is here, after crossing the single-lane bridge, that the wide open spaces of Botswana are encountered for the first time.

Nata's two lodges are popular among visitors to the pans and offer comfortable accommodation (see page 133). Shopping facilities are basic, although there is a butcher with the unlikely name of Nata Wild Beasts. A new take-away provides a good range of palatable meals. Take-aways are also available from Nata Lodge. There is a mechanic at Nata, but spare parts are not readily available. There are no banking facilities but the village does have a new post office.

The Nata area is cattle-farming country, so do not expect concentrations of game here. The occasional black-backed jackal and springbok may be seen.

A nature sanctuary on the Sowa Pan, established by a committee in Nata village, may be found some 20 kilometres out of town on the Francistown road. Bird life can be spectacular when the pan fills with water.

The western section of Ntwetwe Pan falls within the Makgadikgadi section of the national park (see page 123). Sowa Pan in the east and the larger part of the eastern section of Ntwetwe Pan fall outside the park's boundaries and are open to the public, with the following places of interest in the area:

Sowa Pan

Sowa's barren surface, covering an area of approximately 50 by 100 kilometres, is made up of hard, salt-saturated clay and has its own unique, harsh beauty. A steep escarpment of white calcrete runs along the south-eastern shore of the pans and rises, in places, between 70 and 100 metres above the surface. Here geologists have discovered beaches of rolled quartz that mark the perimeter of the ancient Lake Makgadikgadi, which can be found as high as 20 metres up the cliffs. The beaches, sand spits and white cliffs in this area are reminiscent of a coastal resort, but notably absent is the sound of the rolling breakers.

ABOVE TOP: *Ancient stone walls – remnants of a 'lost city', on Kube Island.*
ABOVE: *The appropriately named Wild Beasts butchery in Nata.*
RIGHT: *Hand-operated petrol pump in Nata.*

Kube Island

On the western side of Sowa Pan is Kube Island, situated on a low and narrow treeless peninsula of grass, the Sowa Spit, that separates Sowa and Ntwetwe pans, and accessible from a road that bisects the two major pans. It can be reached from the old Maun/Nata road via Zoroga and isolated cattle posts or the Francistown/Orapa road, by taking the road via Tlhalamabele veterinary fence where you turn right to Mosu and Mmatshumo. There you descend the escarpment and follow the main tracks heading for the village of Thabatshukulu north of Mmatshumo, until you reach a cairn on the road where you turn right and proceed for 16 kilometres to Kube Island.

This small, rocky island with its huge natural monoliths of granitic boulders deeply fissured by the roots of baobabs, is set in the infinite whiteness of Sowa Pan, and has a history that remains a secret and an aura that defies description. The origin of the low crescent-shaped stone wall on Kube is unknown. It may represent the furthest extension to the

An observation platform at Sua offers visitors a vantage point for viewing game.

west of the Great Zimbabwe Tradition – the powerful dynasty of ancient Zimbabwe to which the famous Zimbabwe ruins are accredited. Neither the pottery shards nor the San ostrich shells left behind have solved the mystery yet as to who lived here and what lifestyle they followed – were they fishermen or hunters? (It is an offence to remove any artefacts as this is a national monument.)

Nata Bird Sanctuary

As a result of the development of the soda ash plant at Sua Town and concern for the negative impact this could have on sensitive areas at Sowa Pan, a sanctuary has been created in the extreme north-east of the pan. This includes the mouth of the Nata River and is designed to shield the flocks of flamingoes that are attracted to this part of the Makgadikgadi Pans when the river flows temporarily. Access is through the new, thatched gateway, 20 kilometres south of Nata Lodge. Near the gate, you will see the famous old baobab that toppled in 1992 and that had previously been used as shelter by many travellers. A wooden look-out affords you a vista over the pan and its extremely beautiful sunsets.

Eastern Ntwetwe Pan

The main roads of Nata to Maun and Nata to Francistown flank the two sections of the fossil lake bed of Makgadikgadi. When dry, which is most of the time, it is 6 500 square kilometres of flat, soda-encrusted surface, overlying treacherous mud. A close-up inspection will reveal a mixture of saline silt and clay, sun-dried and cracked into miniature waves, suspended in time on an ageless beach. Surrealistic mirages of ostrich, springbok and cattle dance on elongated legs – their tracks in the white sand the only proof that you are not dreaming. For a magical journey into a special place, the pans are at their best when they are flooded – never more than calf deep, with water extending to the horizon like a giant mirror. Driving on the pans during the dry season is an unforgettable experience, with the sound of the tyres breaking through the thin salt crust, like soft rain on a tin roof, while the horizon never seems to get any closer. For the ultimate experience visit the pans either at full moon when you can see the sun setting in the far distant west and the moon rising simultaneously in the east; or at new moon when the stars are so bright and seem so close that, according to San folklore, you can hear them whisper to each other.

To access the Pan, take the old Nata/Maun road at Zoroga which cuts across the narrow top of Ntwetwe Pan, approximately 70 kilometres past Nata. You may pull off the road there onto the pan, or follow the old traders' route via Gweta.

Gweta

Gateway to the Makgadikgadi Pan, this attractive village halfway between Nata and Maun, is set amidst mopane and combretum woodland, massive sprawling marula trees, African star chestnut or tick trees and baobabs. During the rainy season this flat calcrete-littered countryside is turned into a massive shallow lake. Small wonder it is named Gweta which means 'place where the big frogs meet'. These bullfrogs (*Pyxicephalus adspersus*) bury themselves in the sand and appear miraculously, in their hundreds, once the rains have provided sufficient surface water.

As Paul Augustinus put it: 'Gweta is nothing special … except that it lies on the edge of beyond … where the scent of freedom is almost intoxicating …' (*Botswana, Brush with the Wild*, Augustinus. Southern Books, 1988.) Horse trails, vehicle and four-wheeler bike excursions to the pans can be arranged through Gweta Rest Camp.

Basic supplies, fuel, ice, bread, as well as a post office with a telephone, are available in town. For details on accommodation, see *Advisory*, page 133.

Green's Baobabs

Situated near Gutsha Pan south of Gweta, Green's Baobabs are of historical importance. The major trading route across the pans to Linyanti ran right through the middle of Ntwetwe Pan. On the northern side of the crossing is a small rocky depression, cut deeply into calcrete that in the past held perennial water. All the hunters, traders, missionaries and adventurers used this route as they had to cross the pan at night to avoid the scorching heat reflecting off the white sand, and to reach the water source by morning.

Close to the pan is the smaller of the two baobabs. It is inscribed with the legend, 'Green's expedition', carved in 1852 by the

Green brothers, Frederick and Charles, who were among the earliest explorers and hunters to visit the area. Names and inscriptions have since been somewhat distorted by the tree's growth, but one can still make out some of them. Hendrik van Zyl, the first Ghanzi settler, also carved his name in 1851, the year David Livingstone first travelled this route. Natal hunter, Fred Drake, crossed here regularly between 1873 and 1879.

Seven kilometres further south-east, you will find the second baobab, which still stands as a beacon of hope in the monotonous waste of salt. Many early travellers have left their inscriptions on its broad trunk: the missionaries, Roger Price and Hellmore (1859), James Chapman, who accompanied Thomas Baines to Victoria Falls (1862), the German naturalist, Oswald Bager (1870), and the hunter/trader, J. Jolley (1875).

Bushman Pits

Between the sandridge and Phuduhudu village, on the original Nata-Maun road is a place where the San used to dig for water in the limestone. Today there are only ruins of an extensive cattle post, remains of the Colonial Development Corporation houses and some huge shady trees to camp under.

Large herds of zebra and wildebeest dot the Makgadikgadi plains when the pans hold water, but later on they move toward the river, often leaving the national park for the sanctuary of the wooded area around Bushman Pits where they are generally under less pressure from hunters.

Motopi

This scenic village, situated on the Boteti River about 70 kilometres east of Maun, offers pleasant picnic spots under huge leadwoods with beautiful views of the river. Motopi is the Tawana name for the locally abundant tree, the shepherd's tree (*Boscia albitrunca*).

ABOVE: *Children queuing for water in Gweta.* BELOW: *Green's Baobabs, inscribed with the names of many famous hunters and explorers.*

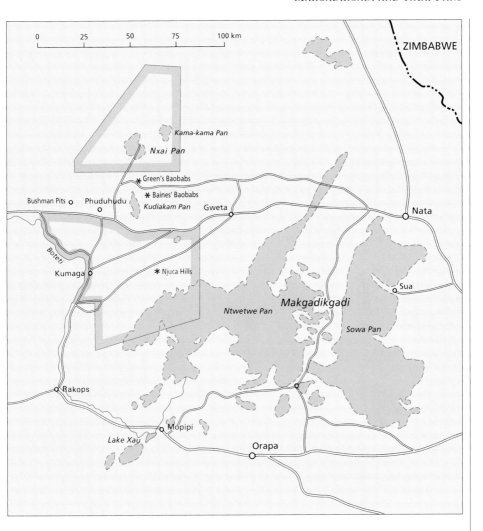

MAKGADIKGADI PANS AREA

The Makgadikgadi Pans area of the national park is situated almost midway between Maun and Nata (158 kilometres from Maun). It includes parts of western Ntwetwe Pan and the area just west of it as far as the Boteti River, which forms the western boundary. Its northern boundary is now adjacent to Nxai Pan, so that the Maun-Nata road separates the two areas of the park. Comprising only 2 500 square kilometres, this section of the national park is relatively small but contains diverse and unique habitats.

Most striking are the salt pans in the southwestern sector of the national park. Clusters of small pans give way to the main Ntwetwe Pan, the larger of the two salt pans that constitute the Makgadikgadi.

Surrounding the pans is flat, open grassland, where the horizon is at eye level in every direction. On the eastern side, the tall grasses are broken by stands of vegetable ivory palms that give the illusion of a tropical island paradise. Further west, the grasslands give way to

123

harsh scrubland, making a formidable and in-hospitable land, which is suddenly broken by dense riverine forest. Beyond lies the Boteti River, the last reach of the Okavango, fringed by phragmites.

GETTING THERE

By air

The only airstrip in the national park is located between the two campsites. As it is a long way from the nearest human habitation, do not try to land there without having organised someone to meet you. Motopi airstrip near the main road, and about 20 kilometres from the western boundary of the reserve, may also be used for access as may Gweta airstrip, 16 kilometres from the eastern boundary.

By road

Travelling along the Maun/Nata road, take the signposted turn-off to the park. The game

BELOW: *Game tracks on the Makgadikgadi Pan.*
ABOVE RIGHT: *Gemsbok and springbok spoor.*
BELOW RIGHT: *On safari in the Makgadikgadi.*

scouts' camp is situated on the old road and it is there that you must pay your park fees before continuing into the park.

From Motopi take the old Nata road east. Eighteen kilometres further on, you will find an oblique turn-off to your right. Nine kilometres down this road, you will come to crossroads. Turn left and follow this road along the Boteti River for 55 kilometres to Kumaga. This is an interesting road, both scenically and in terms of game viewing, but it is very sandy and progress will be slow. A four-wheel drive is essential and three hours should be allowed to travel this section from the main road.

A more direct route is to continue for 6 kilometres beyond Phuduhudu (6 kilometres west of the Nxai Pan turn-off, if you are on the old road), past the turn-off described above. Take the signposted turn to Kumaga for 39 kilometres to camp. Once again, a four-wheel drive is required.

Petrol and supplies are available from Gweta and supplies are obtainable at Mopipi. Basic foodstuffs are available from the village of Kumaga.

WHAT TO SEE AND DO
Western Ntwetwe Pan

The salt pans within this part of the park offer an experience that is totally unique. It is extremely difficult to describe the sense of awe and wonder one experiences in this vast, flat, empty land. Here, nothing grows, nothing but the wind moves, and the land, sky and horizon blur into each other. The illusion of water is everywhere – mirages dance in a heat haze that reflects the sky back upon itself. The knowledge that death would be certain, but for your vehicle, is a constant companion. Yet, leading off into the distance are the mud-encrusted tracks of a hartebeest or a group of zebra.

For a day trip to the Ntwetwe Pans, take the road to the eastern boundary and then turn south. Either take the boundary road onto the pans, or the first road on the right, which leads through some fine country with palms, pans and tall grasses, before it becomes increasingly remote, finally bringing you onto the end of the vast Ntwetwe Pan and, from there, to the southern boundary of the park. Turn right and take the route back to the west, which passes through grassland – there are good prospects of seeing game in this area.

Or if you want to see more of the pans, follow the eastern boundary road back to camp. If you choose this route, be extremely careful not to lose the road or miss the turn at the south-east corner; this is probably the wildest, most empty land you will ever have the privilege to experience.

The Boteti River

Water leaving the Okavango flows through Maun and then heads down the Boteti River, before eventually emptying into the southern Ntwetwe Pan. The banks of the Boteti are steep and offer fine views of the river. As the winter lengthens and the pans begin to dry up, animals are forced to come to the river to drink, so game viewing along this section can be extremely rewarding.

At the Kumaga campsite, which is situated on the Boteti River, you will find a wooden look-out affording a view of the river, while the Njuca Hills are a look-out point in themselves. It is unfortunate that the roads in the park have not been developed with game drives in mind. There are no convenient loops from either of the campsites, which means embarking on very long drives around the park or back-tracking. From Kumaga there are three directions in which to go for short drives. North or south along the river, or east into the park. You are more likely to see game if you choose one of the routes along the river.

DRIVING ON THE SALT PANS

- Let someone know where you are going.
- Take your compass, food and water, vehicle spares and tools, sand mats and a high lift jack.
- **Do not travel on the pans during or shortly after rain**; the crust becomes softened and a vehicle can get irretrievably bogged down, even to the point that it will be sucked down by the deep, saline muds until it eventually vanishes from sight.
- At all times of the year, avoid dark patches on the pans as they are indications of wetter soil.
- Do not stop on the pans unless you are absolutely certain that the crust is strong enough to support the vehicle's weight. If you do stop, check from time to time that the vehicle is not slowly breaking the crust. If the vehicle is settling at all, move immediately.
- Owing to the absence of prominent landmarks, the flat terrain and tracks criss-crossing the area, there is a very real danger of getting lost.
- Dust storms can obliterate your view.
- A four-wheel drive vehicle is essential as some tracks are very sandy and the margins around the pans are often constituted by the powdery black cotton soil that becomes very sticky when wet. It can render areas impassable for weeks at a time for even the most rugged of vehicles.

Zebra running across the vast grass plains of the Makgadikgadi Pans.

Njuca Hills

Nowhere else would a slight rise in the landscape earn itself the title of 'hills', but on these amazingly flat grasslands, this rise provides enough elevation to allow you to see car headlights from more than 15 kilometres away. This is one of the official campsites, so you may stay here but you must be fully self-sufficient. If not, it is nevertheless worth visiting, if only to see the view.

You are centrally situated here but, once again, there are no convenient loop roads. Depending on the rains, the season and your own good fortune, this area can produce the finest game viewing imaginable. At times, however, it can result in a barren game drive. If the pans are holding water, zebra often concentrate around this area, usually between Njuca Hills and the southern boundary. If there is no water for them, they will move toward the river, often staying in the Bushman Pits area outside the reserve.

A full day's drive, incorporating Njuca Hills and the Ntwetwe Pans, is a must. Take a picnic lunch and tell the game scouts where you are going so that they can send a rescue party if you have vehicle problems.

Wildlife

No life is sustained on the pans themselves, although they bear evidence to a lot of animal movement with tracks imprinted in the grey mud. The Makgadikgadi grasslands, however, are home to a wide range of animals, as it incorporates both desert and riverine habitats. From the Kalahari come hartebeest, gemsbok, springbok and the brown hyaena. Also found in the reserve are lion, cheetah, spotted hyaena, kudu, giraffe, zebra, wildebeest, steenbok, black-backed jackal and even elephant in the north-west of the park along the river.

All manner of reptiles may be found here, such as tortoises, rock monitors, snakes and lizards. The Makgadikgadi spiny agama (*Agama hispida* subsp. *makgadikgadiensis*) occurs only in this part of the world around the edges of the pans under the bushes. It is hard to find as it buries itself in the sand during the heat of the day.

Bird-watching

Birdlife in the Makgadikgadi is outstanding. The diverse riverine and desert habitats ensure a wonderful array of resident species. After the rains, water birds of all kinds, undertaking the shorter journey from the Okavango, turn the Makgadikgadi into a birder's paradise. Wattled crane, saddlebilled storks, fish eagles, waders, geese and teals congregate around all the small pans. All year round, the grasslands contain ostrich, coursers and black korhaans. Along the shorelines you will find waders such as avocets, blackwinged stilts and small plovers.

Vegetation

As Lake Makgadikgadi gradually dried up, its salinity increased. The water was at its deepest in Sowa and Ntwetwe, where it was also the last to dry up completely and as a result was the most salty. Today nothing can grow on this saline clay, due to the heat and alkalinity of the soil, and the complete abscence of all flora on the pans proper contributes to their special aura of desolation. However, the shores are rich in flora, which in turn attract wildlife that migrate across the pans in search of water. Tall groves of vegetable ivory palms growing on the northern and eastern grasslands are indicators of fresh water, as these trees require water from a depth of no more than 20 metres. They are used by the greater kestrel as nesting sights.

Baobabs, African star-chestnut, mopane and the grey-looking trumpet thorn (*Catophractes alexandri*) with its snowy white flowers and spiky pods abound beyond the palm belt away from the pans. Prickly salt grass (*Odyssea paucinervis*) with its spiky leaves is often covered in salt crystals and commonly grows on the sandy soil around the pans.

Near the south-eastern corner of the park, are a few of the rare cactus-like hoodii plants (*Hoodia lugardii*) with their one-metre high thorny stems and masses of star-shaped brown flowers that appear in spring.

Summer migrants are attracted in large numbers to the pans.

ACCOMMODATION
There are no lodges in the Makgadikgadi section of the park. The nearest accommodation is at Gweta Rest Camp in the village of Gweta (see page 133). Nata Lodge, 10 kilometres south of Nata village, is also commonly used as a comfortable base from which to explore the Makgadikgadi region (see page 133).

Public campsites
There are two campsites in this part of the park.

Kumaga Campsite
At Kumaga, next to the game scouts' camp, is a pleasant campsite overlooking the Boteti River. A number of large acacias provide shade. A platform overlooks the river, but unfortunately it is not well situated to see game coming down to drink at the waterhole. Cattle and other domestic animals from outside the park cross the river into the park and campsite.
Features:
• Single ablution block with cold showers only • A tap stand with borehole water
• A good supply of firewood in the riverine forest • Look-out platform

PANS OF PINK

Lesser flamingoes flock to the pans after heavy rains.

When the rains are good, the Nata River in the north-east of Sowa Pan and the Boteti in the south of Ntwetwe Pan may flood into the pans and create a shallow flood over a large area. Despite the extreme temperatures during many months, even years of drought, with the first arrival of water, millions of tonnes of tiny shrimps and crustacea hatch from eggs which were buried in the dry saline sands. The legendary flamingoes wing their way to the pans in their thousands in a breathtaking spectacle of long V-shaped skeins. They come from as far afield as East Africa and Namibia. The greater flamingoes are more numerous and feed on the brine shrimps. Algae also flourish in the saline water and form the staple diet of the lesser flamingoes. Although both species breed on Sowa Pan, this is the largest breeding area in Africa for the greater flamingoes. The lesser flamingo is smaller and pinker with a darker bill than the greater. The Setswana name for the flamingo is *'nonyane ya tladi'* which means lightning bird, perhaps because they congregate on the pans after heavy thunderstorms. As their whereabouts are dependent on water levels, some perseverance is required to find them. Appoint a guide from one of the safari companies or lodges to show you the way.

Njuca Hills

At Njuca Hills, 40 kilometres from Kumaga and 20 kilometres from the Makgadikgadi Game Scouts' Camp, two campsites occupy a hill each. No water is available; provide your own adequate supply if you wish to camp here. The nearest source of water is at the game scouts' camp near the main road. This is one of the few campsites in Botswana where firewood is not available, because it is situated in open grassland, so bring your own supply. Should you need to find firewood, the best direction to collect from is some 20 kilometres to the east, where you will find mopane woodland.

Features:

• Pit latrines at each site • Wonderful view

NXAI PAN AREA

Situated north of Makgadikgadi, 136 kilometres from Maun, Nxai Pan supports a strong population of springbok, as the short-cropped grasses can testify. The variety and density of game, mostly desert animals, are surprisingly good, as is the bird life. The vegetation is typical of the Kalahari and, as such, is quite different from the plant life of the Okavango or the Chobe.

The area is conveniently situated 37 kilometres off the main Nata/Maun road and yet is missed by many travellers in their haste to reach the more popular tourist areas. This is a great pity as Nxai Pan is so very different to the other areas in Botswana and it is well worth taking time to visit.

At the end of 1992 the park, which used to cover 2 100 square kilometres, was extended south to the main road to incorporate Baines' Baobabs; this enlarged area has now been incorporated into the Makgadikgadi and Nxai Pan National Park.

GETTING THERE

By air

There is no airstrip at Nxai Pan. The nearest airstrips are at Gweta (90 kilometres away) and Motopi (80 kilometres away).

By road

The road to Nxai Pan is almost midway between Maun and Nata and is clearly signposted. From the main road, there is a straight track that takes you through scrubland before you reach the gate at Nxai Pan. The 35-kilometre road requires a four-wheel drive.

The only turn-off from this road is a crossroad that you will encounter after 15 kilometres. This is the original Nata/Maun road before it was replaced, first by the gravel road and now by the newly tarred road. It is a further 18 kilometres to the gate and game scouts' camp.

To get to Baines' Baobabs, turn right at the crossroads. There is a fork 1 kilometre down the road. If conditions are wet, take the left hand fork for 13,3 kilometres where you will see the baobabs to your right. Turn to the right and follow this road for 3,5 kilometres to reach the baobabs. If the roads are dry, take the shorter and more interesting right-hand fork (11 kilometres), which takes you over small pans and along Kudiakam Pan to the baobabs. Note that Baines' Baobabs are within the national park and a permit to visit them, obtainable from either Nxai Pan or Makgadikgadi gates, is required.

There are a number of detours through the bush. If you decide to leave the main road, select the most recently used track as this is likely to be in the best condition.

LEFT: *San women and children selling melons on the roadside between Maun and Nata.*
RIGHT: *Camping at Nxai Pan.*

Petrol and supplies are available at Gweta; fuel can also be purchased at Mopipi.

WHAT TO SEE AND DO

Nxai Pan, a flat, grass-covered pan dotted with islands of clustered umbrella acacia, was also once a lake. Before reaching the gate, you cross a ridge that was the shoreline of the lake, indicating the depth of water at the time. There is a look-out point on top of the sandridge, providing an excellent view over Nxai Pan. Take the southern road past the South Campsite and then the signposted road to the right. Engage four-wheel drive before attempting the ridge.

Unlike Makgadikgadi, Nxai Pan has an integrated series of loops, allowing various options for game drives. Other than the track leading to Nxai Pan, the roads within the park are generally in good condition due to the hard surface of the pan, and four-wheel drive is not required here. A crisscross of the pans usually yields the best game-viewing results. A drive past the pumped waterhole should be included in a game drive, as the animals must come down here to drink during the winter.

Kudiakam Pan, south of Nxai Pan, is a smaller version of the Sowa and Ntwetwe pans of Makgadikgadi. It is a saline pan on which no vegetation grows. Depending on the rains, it can fill to a shallow depth, creating the illusion that it has once again been restored to its previous glory, when it was indeed a lake. It is on the shores of Kudiakam Pan that the famous Baines' Baobabs are standing. Be wary of driving on this pan when it is wet.

Like Nxai and Kudiakam, Kama-kama Pan, north-east of Nxai Pan, is also a remnant of Lake Makgadikgadi and is now covered in thick entanglements of thornbush. This is most likely as a result of the pan being over-grazed by domestic stock over the last century. During the last century Kama-kama Pan had always held water and it was here that many of the famous explorers rested and replenished their water supplies after journeys across the Kalahari, and before they undertook the next leg to Linyanti. It is possible that Kama-kama got its name from Khama the Great (grand-father of Sir Seretse Khama) who, it is specu-lated, grazed his cattle here. A game drive to Kama-kama Pan is usually only productive in terms of game viewing if the pan holds some water, but it is nevertheless interesting, both from a scenic and an historical perspective.

Wildlife

Springbok and gemsbok are the most common antelope on the pan. Like Etosha Pan in Nami-bia, this is one of the few places where impala and springbok cohabit, as they are normally separated by habitat preference. Here, the mo-pane that surrounds the pan provides the impala with suitable habitat. The park is noted for its many giraffe, sometimes seen in herds of up to 60 animals. This is one of the finest places in Botswana to sight leopard, which often lie out in the open catching the morning sun. Lion, cheetah, spotted and brown hyaena, honey badger, zebra, giraffe, kudu, hartebeest, bat-eared fox, black-backed jackal, wild dog and, in summer, even the occasional elephant are seen in the park.

Bird-watching

The black korhaan, who rises from the bush like a squeaky helicopter when flushed by a vehicle, is the hallmark of Nxai Pan. Raptors, especially smaller ones such as the greater kes-trel and the pale chanting goshawk, abound. The latter is often seen on the ground in asso-ciation with honey badgers who flush out ro-dents which the goshawks are quick to pounce on. The redbilled francolins at South Campsite are particularly tame and if you sit quietly, they will come very close to you. Melba finches and firefinches are attracted by the water spilt at the tap stand. In summer, whydahs with their long tails are conspicuous at the water-hole just before the entrance gate. Barn owls roost in the hollow of one the baobabs at Baines' Baobabs.

Leopard are often sighted at Nxai Pan.

ABOVE TOP: *Wading at Kudiakam Pan.*

ABOVE RIGHT: *The life cycle of the mopane worm – larvae, caterpillar and moth.*

ABOVE: *The black-backed jackal survives in a variety of habitats but prefers open dry terrain.*

RIGHT: *Gemsbok are easily recognised by their magnificent V-shaped horns.*

Vegetation

Nxai Pan, unlike the salt pans of Sowa and Ntwetwe, is covered by short sweet grass that provides the springbok with grazing. Islands of umbrella thorn provide shade and a number of large baobabs dot the pan. Mopane stands are found to the north and the striking purple-pod terminalia (*Terminalia prunioides*) with its conspicuous plum-red pods is found at South Campsite. Blue-green trumpet thorn is prolific in the scrubland area between Nxai Pan and Kama-kama Pan.

ACCOMMODATION

There are no permanent lodges at Nxai Pan. The nearest is 90 kilometres away at Gweta, which is too far to be feasible for daily access to Nxai Pan.

Public campsites

There are two campsites at Nxai Pan.

South Camp

This campsite is closer to the gate and the game scouts' camp. Turn right immediately after passing the gate; the campsite is 2 kilometres down this road. It is situated in a grove of purple-pod terminalias which provide excellent shade in summer. Little firewood is available in the immediate vicinity of the camp.

Features:

• An ablution block with cold showers and flushing toilets • A tap stand for borehole water • Good shade in summer • Observation platform providing a view over Nxai Pan

North Camp

This camp is 8 kilometres from the gate, in a clearing in the mopane forest which provides little shade and no view of the pan. Firewood must be collected away from the camp, as there is a very limited supply in the vicinity.

Features:

• An ablution block with cold showers and flushing toilets • A tap stand for water

THE UPSIDE-DOWN GIANTS

The baobab is the most conspicuous yet peculiar tree in Botswana. It is capable of living for more than 4 000 years, and can attain a height of over 25 metres, with a circumference of some 30 metres. A tree this size would weigh up to 200 tonnes because of its water content, with the wood weighing a mere 50 tonnes.

Baines' Baobabs – little changed since Thomas Baines painted them in 1862.

Carbon dating has showed that a tree with a circumference of 8 metres may well be more than 3 000 years old. The largest baobab in the world is probably the one on the slopes of Mount Kilimanjaro (Northern Tanzania) with a girth of more than 28 metres. The growth rate of the trunks seems to be only 5 millimetres per year and some trees have been known to shrink temporarily during times of drought. The San believe that God up-ended the tree in a fit of anger.

Baobabs pre-date the break-up, 110 million years ago, of Gondwanaland, the super-continent that consisted of all the continents of the southern hemisphere, as well as the Indian sub-continent. This explains why they are also found in Australia and Madagascar. They have been introduced elsewhere in the world, even in cold and wet climates, with great success and apparently will grow from seeds to seven metres within 20 years. Strictly speaking, it is better classified as a succulent than a tree, for it transports nutrients through the pulpy wood, rather than through its inner bark. The outer bark has the ability to re-grow, the practical advantage being that the tree cannot be ring-barked by elephants who favour the bark and tear it off in long strips. The flowers last for less than 24 hours and have an unpleasant smell that attracts bats, bush babies and moths.

The baobab is the ultimate survival tree for which man has found many uses. The trunk is often hollow and fills up with rainwater. The San tap this water source with grass straws. Rope capable of towing a vehicle can be made from the fibrous inner bark. The pulp of the fruit can be eaten or soaked in water to make a very refreshing drink high in vitamin C and citric acid. The seeds, ground and roasted, make a coffee substitute. Bulbs at the root terminals are dried, ground and used for porridge. The leaves are also eaten.

Over the years, these trees have been used for many purposes. In Kasane a hollow tree was used as a temporary prison. Others are said to have housed a bar, a bus shelter for 40 people, and even a flushing toilet. In the Sudan, baobabs may be inherited or sold as private property with detailed ownership registers held by government.

Baobabs provide shelter for many species of birds and mammals. Elephants often gauge large holes in the trunks in search of the moist, spongy pulp, while, together with giraffe, they have exclusive domain over the lofty leaves. Hollows in the trunk provide sanctuary for many nesting birds.

Baines' Baobabs, or the Seven Sisters as they are also known, were made famous by the watercolour painted by Thomas Baines, artist and explorer, during his expedition in 1862. Baines' expedition started in Walvis Bay in 1861, with one of his expressed intentions being to clear his name with Livingstone, who had unjustly accused him of theft during a previous expedition; however, he did not manage to meet up with Livingstone. His name was only cleared after his death in 1875.

ADVISORY: MAKGADIKGADI AND NXAI PAN NATIONAL PARK

CLIMATE

Days are hot and nights are cold throughout the winter. In summer, days are stiflingly hot, while the nights are cooler. Rains fall from November to April and winds are strong from August to November.

BEST TIMES TO VISIT

In the **Makgadikgadi** section of the park, game viewing is at its best from April to July, after which time the game moves to the Boteti River. In contrast, at **Nxai Pan** game is more abundant from December to April; however, if rains have been heavy, the roads may be difficult to negotiate.

MAIN ATTRACTIONS

The vastness and austere beauty of the pans. Huge flocks of flamingoes and other migrants are a memorable sight. Specials at Nxai Pan include a wide variety of raptors. Desert game such as gemsbok and springbok abounds.

TRAVEL

Most visitors drive from Maun in the west, or Francistown in the east. Scheduled air services fly to these centres, should you wish to hire a vehicle at either of these towns. The roads across the pans are really tracks, so a four-wheel drive vehicle is essential. Fuel is available from Nata, Maun (the region's main supply centre), Gweta, Rakops and Francistown, and basic supplies can also be bought at these towns as well as at Motopi. Ice is available from Francistown, Maun and Gweta.

Driving on the pans can be dangerous so ensure that you are properly equipped before setting out (see checklist on page 36 and follow the guidelines for driving given on page 180. If you intend exploring outside the boundaries of the national park, it is recommended that you take a guide with you.

An unusual but exciting way to explore the pans is by participating in a motorbike safari. For details, see *Safari Options*, page 33.

ACCOMMODATION

Nata

Nata Lodge Ten kilometres south of Nata on the Francistown road, this comfortable lodge offers pleasant accommodation under huge marula and vegetable ivory trees. Accommodation is in thatched A-frame chalets with *en suite* facilities or Meru tents. Facilities include a restaurant and bar, a swimming pool and curio shop. Petrol is available and excursions to the pans can be organised. Private Bag 10, Nata; Tel/fax: 611-210.

Sua Pan Lodge Conviently situated at the crossroads to Maun and Kasane, this lodge is suitable for the budget-conscious traveller. Offers 14 thatched chalets with *en suite* facilities, a swimming pool, restaurant and bar, shops and petrol. Private Bag 1, Nata; Tel/fax: 611-220.

Campsites

Nata Lodge Has ablution facilities, braai stands and firewood for sale. Guests have access to the Lodge amenities. Private Bag 10, Nata; Tel/fax: 611-210.

Nata Sanctuary Campsite situated 11 kilometres south of Nata, set amongst mopane woodland near the entrance to Sowa Pan. Has new ablutions with hot showers.

Sua Pan Lodge Camping is permitted here, although there are minimal facilities – a tap stand and toilets. Guests can use the lodge amenities. Private Bag 1, Nata; Tel/fax: 611-220.

Gweta

Gweta Rest Camp A pleasant little oasis in the desert to break the journey to or from Maun. Offers self-catering accommodation in thatched rondavels and campsites. On site are an open-air thatched restaurant and bar, a swimming pool, curio shop and liquor store. Excursions to the pans, horse trails and four-wheeler bike trips can be arranged.

The only accommodation available within the parks are campsites administered by the Department of Wildlife and National Parks. Reservations cannot be made for these sites, but for further information, contact the Department at PO Box 131, Gaborone; Tel: 371-405. Opening times for the parks are:
1 April to 30 September 06h00 to 18h30
1 October to 31 March 05h30 to 19h00

Makgadikgadi (see pages 127 to 128)
Kumaga Campsite Overlooks the Boteti River. Offers an ablution block, water, firewood and views from a look-out platform.
Njuca Hills Two campsites, both situated on top of a hill. Pit latrines are provided, but you must be totally self-sufficient to camp at these sites.

Nxai Pans (see page 131)
South Camp Has ablution facilities, water and an observation platform.
North Camp Offers ablution facilities and a tap stand for water.

HEALTH HAZARDS

Malaria and potentially dangerous animals. Keep to the main tracks on the pans, as it is extremely easy to get lost.

ANNUAL EVENTS

Thousands of flamingoes on the pans during the rainy months.

THE KALAHARI

The Kalahari, which comprises over two thirds of Botswana, is not truly a desert because its average annual rainfall exceeds the maximum rainfall normally experienced in a desert. It is well vegetated, but lacks permanent surface water and, as a result, was regarded as a desert by early travellers. Rainfall is low throughout the Kalahari, with the southern parts of the area being the driest and most susceptible to drought. The northern section is richer in water, vegetation and game, and therefore is more appealing to visitors. Four of Africa's most remote game reserves are situated in the vast Kalahari and it is home to the hunter-gatherer people, the San.

Due to the Kalahari's harsh nature, it does not support large numbers of people. There are, however, small settlements dotted across this vast landscape, which are a welcome sight for any weary traveller after a long day's drive.

Ghanzi

A true frontier town near Botswana's western border, Ghanzi is the supply centre for the small but thriving cattle-ranching community. Situated on a limestone ridge, is has an abundant supply of underground water on which the farms are reliant. Do not expect to see much other than the 190 cattle farms and Van Zyl's cutting, a 3 by 12 metre cutting out of solid rock used to catch rainwater. Hendrik van Zyl was the first European to take up residence here in 1874 on what is now Ghanzi Farm Number One. Petrol, spare parts, ice and basic supplies can be obtained. Accommodation is also available (see *Advisory*, page 159).

A craft shop was set up in Ghanzi to assist the San to earn a livelihood from their crafts. Situated next to the Kalahari Arms Hotel, it offers the best variety of San crafts in Botswana; contact Ghanzicraft, PO Box 196, Ghanzi; Tel: 596-241; Fax: 596-166.

Kalahari scrublands provide an ample source of food for many grazing animals.

Jwaneng

Once a cattle post and now home to one of the world's richest diamond mines, Jwaneng is situated 120 kilometres west of Lobatse. If you wish to visit the diamond mine, apply for a permit from Debswana (see page 137). Jwaneng has modern shops, sporting facilities and an airstrip.

Serowe

Beautiful Serowe lies 51 kilometres west of Palapye *en route* to Orapa and Central Kalahari Game Reserve. The traditional home of the late Sir Seretse Khama, this typical Tswana village sprawls over a considerable area of rocky hills. The village was further immortalised in the writings of the late Bessie Head, Botswana's only internationally recognised author, who fled South Africa to settle in Serowe. Khama family members are traditionally buried on the hill above the *kgotla*. Here Anton van Wouw's *Little Bronze Duiker* (totem animal of the Bangwato tribe) rests on the grave of Khama III, Grandfather to Seretse. The Khama III Memorial Museum in the Red House is worth a visit as it holds memorabilia of the Khama family. There is a national monument site on the flat-topped Thathaganyane Hill. Although there is not much to see from an archaeological perspective, the view from the top of the hill is spectacular.

The newly declared (1993) rhino sanctuary is situated 30 kilometres north of Serowe on the Orapa road. At present there are three white rhinos with a further two black rhinos of a sub-species that occur only in Chobe and Caprivi to arrive later. Plans are afoot to establish a lodge and campsite there, but priorities are to fence the 12 000 hectare sanctuary first. To date there are no tourist facilities available but tourists are welcome. Visitors should announce their intended visit to staff of the Toyota garage in Serowe.

Local guides will escort you from the sanctuary's carpark to the bomas and answer your questions about these animals. Although no entrance fee is charged yet, all donations are very welcome.

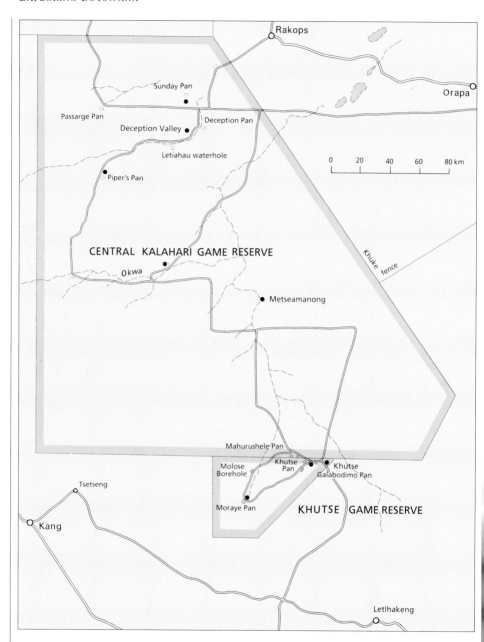

Rakops

A quaint little village located to the east of the Central Kalahari Game Reserve. Stragglers from many groups settled here to build their strange-looking houses and granaries. Life in the village is still very primitive, but basic supplies and fuel can be obtained. The water here is brackish. There is no accommodation.

Orapa

A diamond-mining town at the end of the tarred road *en route* to Central Kalahari Game

ABOVE: *The entrance to the Central Kalahari Game Reserve.*
ABOVE RIGHT: *Airstrip in Deception Pan next to the Owens' old campsite.*
RIGHT: *Driving on safari across Deception Pan.*

Reserve of Makgadikgadi. Permits must be obtained to visit the diamond mine; contact Debswana, PO Box 329, Gaborone; Tel: 351-131; Fax: 352-941. Although Orapa is not open to the public, the hospital will deal sympathetically with emergency cases.

CENTRAL KALAHARI GAME RESERVE

Covering an area of 51 800 square kilometres, the Central Kalahari Game Reserve is the second largest protected area in the world. It encompasses some of the most harsh, inhospitable and undeveloped territory in Botswana, yet also some of the most beautiful.

In 1961, the Central Kalahari Game Reserve was established as a preserve where the San could continue their traditional lifestyle. Because of its remoteness, as well as the fact that it was used by them as hunting ground, it was closed to the public until recently. As a result of social changes among the San and pressure from conservation circles, the government decided in the late 1980s to encourage the San to leave the reserve and to preserve it solely for the use of animals. The San have resisted the move and a situation exists at the moment where the reserve is still the domain of the San, who mostly inhabit the southern parts, while

the north is being developed for tourism. There is speculation that this distinction may be formalised.

GETTING THERE

By air
The airstrip at Deception Pan is mainly used by the more exclusive mobile safari operators.

By road
Central Kalahari Game Reserve is best approached from Rakops, although it can be reached from Ghanzi or Maun, and from the south through Khutse Game Reserve (some 300 kilometres from Gaborone).

From Rakops, a signposted road at the western end of town leads through some attractive countryside to Matswere Game Scouts' Camp, where permits and water can be obtained. The 55-kilometre road is generally in good condition, although it is windy and there are a few sandy patches. Four-wheel drive is advisable.

From Maun, take the Nata road for 50 kilometres until you see the signpost to Makalamabedi. Turn right onto the tar road and follow this to Makalamabedi village. Turn

ABOVE: *Waterhole and camphor trees at Sunday Pan. The pumphouse ensures a regular supply of water.*
LEFT: *Hyaenas and black-backed jackal devour a springbok carcass.*

right at the fence (either side will do) and follow it south for 90 kilometres. This road is very sandy and progress is slow. Go through the gate here, if you have travelled on the western side of the fence. Continue in a south along the fence, until you reach the Matswere entrance gate on the north-eastern side of the reserve, 18 kilometres further on. Turn into the reserve and head west for 10 kilometres, until you reach the Matswere Game Scouts' Camp. Four-wheel drive is required.

From Ghanzi, have a guide direct you onto the correct track for Xade. This is a 210-kilometre stretch of road, and it is a further 141 kilometres to Deception Pan. Allow two days for this journey, although the road is in reasonable condition beyond Piper's Pan. Four-wheel drive is essential.

Generally, all the roads in the north of the reserve are in good condition, but are covered with tall grass that sometimes clogs up radiators. Roads in the southern part (Xade/Khutse and along the cut-lines) go through extremely loose thick sand, where low-range gears are needed most of the way. Maps are available from the game scouts.

Do not drive off-road as the short grass pans and fossil valleys are extremely fragile and the surfaces scar easily. Carry plenty of water with you; being in a desert environment, a reliable water supply is never guaranteed. You should carry at least 5 litres per person per day for drinking and extra for washing, cooking, vehicle emergencies, or in case you come upon someone else in dire need.

Petrol, supplies and very basic vehicle spares are available at Rakops, although on occasion the petrol pumps run dry. If this happens, try Mopipi, although they often seem to run out at the same time! Ensure that you have sufficient petrol to get to one of the larger centres, as there are no supplies or petrol available in the reserve.

WHAT TO SEE AND DO

The Central Kalahari has a mostly flat surface, except for one rocky outcrop named Tsau Hill, on the north-western border of the reserve. The rest of the landscape is thick sand overlying a layer of basalt rock between 200 and 400 metres deep where the water table is generally situated. It has four major fossil river systems – the Passarge, the Letiahau or Deception, the Okwa and the Quoxo. The latter two are narrow with steep banks and tall, harsh grasses growing on soft, thick sand. The wide swathes that were cut by the rivers on their gentle descent into the engulfing sands of the Kalahari provide the opportunity for nutritious grasses to grow in their beds, ensuring food for the animals.

There are not as many sand dunes in the Central Kalahari as one may expect. Those that do occur are mostly well-vegetated linear dunes in the northern section of the reserve. An attractive example of such dunes are those visible on the way to Sunday Pan.

The northern section of the Central Kalahari is dotted with numerous pans of varying sizes. Many of these are grassed, albeit lightly, while the ungrassed pans generally have saline surfaces. These pans play a major role in determining the movement of game, with the greatest concentrations of wildlife typically found on or near a pan.

Deception Pan is situated in the north-west corner of the 80-kilometre long Deception Valley. The bed of the wide sprawling river that flowed through the Kalahari until about 16 000 years ago is now covered by short grasses with islands of trees scattered along its length. The pan became famous due to the book *Cry of the Kalahari*, by Mark and Delia Owens in 1985, who researched brown hyaena from 1974 to 1981. The airstrip, next to their camp, was built by them and is now a popular campsite with visitors to Deception Pan.

RIGHT: *The Kalahari tent tortoise has an attractively patterned shell.*

BELOW: *Springbok are gregarious creatures and roam in large herds.*

The pan is filled with game, particularly in the months following the rains. If you camp on the pan, game drives can be taken in either direction. Unfortunately, there are no loop roads so you are obliged to return to camp via the same route. A game drive to Sunday Pan, 21 kilometres from the top of Deception Pan, is feasible. Game is attracted to the waterhole, particularly later in winter. The pump is driven by a diesel engine, but because it does not operate regularly, animals cannot rely on it as a constant source of water.

The road continues past Sunday Pan for 50 kilometres to Passarge Pan and on to the Khuke fence.

Fifteen kilometres beyond the point where the road first leaves Deception Valley in the south, you will find Letiahau waterhole which is also pumped on an irregular basis. If it holds water, or if you can get permission to operate this pump, game viewing from this point is worthwhile as the animals will very quickly come to use it.

Fifty-six kilometres beyond Letiahau lies Piper's Pan. This is worth visiting, if only for the unusual atmosphere created by the grotesque commiphora trees covering the ridges around the pans. A solar-powered water pump ensures a regular supply of water.

Wildlife

The species that survive this harsh arid land need to be specially adapted. Animals found in this reserve include gemsbok, with their remarkable capacity to survive without water, as well as springbok, hartebeest and caracal. Giraffe, cheetah, wildebeest and kudu have also found a home in this dry wilderness. Lion and honey badger are often seen on Deception Pan. The best chance of seeing brown hyaena is to return to camp as late as regulations permit, as these animals start their rounds soon after dark. The pans are dotted with families of ground squirrels and suricates, a species of mongoose, that dive into their burrows for cover as you drive past.

There are no constructed hides, but the waterholes make for superb game watching.

Choose a shaded spot, far enough away from the waterhole not to disturb the game, and watch the animals come to drink. Take a book with you, as you will experience long, slow periods of little action. Your patience will be tested, but certainly rewarded!

Bird-watching

The birds of the Central Kalahari are dry savanna species. Ostrich, kori bustards, secretary birds, korhaan, guinea fowl and francolins are the larger terrestrial birds of the region. Raptors such as blackbreasted snake eagles, pale chanting goshawks and blackshouldered kites in search of rodents are plentiful, as are larks. Colour is provided by the lilacbreasted roller, swallowtailed bee-eater and lesser masked weaver. Other birds you can expect to see include pied barbets, Cape turtle doves, black crows, Kalahari robins, Marico flycatchers and scalyfeathered finches. The birds around Deception Valley are extremely tame, considering the small number of visitors they encounter. The titbabblers (small grey birds with black and white streaked chests and rust undertails) at Owens' Camp will often hop around the bushes and approach visitors.

Vegetation

The term 'desert' conjures up images of sand dunes and barren wastelands. The Kalahari is not like that at all. It is, in fact, well vegetated and its vast size incorporates a wide diversity of habitats. Tall grasses, open woodland, scrubland and mature forests are found here.

Animals may survive without water by feeding at night from plants wet with dew, as well as from plants that gain their moisture from deep tap-root systems. The swollen tubers are favourites with San and animal alike, and after veld fires the young shoots provide the animals with sustenance.

During years of adequate rainfall the old river channels are covered in short nutritious grasses. The dunes are topped with woodland where silver-leafed terminilia, and Kalahari sand raisin (*Grewia retinervis*), stabilise the dunes and prevent them from shifting.

ABOVE: *Scenes such as this one are typical of the Central Kalahari Game Reserve.*
RIGHT: *Common commiphora are also known as 'ghost trees'.*

The vegetation is amazingly well adapted to survive this harsh climate. Tree roots go down to the rockbed to reach the water table. Shrubs do not cope as well in times of drought as their roots are not as deep, so they drop their leaves and pods to decrease evapo-transpiration. This explains all the scraggly, seemingly dead bushes one sees during the winter months. The grasses and smaller plants however die right down to the roots to wait for the next rains. Clusters of umbrella thorn (*Acacia tortilis*) and buffalo thorn (*Ziziphus mucronata*) form shady thickets around most of the pans. At Sunday Pan, there are some sweet-smelling camphor bush (*Tarchonanthus camphoratus*), while the most noticeable trees at Piper's Pan are common commiphora (*Commiphora pyracanthoides)* and very stunted shepherd's trees.

The People

The Central Kalahari Game Reserve is inhabited by approximately 900 people, of which 50 per cent are San, 35 per cent Bakgalagadi and 15 per cent of a mixed race between these two. The San live mostly in the southern parts of the reserve, in villages such as Xade.

Their housing, although in the bee-hive shape typical of San dwellings, is very different in size and building materials to those of the western Kalahari San. Made of flexible branches of trees such as Kalahari apple-leaf, some are as much as three metres tall – quite a height for such small people. These huts are especially noticeable in Xaka on the banks of the Okwa River.

ACCOMMODATION

There are no lodges in or near the Central Kalahari Game Reserve. The nearest accommodation is in Maun or Ghanzi, both towns being over 200 kilometres away.

Public campsites

Camping is permitted at Deception Valley, Sunday Pans and Piper's Pan. As there is no water at the campsites, you must be self-sufficient; water can be obtained from Matswere Game Scouts' Camp.

Deception Valley

Popular campsites in this area include the Owens' old camp on the pan and the acacia groves in the valley.

Features:
- Shady campsites • Flat, hard surface
- Good view over the grassy plain

There is no firewood on Deception or Piper's Pan. Leave the pans and look in the wooded areas to the east and west. Remember that this is an arid region where man's impact is easily felt. Do not waste wood on huge bonfires and do not collect wood, even the smallest branches, from the tree islands in the fossil rivers as this is a very fragile environment.

Piper's Pan

There is a solar-powered pump at Piper's Pan waterhole with the result that this is an excellent game-viewing area. Make sure that you do not hinder the animals' access to water. There are no shady spots here.

Features:
- Near waterhole

Sunday Pan

This campsite offers shaded spots far enough from the waterhole to ensure that you do not interfere with the game's access to water.

Features:
- Shady campsite • Flat, hard surface
- Near waterhole

KHUTSE GAME RESERVE

This small reserve (2 590 square kilometres) abuts the Central Kalahari Game Reserve to the north and consists of rolling grasslands, savanna woodlands and scrub savanna, well vegetated fossil dunes and dry river beds. The complex of about 60 seasonal pans of varying sizes were part of a river system that flowed north to Makgadikgadi long ago. The Sebolaongwa word *Khutse* means 'place where you can kneel down to drink'. A San settlement is located near the Khutse entrance gate where visitors may stop off to hire a guide, who will show them around the reserve. Visitors are requested to respect the villager's privacy. After greeting the people, wait at the fence around the village until you are asked to enter. It is considered courteous to leave a small gift.

GETTING THERE
By air
There is no airstrip at Khutse.

By road
This is the closest reserve to Gaborone and is accessible via Molepolole. The road is tarred as far as Letlhakeng, but four-wheel drive is essential from there on, as the 100 kilometres to the Khutse San settlement leads through thick red sand and along washed away riverbeds. The soil then changes to more compact white Kalahari sand. Sufficient fuel for approximately 650 kilometres should be carried to enable you to get back to Gaborone.

WHAT TO SEE AND DO
Comprising vast open savanna plains dotted with dry, white sandy pans – often with a little moisture in the bottom – this area affords the visitor true peace and quiet.

Maps are available at the gate from the game scouts. There is only one circular road in the reserve and it forks 12 kilometres after the

The Owens' old campsite at Deception Pan.

ABOVE: *On safari in the Kalahari.*
ABOVE RIGHT: *A Kori bustard.*
BELOW: *The bat-eared fox has an extraordinarily acute sense of hearing.*

game scouts' camp at Khutse Pan. The left-hand road goes to Moraye (also called Moreswe) Pan, 52 kilometres further on. From the Moraye campsite, you can do a long loop north to Molose borehole (24 kilometres), continue south-east to the Khutse/Moraye road (21 kilometres) then back to Moraye.

The right-hand fork after Khutse Pan continues for 12 kilometres through the park and the reserve boundary to Mahurushele Pan and then a further 4 kilometres to the Central Kalahari Game Reserve, or south-west to Molose borehole (24 kilometres).

Wildlife

Most of the desert herbivores such as kudu, gemsbok, hartebeest, wildebeest, springbok, steenbok and herds of eland may be seen here, but they are generally concentrated around the pans when these are filled with rain-water, or at Molose Pan where water is pumped. Cheetah, lion and leopard also occur here. Smaller animals such as black-backed jackal, caracal, porcupine, brown and spotted hyaena, mongoose, bat-eared fox and ground squirrels are abundant. Do not expect to see large herds of game, but rather a variety of different species in smaller numbers.

Bird-watching

Khutse is renowned for its bird life, which is dominated by the dryland savanna species typical of the Kalahari. Larks, whitebacked vultures, greater kestrels, chanting goshawks, ostrich and Kori bustards are some of the over 150 species recorded.

ACCOMMODATION

There are no lodges or permanent camps in this reserve.

Public campsites

Six new campsites have been designated, but only the campsite at the gate has cold showers and toilet facilities. Money has been allocated to build more ablution blocks, but this development is still in the planning phase. There is a borehole at the Golalabadimo Pan game scouts' camp at the gate, but the water from it is slightly salty in taste.

GEMSBOK NATIONAL PARK

One of the most interesting but lesser known regions in Botswana, the Gemsbok National Park is set in the remote south-western corner of Botswana, where the annual rainfall seldom exceeds 125 millimetres. Closer to the traditional image of a desert, it consists of gently undulating sand dunes that are sparsely vegetated and criss-crossed by fossil rivers.

There are two Gemsbok parks: the larger, Gemsbok National Park (26 000 square kilometres) is in Botswana and the smaller adjacent Kalahari Gemsbok Park (9 600 square kilometres) is in South Africa. Although they are separated by the ancient riverbed of the Nossob, both parks are conserved as a single ecological unit of 36 000 square kilometres. There are no boundaries between the parks which enables game to move freely from one country to the other.

This is the oldest park in Botswana, having been created in 1937. Originally, it consisted of a number of farms on the South African side,

Resembling an abstract sculpture, a dead tree is a victim of drought in the Nossob River Valley.

and some small settlements in Botswana. Over-grazing of the area by domestic stock prompted the governments of South Africa and Botswana to create a game reserve, not as a tourist attraction, but to use the water resources to stabilise and control the wildlife. In 1967, Botswana's government increased its part of the reserve almost four-fold. Until recently, the whole park was administered and run by the South African National Parks Board, with Botswana's section of the park closed to the general public. However, this has now been opened to the public and development plans, which include the introduction of camel trails, are in the pipeline.

GETTING THERE

By air
There is an airstrip at Tshabong.

By road
The Gemsbok National Park is best approached from the south via the tarred road to Tshabong, after which a four-wheel drive is necessary. Past Tshabong, the road forks and the signposted left-hand route leads to the Gemsbok National Park. Maps are available from the game scouts.

ABOVE: *When threatened, the pangolin rolls into a defensive ball.*
ABOVE RIGHT: *Despite its name the Cape cobra is found in many parts of southern Africa.*

WHAT TO SEE AND DO

The south-eastern Kalahari is dominated by extensive ochre dune fields, sparsely covered by thornscrub. The pink to red colour of the soil is caused by the ferric oxide imbedded on the quartzite grains. Ancient riverbeds cut through this totally arid area and may carry water only once every 20 years. In the 1992/93 summer, the Molopo/Nossob rivers flowed again for the first time in three years after good rains. There are numerous pans in the north and east of the park, towards Union's End. The Kalahari is most spectacular after good rains, usually in late summer (from March to May).

There are limited options for game drives in Botswana's section of the park. The present road system runs along the ancient riverbeds of the Nossob and if the rains are exceptionally heavy, access to the park becomes impossible. If you are travelling in summer months you are advised to check with the Department of Wildlife and National Parks (See *Advisory,* page 159) as to the state of the roads before you embark on your journey. Options may be extended by utilising the park and facilities on the South African side of the border.

Wildlife

One of the greatest attractions of the south-western Kalahari is its stunning variety of mammals. Large herds of springbok are found along the riverbeds and pans as they prefer the short grasses that grow there. Gemsbok are generally attracted to the mature grasses in the riverbeds at the end of the rainy season, and as it becomes drier they move into the dunes in search of food. Red hartebeest are found in small herds on the flat open plains of the Nossob and are more common in the wooded areas further north. As conditions become drier they also disperse into the dunes. Eland prefer to roam the dunes and are seldom spotted. Kudu can be seen in the Botswanan section of the park as well as wildebeest, grey duiker and steenbok. Impala have been sighted in the past but are now very rare. Predators, such as lion, cheetah and leopard are commonly seen. Brown hyaena are prevalent between Nossob and Union's End and may be spotted on early morning game drives. Spotted hyaena are less common but do occur and wild dogs are known to exist here. Cape and bat-eared fox are abundant, as are suricate in the Nossob River, whereas yellow and slender mongoose prefer the dune grasses in the south. Banded mongoose, honey badger, aardwolf, pangolin, striped polecat and small spotted genet also occur. The African wild cat is common, whereas the small spotted cat is more secretive and rare.

Cape cobras can sometimes be seen raiding the weaver's nests.

Bird-watching

Over 264 species have been recorded in this park. Sociable weavers are common with as many as 300 birds using one nest, each pair living in an individual chamber. Some weavers' nests are the size of small rooms and

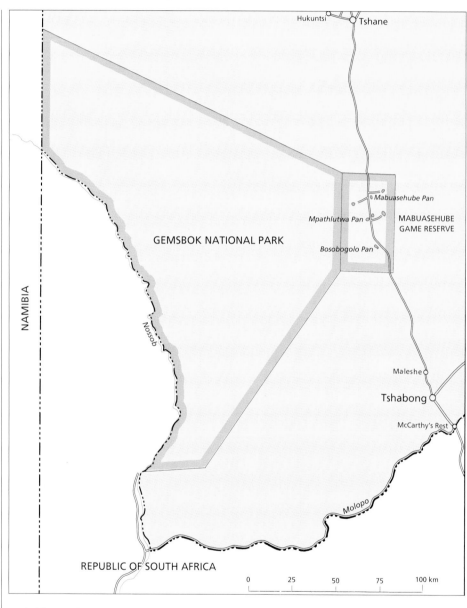

probably weigh more than a tonne. They last as long as the trees that they are built in, and get added to and repaired each year.

This is one of the most favoured places in southern Africa for raptors – of the 80 species recorded in the region, 52 have been observed in this park. The best places to see them are around the waterholes in the northern Nossob

Valley, especially in late summer when the raptors congregate for the termite eruptions – as the insects emerge from the termitaries, they are snapped up by the voracious birds. Some of the most common and widespread raptors are secretary birds, pale chanting goshawks, gaber goshawks and greater kestrels. Lanner falcons are often seen hunting doves when they come to drink at the pans. Pygmy falcons live in the sociable weaver's nests and it is said that one in every four nests contains a resident falcon; a tell-tale sign of their presence is a ring of white droppings at the entrance. They are mostly seen hunting sand lizards – their favourite food.

Tawny, martial and blackbreasted eagles are often encountered. Vultures are often sighted, with the whitebacked vulture nesting prominantly in the taller trees north of Nossob. Seven species of owl have been recorded.

Larger birds include ostrich, Kori bustards, Ludwig's bustards and korhaans. Lilacbreasted rollers, redheaded finches and yellow canaries add splashes of colour to the landscape.

Vegetation

Vegetation is scant and many dunes have been badly denuded by over-grazing in the past. Camelthorn acacias occur in the riverbeds, often covered by sociable weavers' nests.

On the dune slopes grow shepherd's trees, umbrella thorns, Kalahari sand acacia (*Acacia luederitzii* subsp. *luederitzii*) with its purplish-red pods, and velvet raisin bushes (*Grewia flava*). The dune crests are often covered in grey camelthorn bushes and Kalahari couch grass (*Stipagrostis amabilis*).

In the north-eastern parts of the park, the untidy looking bushes, worm-cure albizia (*Albizia anthelmintica*) and silver terminalia are quite common.

In summer, an attractive yellow flower covers the ground, which has as its fruit a nasty three-sided thorn, with one of its prongs always facing upward. It is known as devil's thorn (*Tribulus zeyheri*), which is one of the first plants to appear after an area has been denuded and, as such, is a sign of the previous over-utilisation of the area. During the long dry season in this extremely arid region, much of the moisture needed by the animals for survival, comes from two wild vines – the tsamma melon (*Citrullus lanatus*) and the gemsbok cucumber (*Cucumis metuliferus*).

The bare essentials for a successful camp.

ACCOMMODATION

There are no lodges and permanent camps in the vicinity. However, there are three camps – Twee Rivieren, Mata Mata and Nossob – with fully equipped, air-conditioned chalets on the South African side of the border. To get there, cross the border post at Bokspits which is open between 08h00 and 16h00.

Public campsites

There are three campsites in the park at present: one at the game scouts' camp at the Twee Rivieren entrance, with ablution facilities (cold showers and toilet), the other 300 kilometres further at Swartpan but with no facilities available. There are two designated but undeveloped campsites within the park. Palanjwe is 55 kilometres north of Nossob camp and Rooiputs is 28 kilometres north of Twee Rivieren. You have to be self-sufficient to camp at these sites, although the game scouts will drop off a drum of water and firewood for your use. The three camps on the South African side may also be used, but you have to cross the border to do so. You can buy basic supplies at all of the South African camps and fuel is available at Mata Mata. Firewood must be pur-

ABOVE: *Young cheetahs rest on the roadside.*
LEFT: *A white-backed vulture perched on high.*

MABUASEHUBE GAME RESERVE

The 1 792 square kilometre reserve abuts the Gemsbok National Park to the west and there is talk of these two reserves being amalgamated. Although remote and costly to reach in terms of time and fuel, it is well worth a visit.

The Kgalagadi word, *mabuasheube*, means 'place of red earth'. The reserve consists of six large pans and a myriad of smaller ones, with a good variety of game, although these animals may migrate during times of drought. There are typical sand dunes at the south/south-west side of each pan, some reaching as high as 20 to 30 metres. The pans themselves hold water for some months of the year and attract plenty of wildlife.

chased at the camps as you may not take in your own supply or collect any from the park.

Contact the South African National Parks Board (PO Box 787, Pretoria 0001; Tel: (012) 343-1991, Fax: 343-0905) for reservations and details on their section of the park.

GETTING THERE
By air
There is an airstrip on the pan at Tshabong, south of the reserve.

By road

The most commonly used road to Mabuasehube is from the south, via Tshabong, some 120 kilometres north of McCarthy's Rest border post near Kuruman in South Africa. Continue on the extremely sandy road, where four-wheel drive is required, across long ranges of gently undulating dunes. You will reach a fork in the road; the route to the left goes into the reserve, while the right-hand turn runs along the boundary, by-passing the reserve towards Ghanzi. Allow four hours to drive from Tshabong to Mabuasehube.

If you are approaching from the north, use the Tshane road. It is 125 kilometres from Tshane to the northern boundary of the reserve over a badly corrugated surface and the journey should take four hours to complete.

The third route, although seldom used, is in the best condition. On the Khakhea road, 20 kilometres north of Werda, is a turn-off to the west, 1,5 kilometres after the road that crosses the Moselebe riverbed. This 145-kilometre stretch of road leads through typical Kalahari countryside to Mabuasehube.

WHAT TO SEE AND DO

Mabuasehube is typical of a more desert-like landscape with sparsely vegetated dunes and a few white pans dotted about. Although plain and bare in appearance, the pans have an aura and a beauty that is unique.

The road passes three very large pans, while another three are set back not more than ten kilometres from the road: Monamudi and Lesholoago to the east and Khiding to the west. The two pans in the south, Mpaathutlwa and Bosobogolo are covered with grass, while Mabuasehube Pan in the north is an almost bare surface of salty white clay.

Wildlife

Large herds of springbok, gemsbok, red hartebeest, wildebeest and eland attract predators such as lion, leopard, brown hyaena and caracal. You can also expect to see Cape fox, bat-eared fox, suricate, yellow and slender mongoose and even wild dogs.

There are some good viewing points over the pans, but no formal look-out structures.

Bird-watching

The bird life is typical of the semi-arid bush and scrub savanna of the region, with records listing 170 species. The most rewarding place to look for birds is on the dunes to the southeast of the pans. Large birds include the Kori bustard, secretary bird and black korhaan, as well as a large variety of raptors and vultures. Other species you can expect to see include redcapped lark, greybacked finchlark, capped wheater, redeyed bulbul, pied barbet and crimsonbreasted boubou. When the pans fill with rain-water all manner of water fowl are attracted to the reserve.

ACCOMMODATION

There are no lodges in the vicinity.

Public campsites

The only designated campsite in the reserve is located at the game scouts' camp. There are ablution facilities and water should be available, but it is not advisable rely on this. Ensure that you are completely self-sufficient. Camping anywhere else within the reserve's boundaries is not permitted.

WESTERN KALAHARI

There are no protected reserves in the western Kalahari. It is the historical, anthropological and geological aspects of this region that make it worth visiting. The main attraction is Tsodilo Hills, with its rock art and imposing presence, while the sandstone caves of Drotsky's Caverns are as large as they are unexpected. There is no charge and no restriction on visiting either of these places. Apart from these two features, the hills at Aha are interesting only for their rarity in a land so flat. The area is populated mainly by the San and the Ovaherero peoples and visitors to the region are certain to come into contact with both these groups.

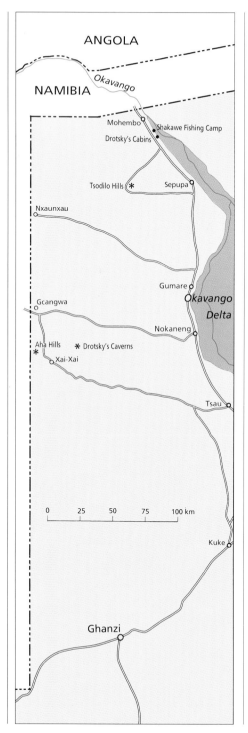

TSODILO HILLS

The word Tsodilo is derived from the Hambu-kushu word *sorile*, meaning 'sheer'. Rising out of the flat Kalahari terrain like a volcanic island in a calm sea, Tsodilo Hills dominate their surroundings completely. The hills are rocky outcrops of micaceous quartzite schist known as *Inselbergs*, formed a relatively recent 450 million years ago, in the same sequence as that of the Aha Hills and Gwcihaba. The sheer western face of the Male hill juts 420 metres above the horizon and is clearly visible from points in the Delta over 50 kilometres away.

GETTING THERE

By air

There is an airstrip west of the Male hill (see below) which makes day trips to Tsodilo Hills feasible. Be warned, however: if you do not have transport waiting for you (which may be arranged through Drotsky's Cabins or Shakawe Fishing Camp, see page 90), you will be in for a very long walk!

It is important to start as early as possible to avoid spending too much time walking through thick sand in the heat of the day. Ensure that you have drinks at the plane for your return and that you take water with you for the walk.

By road

The approach to Tsodilo Hills, which can only be attempted in a four-wheel drive vehicle, is a journey not likely to be forgotten. Whether you use the road from Sepupa to the south-east, or the shorter road from Shakawe, you will experience some of the worst roads in the country, particularly if you happen to be the first vehicle to follow after a government truck with a wider wheel-base. Unskilled drivers have churned up the sand, causing very bad corrugations to line the roads and making it impossible to build up any speed. Crossing these dunes in the dry months when the sand is soft and loose may require a great deal of digging and pushing.

ABOVE: *A traditional San settlement is overshadowed by the Tsodilo Hills.*
RIGHT: *The village well – source of the local people's most precious commodity.*

From Sepupa to Tsodilo is 53 kilometres. The turn-off is a few kilometres south of Sepupa village and is signposted with the zebra-striped logo of the Botswana National Museum and Art Gallery. Allow three hours for the trip.

The 41 kilometre road from Shakawe starts near the turn-off to Shakawe Fishing Camp – watch for the signpost. The road is extremely bumpy and even where it is not sandy, you will seldom get out of low gear. Set aside four hours for this particular nightmare.

WHAT TO SEE AND DO

The hills are the subject of many myths and legends. To the !Kung San, (the San tribe that lives north of Ghanzi and west of the Okavango Delta) they are the birth place of man, the tomb of the gods and the home of the serpent monster. By air or road it seems to take an eternity to reach the foot of the hills.

The Tsodilo group comprises four individual hills, the largest of which is known by the

San as the Male hill. Approximately one kilometre beyond this is a conglomeration of smaller outcrops which are collectively known as the Female hill (approximately 250 metres high) and further away is the Child. The fourth and smallest hill is not named.

151

HILLS OF LEGEND

The Story of the Male and Female

The male and the female are man and wife and the closest of the smaller hills is their child. One legend has it that the furthest hill is the male's first wife, who had been cast aside by him since the arrival of his new and younger wife.

The Horned Serpent Monster

There is a cave in the western face of the Female hill which holds water all year round. The San will tell you that it is inhabited by a large serpent with horns like a kudu, which are long enough to reach the bottom of the hill and beyond. Your San guide will always throw a stone into the water to ward off the serpent before allowing you to approach.

The Birthplace of Man

The Hambukushu believe that when their tribe, complete with livestock, was first lowered to earth, it was onto the Female hill by their god, Nyambe. As evidence, they point to the hoof-prints which are clearly visible in the rock, high on the hill. Some modern theorists believe that these prints may well be ancient dinosaur tracks, while others consider them to be merely erosion marks etched into the rock.

The Gods that Fill the Hills

The San believe that the gods reside in the Female hill, each in his own compartment, and it is from here that they rule over the mortal world.

Bad Luck to Hunt

The gods will be angered if you bring death to their home and bad luck will befall you. Sir Laurens van der Post tells of an early incident in his book *The Lost World of the Kalahari* when one of his party ignored the warnings and hunted a steenbok. All manner of mysterious misfortunes plagued the crew during the time they stayed at the hills, including their cameras refusing to work and then inexplicably operating normally again once they left the hills.

San paintings

There are over 3 500 individual rock paintings in more than 350 sites at Tsodilo Hills. The exact age of the paintings is not known for sure. The most recent may be only 100 years old, although when a geologist visited the hills in 1898, none of inhabitants knew the origin of the paintings.

Most of the rock paintings are to be found on the Female hill and many can be seen without too much climbing, if you are short of time or breath. Some particularly interesting paintings include what appears to be a perfect depiction of a whale or a fish. The nearest ocean is over 600 kilometres away and to get there the ancient artist would have had to cross both the Kalahari and the extremely harsh Namib deserts! High on the Female hill is an over-hanging rock on which is depicted a collection of hunters, each with a prominent, erect penis. Alec Campbell, the curator of the National Museum, dubbed this 'The Valley of the Dancing Penises'. A large panel on the western face of the Female hill contains a number of well-executed paintings that were first described by Sir Laurens van der Post and subsequently named 'Van der Post's Panel' in his honour. This famous feature was defaced by vandals, but is has recently been completely restored and all graffiti has been very carefully removed. For further reading, see *Kalahari; Life's Variety in Dune and Delta*, Main. Southern Books, 1987.

On your arrival at Tsodilo Hills, contact the Monuments Officer, who lives at the end of the airstrip and will appoint a San guide to show you around. He will be able to point out the perennial spring which is believed to be the home of the serpent monster, and other local points of interest.

RIGHT: *View from the top of Tsodilo Hills.*
BELOW: *Some of the many San paintings at Tsodilo Hills.*

There is a trail on the Female hill that starts just beyond the tall baobab and takes you past an old well to the 'dinosaur footprints'. You will pass numerous San paintings on the way. From the top of the hill there is a wonderful view over the flat, seemingly endless land surrounding the hills. The descent on the other side of the hill takes you through a natural amphitheatre and down to the 'Valley of the Dancing Penises' beyond which you will find the paintings of the two rhinos and a calf. These are the only polychrome paintings in the hills, the colouring of which has created a three dimensional effect. Around the corner is the puzzling whale painting and further down the road is the famous Van der Post Panel.

If this walk is too strenuous, you can see the rhino, the whale, Van der Post's Panel and a number of other paintings from ground level by walking around the base of the Female hill.

The northern part of the Female hill also has interesting paintings on the loose boulders at the foot of the hill, but is too long a trip to do on foot. If you have transport or more time, explore the western face of the Female hill, which is rewarding in terms of the number of paintings that adorn the lower rocks.

There are about 250 paintings on the Male hill, but if it is exercise and a view you are after, this is the hill to climb. Rock climbing is possible on the Male hill, but is only suitable for experienced climbers and requires the correct equipment. There have been bad accidents at this site in the past.

Wildlife

Except for kudu, steenbok and duiker who have the ability to live in waterless areas, do not expect to see much large game in this area. Although leopard tracks are often seen in the hills, the animals themselves are masters of stealth who can live in settled areas for years without being noticed. A small nocturnal gecko with brown and yellow stripes called the

Tsodilo gecko (*Pachydactylus tsodiloensis*), part of the lizard family, is found in these hills only and nowhere else in the world.

Bird-watching

Birding at Tsodilo Hills is reasonable, but if you fly in for the day you are unlikely to see very much, as most of the birds are to be found in the mixed woodland further away from the hills. In the scrub between the airstrip and the Female hill you are likely to see yellowbilled hornbills, grey louries, Melba finches and blackheaded orioles.

Vegetation

The mixed woodland and tree savanna surrounding the hill is a tree lover's paradise. A lasting impression will remain of the many different types of tall trees which provide a canopy around the base of the Female hill.

153

Groves of massive mongongo or manketti trees (*Ricinodendron rautanenii*) can be identified by their sprays of yellow flowers and grey-green egg-shaped fruits, the kernels of which are much loved by the San. In the winter the stout bare trunks and branches stand out above the surrounding vegetation and may be mistaken for baobabs, which also occur in the area. Bird plums (*Berchemia discolor*) with their single stems and dense crowns of large brilliant green leaves with prominent herringbone veining are found around the base of the hills. Monkey-orange (*Strychnos cocculoides*), mukwa or kiaat, red syringa, marula, grewia and acacia species are all found in this part of the desert.

The People
Two groups of people live at Tsodilo hills, the Hambukushu and the San. Despite claims made by the Hambukushu that they have lived here since time immemorial, historians maintain that the Hambukushu arrived in Botswana only in the early 19th century, but concede that they have found signs of early Bantu tribes at the hills going back some 1 400 years.

The San have lived almost permanently at the hills for at least 25 000 years and have left behind much of archaeological interest.

ACCOMMODATION
There are no lodges at Tsodilo Hills. The nearest accommodation is at Shakawe, which is a four-hour drive away. Drotsky's Cabins and Shakawe Fishing Camp cater for day trips to Tsodilo Hills.

Public campsites
There are no official campsites in the area and you are permitted to camp wherever you like. A favourite spot is next to the cave between the Male and Female hills, particularly during hot weather as the cave provides cool shelter from the stifling heat outside. Another popular site is just around the corner to the east where the wonderful rhino paintings are, and another to the west where the trail commences. There are no facilities and to stay here you must be completely self-sufficient.

Firewood should be gathered away from the hills, as the local people do not have the necessary transport to collect wood and they will suffer if the source around their village is denuded by tourists. There is a well near the airstrip, from where water may be drawn in an old bucket.

LEFT: *The styles on the Namibia/Botswana border allow the San access to both countries.*
BELOW LEFT: *Mongongo nuts.*
BELOW: *Driving through thick bush on sandy Kalahari roads.*

AHA HILLS AND DROTSKY'S CAVERNS

Aha Hills and Drotsky's Caverns are set in one of the remotest areas of north-western Botswana, near the Namibian border. *Aha* means 'small rocks' and is the name of the largest range of hills in northern Botswana. Drotsky's Caverns are also known as Gcwihaba Caverns – *Gcwihaba* is the name of the ancient river that flowed through the caves and is !Kung for 'the hyaena's lair'.

GETTING THERE

By air

Fashioned from the riverbed running past Xai-Xai is a serviceable airstrip – provided the livestock are removed from the landing area! Xai-Xai lies between Aha Hills and Drotsky's Caverns and is the closest airstrip to both of these places. It is a small San/Ovaherero village and neither shops, petrol nor accommodation are available.

Gcangwa, 30 kilometres north of Aha Hills, also has an airstrip. It is considerably larger than Xai-Xai and has shops with basic supplies, a police station and clinic.

By road

The drive to Aha Hills and Drotsky's Caverns is long regardless of whether you set off from Maun or from Shakawe. From Maun, take the road to Sehithwa and then north to Tsau or Nokaneng; from Shakawe, travel south to these towns.

The road from Tsau to Xai-Xai is in fair condition, but not often used. Should you experience problems here, assistance may be a long time coming. The turn-off to the caves is 153 kilometres south along this road. You should allow 10-12 hours for the journey, which would usually mean camping *en route*. Four-wheel drive is required.

The alternative road is from Nokaneng to Gcangwa and then south to Xai-Xai and Drotsky's Caverns. This sandy road is a route favoured by government vehicles, and therefore assistance would be more readily available

Stalactites and stalagmites within the magnificent Drotsky Caverns.

should you need it. The distance from Nokaneng to Gcangwa is about 120 kilometres and from Gcangwa to Xai-Xai a further 60 kilometres, which covers a stretch of very thick sand. Four-wheel drive is essential.

To get from Xai-Xai to Drotsky's Caverns, take the Tsau road for 42 kilometres to the signpost sporting the logo of the National Museum and turn south. Continue on this road for 27 kilometres to the caverns.

No petrol is available anywhere in the western Kalahari, so take all your requirements with you. Fuel consumption is heavy in the long stretches of thick sand and food supplies are almost non-existent, so ensure you have plenty of both.

Some maps indicate a road between Dobe and Tsodilo Hills via Nxaunxau, but this road in fact takes you along the Xaudum riverbed from the boundary fence and Nxaunxau, and is so seldom used that it has become overgrown with thick acacia bush. The roads north of Nxaunxau are very sandy and four-wheel drive is essential. Should you choose to take this extremely remote route, do not attempt it with only one vehicle and be prepared for two long days of travel.

WHAT TO SEE AND DO

Aha Hills

Situated anywhere else, the Aha Hills would probably appear insignificant, but the range is interesting for its remoteness and for materialising, as it does, from an otherwise flat and sandy land, forming a low plateau of approximately 250 square kilometres. The hills consist almost entirely of limestone, dolomite and marble which lends them a soft pink hue. Isolated pans hold rain-water for short periods and attract what little game has not already been hunted. You are more likely to encounter cattle, goats and donkeys than wildlife. Appoint a guide from Xai-Xai if you want to explore the hills. Straddling the Namibian border, they are part of the same formation as Drotsky's Caverns and the possibility exists that further caves may be discovered. Two sinkholes of 35 and 75 metres deep have been found, but neither appear to be linked to a cavern system. The top of Aha Hills offers some outstanding views of the whole range stretching west into Namibia and of the flatland, valleys and dunes to the east and south.

Drotsky's Caverns

The low knoll, one of six in the immediate area, that houses the caves would scarcely warrant a second glance from the outside – certainly it would never be suspected of concealing such magnificent limestone caves. The knoll is situated south-east of Aha Hills within a shallow fossil river valley that cuts its way through row after row of incomplete sand dunes. The caves are part of the same dolomite formation that includes the Aha and Tsodilo Hills, dated at 800 to 1 000 million years old. They were gouged out by the Gcwihaba River during successive dry and wet periods over the millennia.

They became known to the world after being shown to Martinus Drotsky in 1932 by the San, and today they bear his name. After his first visit he described the area as being full of natural springs but these have long since dried up, indicating a general drop in the water table of the region. Hendrick van Zyl, the maverick founder of Ghanzi who was believed to have amassed a fortune that was never found after his death, is rumoured to have stashed his millions here.

These caves were never used as dwellings by the San and consequently no rock paintings are to be found in them.

There are two entrances into the caves, the first behind the information board and the other approximately 250 metres further along the ridge of the hill (a map of the caves is available from the Department of Geological Survey, Private Bag 0014, Gaborone). It is possible to work your way from one to the other by following the string indicating the route. Impressive stalagmites, stalactites and flowstone formations abound. Towards the centre of the caves, you will come across a very large cavern and encounter the bats that inhabit the caves. Although not all the species have yet been identified, one species that does occur is the highly gregarious Commerson's leaf-nosed bat, which may be identified by its large size, pointed ears and white shoulder flash. Be prepared to wade knee-deep in bat dung and debris in some places! Also make sure that you are properly prepared to venture in here, with back-up light sources.

As you arrive at Drotsky's Caverns the road splits, the right hand fork leading straight to the caves. The left fork follows the riverbed through a steep-sided valley to the San village of Ncwama. This is a very scenic journey and the village itself is interesting, so allow a full morning for the outing.

The distance from Drotsky's Caverns to Aha Hills is 85 kilometres and the trip will take two to three hours. Follow the 27-kilometre road from the caves back to the Tsau/Xai-Xai road and then travel 42 kilometres to Xai-Xai. The hills are 15 kilometres to the north over deeply corrugated, sandy roads where a four-wheel drive is required.

If you are travelling to Gcangwa, the diversion to Dobe is interesting. It is a small San settlement numbering a hundred or so people with none of the modern trappings of Xai-Xai or Gcangwa.

ABOVE: *Bullfrogs emerging from the clay after the rains in the Kalahari.*
RIGHT: *The bright yellow flowers of the western rhigazum, which thrives in this region.*

Wildlife

Game is widely distributed and seldom found in large concentrations in this arid region. However, as the traditional hunting ground of the !Kung, game can definitely be spotted here. Gemsbok, eland, steenbok, duiker and kudu are the most common antelope. Predators including lion, leopard, wild dog and cheetah are all found in the western Kalahari.

After the rains, thousands of bullfrogs (*Pyxicephalus adspersus*) may be seen around every pan and depression. They burrow into the soil when the pans dry out and lie dormant and emerge when the rains come again.

In the early evening the valleys ring with yapping of the little barking geckos (*Ptenopus garrulus*) whose incessant and rapid clicks break the stillness of the desert; however, it is only the territorial males who are vocal.

The smaller Kalahari tent tortoise or serrated tortoise (*Psammobates oculifer*) with its beautifully scalloped dome inhabits this area. The San eat the flesh and the women use the shells as a carry pouch for sweet-smelling herbs.

Bird-watching

For keen birders the north-western Kalahari is another commmendable area for the dryland species, especially during the summer when the migrants, waders and water fowl are attracted to the rain-filled pans. Pale chanting goshawks, Stanley's bustard, blackbellied korhaan and ostrich are some of the larger birds commonly encountered throughout the year in the bush savanna. Barn owls are permanently resident at Drotsky's Caverns. A true spectacle are the phenomenal numbers of Cape turtle doves and laughing doves that are attracted to the waterholes. Some of the smaller birds include doublebanded coursers, cutthroat finches, chestnutbacked finchlarks, Sabota larks and penduline tits.

Vegetation

This area is dominated by tree and scrub savanna that covers the ancient dune fields.

North-western Botswana has a tremendous variety of trees, that give much denser cover than that of the southern Kalahari. The vegetation provides the San with the bulk of their diet, by way of tubers, roots, berries, fruits and leaves. Species that abound and the fruits of which are used by the San include mongongo and the white bauhinia or coffee-bean and the various grewia species. Kalahari apple-leaf, blackthorn and candle-pod acacias are common throughout this region. The peeling-bark ochna (*Ochna pulchra*) is used by the San to brush their teeth. The grapple or devil's claw (*Harpogophytum procumbens*) is a ground creeper with red tubular flowers and a large grapple-like thorn often seen in the Kalahari. The tubers are harvested and sold in most market places as a remedy against arthritis and many of other ailments.

On top of the knoll that houses the caverns are some mopane aloes (*Aloe littoralis*) and Namaqua fig trees (*Ficus cordata*), not recorded elsewhere in Botswana.

The People
The San

The western Kalahari is the home of the !Kung San. Traditionally they are hunter-gatherers, the men being responsible for hunting and the women for gathering fruits and tubers. Traditional ways among the San, as with most other peoples, are giving way to more modern lifestyles. The schools at Xai-Xai and Gcangwa symbolise this change as the government continues with its policy of integrating them into mainstream society. The provision of water and the supply of drought relief food-aid have

had the effect of attracting San bands to the permanent villages. The international boundary fence between Botswana and Namibia splits the !Kung groups in half, but styles have been erected along the fences for their use so that they may cross the boundary unhindered by customs and immigration formalities.

Ovaherero

The Ovaherero probably arrived in Botswana in about 1810, and many more fled from the German/Ovaherero War of 1904 to 1905. When they arrived as refugees, they left their wealth behind and worked as servants. However, they slowly built up their resources until, today, they are among the wealthiest cattle owners in the country. The distinctive traditional dress of the women stems from German missionary influence during the Victorian era.

Following an agreement between the Botswana and Namibian governments, the Ovaherero were given the option of returning, with all their cattle, to their ancestral homes in Namibia. About 750 people, most of these recent refugees to Botswana, accepted the offer and left for Namibia in May 1993, but most of the population elected to remain in Botswana.

ACCOMMODATION

There are no lodges within a comfortable day's drive from Aha Hills or Drotsky's Caverns, so you must be prepared to camp.

Public campsites

There is no development for tourism in the western Kalahari, hence you may camp where you like. There are some shady sites at Aha Hills, but take care not to get stuck in the thick sand around the hills. There is little shade around Drotsky's Caverns. Water is available from Xai-Xai and Gcangwa but there is no water at the caverns or the hills. Make sure you are completely self-sufficient.

ABOVE LEFT: *Traditional temporary shelters erected by a San hunting party.*
BELOW: *Digging and finding fresh water in seemingly dry terrain.*

ADVISORY: THE KALAHARI

CLIMATE

In winter, the days are hot and the nights bitterly cold. Temperatures can drop as low as -12 °C, while day-time temperatures may hover in the high thirties.

In summer, the days are scorching and the cooler nights are most welcome.

Best times to visit
Central Kalahari Game Reserve
Game viewing is best form March to June.
Khutse Game Reserve
The area has still not fully recovered from the droughts of the eighties, large concentrations of animals have been absent, but birding is worthwhile.
Gemsbok National Park
Game viewing is at its best here from March to early May, when game comes to the riverbeds for food and water. However, viewing is reasonable all year round.
Mabuasehube Game Reserve
September to April or May is when the large concentrations of eland and red hartebeest can be found.
Western Kalahari
Tsodilo Hills and Drotsky's Caverns are worth a visit any time of year. The sandy roads leading there are best after the rains, but you must cross many pans filled with water. The summer months are best for birding when the migrants are still around.

MAIN ATTRACTIONS

Because of its great size and inhospitable nature, much of the Kalahari is undeveloped and it offers visitors the ultimate wilderness experience. It is home to many varieties of bird and animal life, as well as some of the last traditional San communities in Botswana. Fine examples of their paintings can be seen at Tsodilo Hills. Sheltering magnificent stalactites and stalagmites, Drotsky's Caverns are one of the country's natural wonders.

TRAVEL

The parks are very remote and, apart from the Central Kalahari, are seldom visited on an organised basis by any safari operators. To visit these areas, you will need to contact a mobile operator specialising in tailored safaris (see page 183).

Most visitors to the Kalahari organise their own safari. Any trip into this region must be very carefully planned. For safety, travel in a convoy of at least two vehicles. Take a map – a hand-drawn one from the game scouts' camps will suffice if nothing else is available – and a compass. Carry a complete set of spares and tools (see page 38 for suggested list). It is common courtesy to assist anyone who is stranded .

Basic foodstuffs and fuel are available from Tshabong, Jwaneng, Werda, Ghanzi, Rakops and Etsha.

Ice is only available in Ghanzi. There are no facilities in the reserves and visitors must be self-sufficient .

ACCOMMODATION

Ghanzi (see page 135)
Kalahari Arms Hotel A typical small town hotel located in the centre of Ghanzi. Offers comfortable new rondavels with private facilities, a restaurant that serves wholesome meals, a bar and a swimming pool. PO Box 29, Ghanzi; Tel: 596-311.
Kanana Game Lodge A new lodge 55 kilometres west of Ghanzi on the road to Gobabis, Namibia. Accommodation and dining room built around a waterhole. Game drives and walks can be arranged. PO Box 2, Ghanzi; Tel/fax: 596-166.

Campsites
Kalahari Arms Hotel There is a public campsite at the hotel, but facilities are minimal. Hotel amenities may be used. PO Box 29, Ghanzi; Tel: 596-311.
Jakkalsputs Camping is permitted on this farm, which is owned by John Hardbattle. The signposted turnoff is 70 kilometres west of Ghanzi. Offers ablution facilities, braai stands, a swimming pool and meals by arrangement. PO Box 173, Ghanzi. Tel: 596-241; Fax: 596-166.

Serowe(see page 135)
The accommodation in both of Serowe's hotels is below normal economy standard, but is available should you need it.
Serowe Hotel Offers 6 double and 5 single rooms with *en suite* bathrooms, a bar/restaurant and bottle store. PO Box 150, Serowe; Tel: 430-234.
Tswaragano Hotel Has thatched rondavels with *en suite* bathrooms and a bar/restaurant. PO Box 102, Serowe; Tel: 430-377.

Public campsites are the only accommodation available in the Kalahari parks. All of these are managed by the Department of Wildlife and National Parks, PO Box 131, Gaborone; Tel: 371-405. Bookings are not necessary, and entry permits and fees are payable at the entrance gates. In the Western Kalahari at Tsodilo Hills and Drotsky's Caverns, there are no designated campsites and visitors are allowed to camp wherever they choose. Opening times are:
1 April to 30 September 06h00 to 18h00
1 October to 31 March 05h30 to 19h00

Tsodilo Hills and Drotsky's Caverns
Both places have been declared national monuments and are protected by law. Further information can be obtained from the Gaborone National Museum and Art Gallery, PO Box 00114, Gaborone; Tel: 374-616.

HEALTH HAZARDS

Malaria. Potentially dangerous animals. It is very easy to get lost in these reserves, so a map and compass are essential, as well as adequate supplies.

EASTERN BOTSWANA AND
THE TULI BLOCK

Eastern Botswana, also known as the Hardveld, lies between the Limpopo River and the eastern boundary of the Kalahari Sandveld. It roughly encompasses everything east of the main Gaborone/Kasane highway, from the Tropic of Capricorn in the south as far north as the Dukwe veterinary fence. The Tuli Block is a strip of land following the contours of south-eastern Botswana that wedges in between Transvaal in South Africa and Zimbabwe and takes its name from the Zimbabwean Tuli River. The Tuli Circle, a semicircle with a radius of approximately 16 kilometres and still incorporated in Botswana's easternmost borderline, was granted to the BSAC (see page 24) by King Khama III in 1891, to ensure that lung sickness, which had stricken the Bangwato herds, did not reach the animals at Fort Tuli.

This boulder-strewn part of the world is the 'Cinderella' of Botswana, unexplored by most visitors as it is not on the well-trodden paths to the north. It deserves a lot more attention, however, as it has its own beauty and is of great historical and archaeological importance.

Tourists approaching Botswana from the south on the main highway will pass through a number of cities and towns along their way. The following places can be used as stopping points to break the journey north.

Lobatse

A pleasant town set among the hills 65 kilometres south of Gaborone, houses the High Court of Botswana. The first abattoir was built here in 1934. A meat canning factory was added in 1954 and it is now one of the largest meat- processing plants in Africa. The highest point in Botswana, Otse Hill (1 489 metres above sea level) is set north of Lobatse on the

Walking beneath a sandstone massif in Eastern Botswana.

road to Gaborone. There is one hotel in the centre of town (see *Advisory*, page 172).

Gaborone

Capital of Botswana, Gaborone is situated in the south-east of the country on the Ngotwane River within a few kilometres of the South African border.

Before independence in 1966 the country's administrative headquarters were in Mafikeng in South Africa. It was then decided to build a new town on the site of the old district headquarters (Gaberones, as it was then called) and to name it after Chief Gaborone of the Batlokwa tribe.

Declared a city in 1986, Gaborone is the fastest growing settlement in Africa today with a growth rate of 10,3 per cent per year and a population of 150 000. Rapid expansion has taken place in every sphere of community life. Glass and concrete high-rise buildings tower above neat suburban houses. Residents are proud of the new modern shopping areas, the public library, the Botswana University, the National Museum and Art Gallery and the National Sports Stadium, which has facilities for international sports events and shows. The National Assembly, the office of the President and all government ministries and department headquarters are housed in Gaborone, and employ half of all the working people in the city.

Roads can be a nightmare at rush hour and accompanying bottle-neck problems are as inevitable as they are inconvenient.

Today, Gaborone offers every amenity you could hope to find in a modern city, in good and constant supply. These include banks, all manner of food and fresh supplies, hospitals, doctors and dentists, garages and mechanics, as well as bookstores, handicraft outlets and other speciality shops.

Visitors to Gaborone have a choice of six hotels offering pleasant modern facilities as well as several standard hotels that are, unfortunately, situated out of town and inconvenient to reach without transport (see *Advisory*, page 172).

GABORONE STREET MAP

Places of interest to visit in and around Gaborone include:

The National Museum and Art Gallery, open Tuesdays to Fridays from 09h00 to 18h00, and on weekends and public holidays from 09h00 to 17h00. Closed over Easter and on Christmas and Boxing days. Entry is free. It is well worth making time to visit this museum, which specialises in information on fauna and ethnographic material. It provides an opportunity to familiarise yourself with the wildlife and customs of the country. The gallery houses paintings by local artists, South Africans and, most interestingly, from some of the original European explorers including Thomas Baines.

St Clair Lion Park, set on the banks of the Ngotwane River, 18 kilometres south of Gaborone on the Lobatse road. It is open from 10h00 to 18h00 every day and a small entry fee is charged. Popular for weekend getaways, the park caters for families and offers a restaurant and bar, picnic spots, train and motorbike rides for children, horse trails and swimming.

It also has the only camping facilities around Gaborone as well as a range of amenities (see *Advisory*, page 172 for details).

The lions and their cubs are the main attraction, but the park is also home to other species of wildlife that includes impala, kuku, zebra, warthog, duiker and even the occasional leopard. A variety of birds are attracted to the trees along the river. Enjoy a game drive through the park, either in your own four-wheel drive or join an organised trip in a park vehicle.

Gaborone Game Reserve, located on the edge of town just off Limpopo road, comprises 550 hectare (5 square kilometres) of bush. A rhino as well as antelope such as kudu, eland, wildebeest, impala, gemsbok, zebra are the main attractions. It is open between 06h30 and 18h30 and normal park fees are payable, as it is administered by the Department of Wildlife and National Parks.

Manyelanong Game Reserve is situated a few kilometres from the village of Otse *en route* to Lobatse. Late May to September/October is the best time to visit this Cape vulture breeding colony. The birds are in a fenced area where entry is not allowed as it disturbs the vultures. A minimal entry fee is payable to the reserve attendant.

Kolobeng, half an hour's drive west of Gaborone on the Thamaga road, is the ruins of the mission where David Livingstone lived in the 1840s. It is here that he planned his travels to the interior and converted Chief Sechele to Christianity. This is the site of many firsts in Botswana: the first church, the first doctor of western medicine, the first irrigation project and buildings built by European methods. All that remains of Livingstone's mission station is the floor of his house and some graves; his daughter and the artist Thomas Dolman are both buried here. A National Museum information board provides details of local history and a site museum is currently being planned.

Gaborone Dam is the place for windsurfing, fishing and sailing. Picnic and braai spots are available to the public, but are some distance from the water's edge. Entry and fishing permits are available at a nominal fee from the

Department of Water Affairs, Private Bag 0029, Gaborone; Tel: 352-241.

Gabane Village, a scenic spot, hidden in the rocky outcrops about ten kilometres west of Gaborone *en route* to Kolobeng. Here you will find Pelegano Village Industries, best known for its unusual pottery (see page 188).

Lentswe-La-Oodi Weavers, a village workshop 18 kilometres north of Gaborone, where woven tapestries and wall hangings are made and sold to the public (see page 188).

Mokolodi Crafts, located 15 kilometres south of Gaborone on the Lobatse road, is famous for ceramic and carved bone jewellery (see page 188).

Mochudi

Another of Botswana's very scenic and traditional villages nestling among a range of hills 40 kilometres north of Gaborone. There are many interesting sites around Mochudi other than the graphically decorated courtyards in front of houses with huge thatched roofs. Look out for the two colonial-style buildings (an historical rarity in a country where there was little colonial development), the Dutch Reformed Church and the Mochudi National School. Here, you will find the two southernmost baobabs in Botswana and the Phuthadikobo Museum, originally a school built and sponsored by the people themselves to further practical secondary education. The museum houses the silkscreen workshop. It is open weekdays 08h00 to 17h00 and weekends 14h00 to 17h00; an entrance fee is charged.

Mahalapye

This is the first town past Mochudi *en route* from Gaborone to Francistown and North-east Tuli Game Reserve. It is another picturesque town beneath shady trees and rocky outcrops towering above the railway line and shops. At Shoshong, a village in the hills 25 kilometres west of Mahalapye, are the remains of an old church where the missionary John Mackenzie lived for 14 years. He played a major rôle in assisting the chiefs in bringing Bechuanaland under British rule and opposing the Batswana

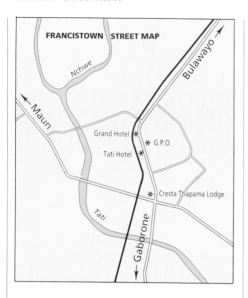

FRANCISTOWN STREET MAP

Nchwe

Bulawayo →

← Maun

Grand Hotel *

* G.P.O.

Tati Hotel *

* Cresta Thapama Lodge

Tati

Gabbrone

← Gabrone

ABOVE: *The Marang Motel set amid shady attractive gardens.*
OPPOSITE RIGHT: *Francistown's modern and well-utilised Civic Centre.*

and a bookshop. There are two hotels in town (see *Advisory*, page 173). Curios and crafts are available from the Handicrafts Club or from Bushman Craft at Tonota, a village north of Selebi-Phikwe on the road to Francistown.

territory being colonised by the Boers. There is a large flat stone that served as a bell to hail the people to church. When the stone is struck by another rock, it sounds just like a church bell.

Mahalapye is the new Railway Headquarters of Botswana. Accommodation is available at the hotel (see *Advisory*, page 173).

Palapye

At the crossroads to Francistown and Orapa, Palapye was once the capital of Khama III before he moved to nearby Serowe. It boasts a new modern shopping centre and hotel (see *Advisory*, page 173).

Selebi-Phikwe

Until 1992, Selebi-Phikwe was a remote place, but thanks to the new tarred road via Ellisras and Martin's Drift, this growing industrial centre is now halfway between Kasane and Johannesburg. Despite the fact that this copper and nickel mining town is so young – it was only established in 1967 – it has grown to be the third largest town in Botswana.

It offers all the supplies and services you may need: fuel, garages, banks, take-aways,

Francistown

The oldest and second largest town in Botswana derives its name from an English prospector, miner and entrepreneur, Daniel Francis, who was first attracted to the region in the gold rush of 1869. Francistown, split in two by the Tati River, developed primarily as a town to service the mineral extraction industry. Gold, copper and nickel are still mined in the vicinity, although the diamond mine at Orapa and soda ash plant at Sowa have now eclipsed the mines at Francistown in importance to the national economy.

Francistown grew to be the capital of the north and the last staging post for supplies and a touch of civilisation. Although it has expanded in recent years into a sizeable town with a population of over 60 000, it is no longer your last chance to stock up on necessary goods for the journey north, as Maun has now become totally self-sufficient in this respect. It is, however, the last train stop in Botswana and the crossroads for all Botswana's major international transport routes. Francistown is the main point of entry to Bulawayo in Zimbabwe, three hours' drive away, and is a popular and

convenient overnight stop on many tourist routes. There are four hotels in Francistown (see *Advisory*, page 173).

Here you will be able to purchase everything you may need. Shops include well stocked supermarkets, an excellent butchery and bakery, and take-away and fast food outlets. Fuel, vehicle spares and tyres, mechanics and workshops are also available. There are two banks. The largest referral hospital in Botswana was recently completed here so doctors, pharmacies and dentists are at hand. Places of interest include:

Supa-Ngwao Museum Recently opened and centrally situated, this museum is the cultural centre of north-eastern Botswana and also houses a tourist information centre.

NORTH-EAST TULI GAME RESERVE

No visit to the eastern Botswana can be considered complete without a trip to the North-east Tuli Game Reserve. It is located between the Limpopo, Motloutse (Great Elephant) and Shashe rivers, and is the largest privately owned conservation area in southern Africa. It is home to the largest herd of elephant on privately owned land in the world.

The 90 000-hectare reserve comprises the 46 000-hectare Mashatu Game Reserve, and Tuli Lodge. However, with the adjoining farms from the Tuli Circle and Jwala, the region covers a total of 120 000 hectares, and is rich in game that have free reign over the whole unfenced area.

GETTING THERE

By air

North-east Tuli Game Reserve, commonly called Tuli Game Reserve, has an airstrip at Tuli Lodge where you can attend to customs and immigration formalities. The lodges will alert the authorities to your arrival. Air Botswana flies to Tuli from Gaborone, Maun and Victoria Falls on Fridays and Sundays. Other airstrips in the area are at Jwala and all the towns in the vicinity, Selebi-Phikwe and Palapye being the closest. Customs can also be cleared at Francistown. Private charters must get clearance from the Department of Civil Aviation (PO Box 250, Gaborone; Tel: 371-397). Landing fees and airport tax are payable at the lodges.

By road

Tuli Game Reserve is a five-hour drive from both Johannesburg and Gaborone. Visitors from South Africa should consider commencing their tour of Botswana at Tuli. The tarred road via Ellisras and Martin's Drift makes this the shortest route to northern Botswana.

During the rainy season (December to April) when the Limpopo and Motloutse are in flood, Pont Drift is not fordable and the only way to cross the river is by cable car, for which a small fee is payable. Collection from there by the respective lodges has to be pre-arranged, but it is usually done at 12h00 and at 15h00. Vehicles are left in a secure area, which is locked at night. Customs and immigration must be cleared at the border post, which closes at 16h00.

The best route to Tuli and Mashatu from Gaborone is to turn right at Mahalapye then travel 102 kilometres to Machaneng, followed by a further 170 kilometres to Baines Drift. From there, it is 40 kilometres to Pont Drift. The roads are graded gravel and can be negotiated by a two-wheel drive vehicle.

To reach Mashatu and Tuli from Francistown, travel via Selebi-Phikwe (144 kilometres) towards Bobonong (79 kilometres) and then on to Pont Drift (120 kilometres). While four-wheel drive is not essential except to cross the seasonally flooded Motloutse

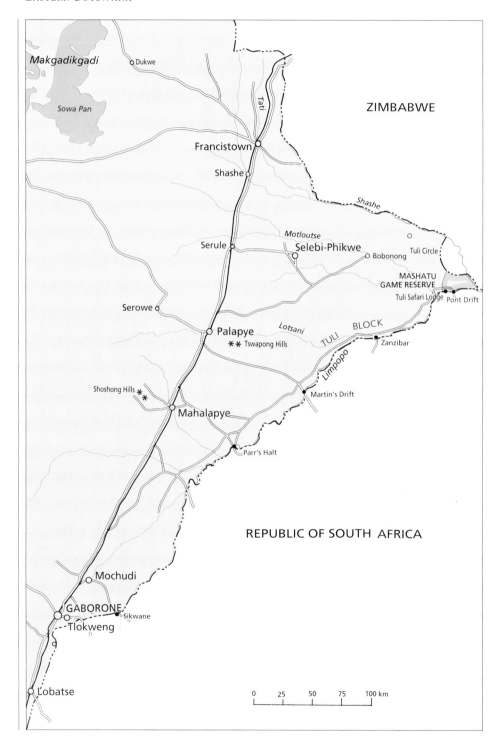

River, the riverbed can become extremely sandy in the late dry season and can also be impassable due to flooding after heavy rains. Contact your lodge about the road conditions before starting your journey.

Tuli Lodge is approximately 7 kilometres west of the border at Pont Drift. Follow the well signposted road from the border.

The Selous/Makamana Road

This is the 70-kilometre road built in 1890 by the famous hunter Frederick Courtney Selous, who was intelligence officer and path finder to the Pioneer Column at the time (see page 24 for details). Selous, with the help of the Bangwato headman Makamana and 200 of his followers, built the road between Fort Matlaputla, near Bobonong, and Fort Tuli on the Shashe River. It was completed within two months in order to get supplies and the Pioneer Column to Fort Matlaputla. The present road via Bobonong, Semolale and Gobojango follows the general direction of the old road, which was also used by settler wagons, post riders and pioneers. It then veers south to the Tuli Block.

The Mashatu cableway enables visitors to cross the mighty Limpopo in a most unusual way.

Missionaries Road

This road was used by the London Missionary Society to reach their mission at Inyati in Zimbabwe. Robert Moffat was among the first missionaries to use this road. Hunters, explorers and traders used it to reach the far interior, as did the gold diggers going to Tati (Francistown) and Bulawayo. On one occasion, Selous did the 100 miles from Tati to Old Palapye in 27 hours on his pony, Mars. The present road between Palapye, Selebi-Phikwe, Mmadinare, Makome Hills and Francistown follows the general direction of the old wagon and coach road.

WHAT TO SEE AND DO

Tuli is a place of striking landscapes. The easternmost part of Botswana around Pont Drift offers eroded sandstone massifs that rise from flat, scrub-covered plains. The country surrounding Mashatu Game Reserve is extremely picturesque, with hills, rocky outcrops and lush vegetation along the river. Further north towards Jwala, an area of austere beauty, the landscape changes and is dominated by mopane belts along dry riverbeds with coarse black sand. The whole region north of the Motloutse River is also very attractive with

granite hills and dry river beds, lined with beautiful shady trees.

The Tropic of Capricorn lies south of Mahalapye and is clearly signposted.

Solomon's Wall

Close to the confluence of the Limpopo and Motloutse Rivers, located approximately 24 kilometres west of Pont Drift, is a large dolerite outcrop. The rock strata resembles two massive stone walls some 30 metres high keeping guard on either side of the Motloutse River, like the entrance to an ancient citadel. River water is trapped in deep, clear pools on the sandy riverbed. Fever trees surround this natural beach, making it an idyllic shady picnic spot. A four-wheel drive vehicle is essential for this crossing.

Ancient rock formations of granite gneisses are to be found in the area around Francistown and Modipane, as well as on the farms along the Molopo River. These rocks, often pink in colour, are between 2 700 and 3 500 million years old and are probably the oldest known rocks in the world. They are also of economic importance, as they yield a range of metal ores including gold, copper, nickel, and kimberlite.

There must have been a great lake on the Motloutse at one time, as semi-precious stones such as agate and quartzite can be found along the riverbeds. Indeed, this is where the country's first three diamonds were found in a village called Foley, just south of Francistown.

Prospectors searched for the source of these diamonds for nearly 12 years before they realised that the Motloutse was perhaps once connected to the ancient inland lake of Makgadikgadi. Within six months, prospecting much further west near Orapa revealed the world's second largest kimberlite pipe, a huge source of diamonds.

In the Lepokole Hills, 25 kilometres north of Bobonong, are the southern continuation of the eroded granite formations of Matopos in Zimbabwe. Rocks balanced on top of one another form towers that sometimes reach heights of more than 100 metres, narrow passages and caves.

Archaeological and Historical Sites

Mysteries and legends abound in this historically rich area. Ruin sites are scattered throughout the area with pottery shards and beads that bear testimony to early human presence in the area. It is believed that the peoples who lived here may have given rise to the culture of Great Zimbabwe.

The river basin was probably first occupied by iron age peoples during the 6th century. Ruins indicate that they lived on hill tops and built low protective walls and terraces for their houses. Sites in the area include evidence of smelting activities and granaries. Approximately 30 kilometres west of Mahalapye in the Shoshong Hills, and 40 kilometres north of Palapye at Toutswemogala, are the remains of a few large villages situated on the hill tops. These villages date back to AD 1050 and occupy six or more hectares. Surrounding these, and fairly close to them, were a number of smaller hill-top settlements. Because they are situated on hill tops, these sites are not easy to find and the services of a guide from one of the nearby villages should be engaged.

Other historical sites in the area that show evidence of earlier human habitation are to be found at Pont Drift, Serowe, Mokgware Hills south of Serowe, Serule, Sefophe, on the Lotsane River halfway between Zanzibar and Sherwood Ranch, as well as north and north-east of Francistown.

At Maredi Hill, 1 kilometre south of the Lepokole Hills, is a cave housing fine rock paintings which have been shaded to give a three dimensional perspective. Although the precise age of the paintings is not known, they are thought to be some 2 000 years old. It is not easy to find, as it is high up in the gorge. There are approximately 60 paintings of antelope and human figures in black, white and ochre.

A rock painting of sheep is situated in the hills near Molalatau. Enquiries should be directed to the *kgosi* (chief) if you want to visit it.

Colonial history was also made in eastern Botswana. David Livingstone visited this area during the course of his travels. The artist,

ABOVE: *A vast herd of elephant cross the Matobole River in the Mashatu Game Reserve.*
RIGHT: *Solomon's Wall – an impressive dolerite outcrop.*

naturalist and explorer, Thomas Baines, delighted in this area and painted numerous scenes at Mashatu. Rudyard Kipling, the British author, described the Limpopo in his *Just-so Stories* as '... the great grey green greasy Limpopo all set about with fever trees ...'. It was the setting he used to describe how an elephant child has his nose stretched to a trunk by the crocodile. Do not be surprised to find only a dry river bed with the occasional pool in winter, or turbulent muddy red waters trying to escape their embankments after the summer rains in place of the languid stream described by Kipling.

Frederick Courtney Selous, the most famous of all the 'Great White Hunters', hunted elephant in this area. There were skirmishes during the Anglo-Boer War in the region and remnants, such as bullet cartridges, are still to be found. The Pioneer Column of the British South Africa Company passed just west of the Tuli Block along the Zeederberg trail. South-east of Bobonong at Matlaputla are the ruins of a square 1,5 metre high earthen wall of a Rhodesian pioneer column fort, surrounded by a trench, which dates back to 1890. The remains of a fair-sized hospital, a sports club and an electric light plant may still be found here, as can signs of early telephone contact with Mafikeng.

Remember, all archaeological and historical sites are strictly protected by law and it is an offence to remove or disturb anything.

Wildlife

The North-east Tuli Game Reserve is a delight for anyone keen on game viewing as the animals there are as diverse as they are prolific. There are over 840 elephant, black-maned lions which are the same species as the Kalahari lions, leopard, cheetah, hyaena, aardvark, black-backed jackal, bat-eared fox, African

TOP LEFT: *Look-out bar and waterhole, Mashatu Main Camp.*
BELOW: *Mashatu is one of the few reserves to offer game -viewing walks.*

babbler. Ostriches are commonly seen. Where acacia and combretum woodland take over south of the winter frost line, rich and varied bird life occurs. You can expect to see a variety of raptors, hornbills, woodpeckers, babblers, flycatchers, shrikes, starlings, swallows and waxbills. The Limpopo riverine strip is home to the pygmy kingfisher and longtailed starling, as well as the more usual array of cormorants and darters.

There are breeding colonies of black eagles and lappetfaced vultures in the area. The Tswapong Hills east of Palapye house breeding colonies of Cape vultures, but their numbers are declining as a result of the decrease in the hyaena population caused by increased cattle farming. The hyaenas leave slivers of bone at their kills, which the vultures require to provide calcium for their young. Because of a calcium deficiency, the young lack the bone development to be able to fly.

wild cat, giraffe, eland, kudu, bushbuck, wildebeest, waterbuck, impala, zebra, warthog, serval, crocodile, hippo, baboon, klipspringer, duiker, steenbok and dassie.

Tuli Game Reserve affords all guests an exclusive game-viewing experience as each lodge operates only within their immediate vicinity to avoid over-crowding; therefore it is not open to casual visitors. Mashatu offers day and night game-viewing drives, and walking trails with armed guards. Tuli Lodge offers game drives and walks, also in the company of armed guards.

Mashatu main camp and tented camp both overlook floodlit waterholes.

Bird-watching

The bird life in the whole Tuli area is varied and abundant, with over 350 species recorded. Some experts regard it as one of the top five birding spots in southern Africa. The mopane forests are a favourite place for Arnot's chat and rock pigeons are common in the hills.

It is also well worth searching for the elusive boulder chat among the granite hills, as well as the short-toed rock thrush and the sooty

Vegetation

The area encompasses wide habitat diversity, ranging from sub-tropical river valleys to open savanna, from Kalahari sandveld to combretum/acacia and mopane woodland. The mashatu or nyala tree (*Xanthocercis zambesiaca*) dominates the riverine forests. Commonly seen along the roads in Tuli are the sesame trees (*Sesamothamnus lugardii*), with their fleshy swollen yellow trunks and numerous stiff grey branches. Other predominant species are fever trees (*Acacia xanthophloea*), mopane, baobab, water acacia (*Acacia nebrownii*), zebra corkwood (*Commiphora merkeri*) and both large-leafed rock fig (*Ficus soldanella*) and small-leafed rock fig (*Ficus tettensis*).

Hundreds of years of subsistence farming in the area has, unfortunately, altered the natural vegetation, robbed the rivers of much of their luxuriant plant life, and laid bare large tracts of land.

ACCOMMODATION
Mashatu Game Reserve
This is home to the largest elephant population on freehold land in the world. There are two camps in Mashatu.

Mashatu Main Camp
Conveniently situated 35 minutes from Pont Drift, this camp offers visitors a luxurious wildlife experience. A bar and dining room overlook a spotlit waterhole, from where one can sit in shady comfort and view the animals.
Features:
• Accommodation in ten chalets and five rondavels, all air-conditioned • Swimming pool • *En suite* facilities • Curio shop • Spotlit waterhole • Day and night game-viewing drives • Game walks

Mashatu Tented Camp
Located 7 kilometres north-east of Mashatu main camp.
Features:
• Accommodation in seven comfortable Meru tents • Rustic *en suite* facilities • Solar power only • Plunge pool • Spotlit waterhole and hides • Day and night game-viewing drives • Game walks

Tuli Safari Lodge
Situated within a 7 500-hectare private game reserve, Tuli is the oldest of the lodges on the reserve and is set in lush green gardens close to the Limpopo. Facilities have recently been upgraded to de luxe standard. The bar is built around a 600-year-old mashatu tree. There are two hides built on stilts where guests can overnight and enjoy superb game viewing.
Features:
• Accommodation in thatched chalets • *En suite* facilities • Swimming pool • Well equipped conference centre • Curio shop • 2 hides • Game-viewing drives and walks

Public campsites
Camping is not allowed anywhere within the Tuli Game Reserve.

WILD ANIMALS

The hippo's jaws can easily slice a person or, on occasion, a boat in two.

Should you come across a wild animal in the bush, be it reptile or mammal, the golden rule is never to turn your back on it and run away. Remain absolutely motionless until you can back off slowly and unobtrusively. Move at the animal's pace. Keep your eyes on it without staring directly at the animal as this is frequently regarded as a challenge. Give it plenty of room to go its own way. Never position yourself between a mother and her young or cut animals off from the rest of their herd. Never make an animal feel cornered.
Hippo Never get between hippo and water. When you are in a boat or mekoro on the water, give them fair warning of your presence, either by tapping the side of the vessel or talking loudly. Keep to the shallow edge and allow them plenty of room to get to the deep water where they will feel safe again.
Lion and hyaena Stand your ground if you accidentally encounter one of these animals at close quarters. Do not run. If you run, you are behaving like a prey species and you will be chased. If the animal shows aggression, show aggression in return. Shout, wave your arms and even advance towards the animal. If it charges, charge back and make as much ferocious noise as possible.
Buffalo Look for a suitably sturdy tree and quickly climb it.

ADVISORY: EASTERN BOTSWANA AND TULI BLOCK

CLIMATE

On winter days temperatures can reach 35 °C or more while the nights are very cold. In summer the days are scorchingly hot, making the cooler nights most welcome. October to April is the rainy season.

BEST TIMES TO VISIT

Game viewing is best from April to December.

MAIN ATTRACTIONS

This picturesque area is renowned for its wealth of historical and archaeological sites. Wildlife is prolific and varied, and Mashatu is famous for its large herds of elephant. The region is a bird-watcher's delight, with over 350 species having been identified.

TRAVEL

Most people visiting Tuli Game Reserve choose to fly in to either Mashatu or Francistown on a scheduled Air Botswana service. Charter flights can also be arranged from Gaborone, Maun and Kasane.

Many of the main access roads and bush tracks are normally negotiable by two-wheel drive vehicles. During the dry months some of the dirt roads may be corrugated or very sandy, but passable. However, off these main routes there are some steep gradients, sandy rivers and streams that require four-wheel drive vehicles. Roads may be rocky, or covered in loose grit which causes vehicles to slip and slide down inclines and play havoc with undercarriages, oil sumps and tyres. When crossing the narrow rocky drifts vehicle exhausts, tow bars, trailers and vehicles with low clearance tend to catch on the bottom.

During the rainy season the red clay and black cotton soil turns into muddy quagmires and the roads are sometimes badly washed away in places. Flash floods can occur during storms and you should be very aware of this possibility when crossing the numerous drifts. The Limpopo River is not negotiable during the summer months and tourists are best advised to stay on the main routes.

Supplies and fuel are available from Selebi-Phikwe, Francistown, Palapye and Mahalapye. Ice is available from Francistown and Selebi-Phikwe.

ACCOMMODATION

Lobatse

Cresta Cumberland Hotel In the centre of town, set amidst beautiful gardes. Offers *en suite* rooms, a restaurant and bar, swimming pool, conference centre, tennis court and sauna. PO Box 135, Lobatse; Tel: 330-281; Fax: 332-016; Central Reservations South Africa; Tel: (011) 787-9500; Fax: (011) 787-9757.

Gaborone

Cresta Gaborone Hotel Close to the railway station and bus terminus, this hotel has 44 bedrooms, each with *en suite* shower, TV, telephone, radio, and ceiling fan. Facilities include a restaurant, cocktail bar, take-away service and courtesy transport. Suitable for the budget-conscious traveller. Private Bag 00127, Gaborone; Tel: 375-200; Fax: 375-201.

Cresta Lodge A modern hotel, built to international four-star standard. Centrally situated. Landscaped gardens and nature trails add to its appeal. 80 luxury rooms with *en suite* bathroom, air conditioning, telephone and radio. Swimming pool, restaurant and cocktail bar, courtesy transport and boardroom facilities available. Private Bag 00126, Gaborone; Tel:375-375; Fax: 375-376.

Cresta President Hotel Situated in the Mall in the centre of town. Rooms have *en suite* bathroom, air conditioning, TV, telephone, refrigerator. Three restaurants, conference facilities and courtesy transport available. PO Box 200, Gaborone; Tel: 353-631; Fax: 351-840.

Gaborone Sun Newly expanded and refurbished, this hotel offers 203 *en suite* rooms including four presidential suites. Also on site are a variety of restaurants and bars, a swimming pool, tennis and squash courts, golf course, conference facilities and a casino. Private Bag 0016, Gaborone; Tel: 351-111; Fax: 351-111, ext. 2522.

Oasis Motel Located 4 kilometres from downtown Gaborone on the Tlokweng road to the South African border. Has 50 self-contained chalets with bedroom, lounge and kitchenette. Other amenities include restaurant, swimming pool, gymnasium, conference facilities and courtesy transport. PO Box 30331, Gaborone; Tel: 356-396; Fax: 312-968.

Sheraton Gaborone Situated 4 kilometres out of Gaborone. Set in beautiful gardens with walking trails around a bird pond, this complex offers 199 *en suite* rooms, as well as de luxe suites in true five-star tradition. Also on site are several restaurants and bars, a swimming pool, squash and tennis courts, a sauna, gymnasium, conference facilities, a bank and a curio shop. PO Box 2025, Gaborone; Tel: 312-999; Fax: 312-989.

Campsites

St Clair's Lion Park The only caravan and campsite in and around Gaborone. Offers clean ablution facilities, braai stands, firewood for sale, electric points, shady campsites and a restaurant and bar. PO Box 238, Gaborone; Tel/fax: 372-711.

Mahalapye

Mahalapye Hotel A quaint hotel overlooking a dry riverbed. Has rondavels with *en suite* facilities, a restaurant and bar. Camping facilities also on site. PO Box 526, Mahalapye; Tel: 410-200.

Palapye

Cresta Botsalo Hotel Newly renovated and a handy overnight stop on the way from Gaborone to the Okavango, this hotel offers air-conditioned rooms with TV, a restaurant and cocktail bar, swimming pool and curio shop. PO Box 35, Palapye; Tel: 420-245; Fax: 420-587.

Selebi-Phikwe

Cresta Bosele Hotel Centrally situated, this hotel features rooms with *en suite* facilities, a restaurant and bar, swimming pool and conference facilities. PO Box 177, Selebi-Phikwe; Tel: 810-675; Fax: 811-083.

Syringa Lodge Named after the giant Syringa tree (*Burkea africana*) in the garden and situated on the edge of town on the road to Bobonong. Offers luxury air-conditioned rooms with *en suite* facilities, TV and video, a restaurant serving excellent meals, a bar, swimming pool, hairdresser and curio shop. PO Box 254, Selebi-Phikwe; Tel: 810-444/019; Fax: 810-450.

Francistown

Cresta Thapama Lodge Recently upgraded and now one of the larger hotels in the country. Centrally situated amidst beautifully landscaped gardens, it also has its own shopping centre. 100 air-conditioned rooms with TV, telephone; other amenities include restaurants, bars, a swimming pool, squash courts, a gymnasium and conference facilities. Private Bag 31, Francistown; Tel: 213-991; Fax: 213-766.

Grand Hotel Centrally situated. Although recent renovations have improved the quality of this hotel's facilities, they still fall far short of international standards. Facilities include communal bathrooms and a bar/restaurant. PO Box 30, Francistown; Tel/fax: 212-300.

The Marang Motel Five kilometres south-east of town, this hotel is set in exquisite grounds amidst rolling green lawns and lush gardens on the banks of the Tati River. Accommodation includes family chalets, rondavels and executive rooms with air conditioning, TV, telephone and radio. Other amenities include a restaurant, cocktail bar, swimming pool and conference facilities. PO Box 807, Francistown; Tel: 213-991; Fax: 212-130.

Tati Hotel Centrally located, recently renovated and of a similar standard to the Grand Hotel. Communal bathrooms and a bar/restaurant. PO Box 15, Francistown; Tel: 212-255; Fax: 215-079.

Campsites

The Marang Motel Five kilometres from the centre of town and the only campsite in Francistown. Courtesy transport is not available, but taxis can be hailed and a staff bus in the mornings and evenings will give you a lift. Offers ablution facilities and plenty of shade. PO Box 807, Francistown; Tel: 213-991; Fax: 212-130.

North-east Tuli Game Reserve

For a more detailed description of the establishments listed below, refer to page 171.

Mashatu Game Reserve Guests can be accommodated either at the luxurious lodge or at a small tented camp. Excellent game-viewing opportunities. Rattray Reserves, PO Box 2575, Randburg 2125, South Africa; Tel: (011) 789-2677/9; Fax: (011) 886-4382.

Tuli Safari Lodge Offers luxury accommmodation and a variety of recreational activities. Guests can also overnight at game hides. PO Box 781329, Sandton 2146, South Africa; Tel: (011) 883-4345/6/7; Fax: (011) 883-2556.

Campsites

There are no campsites within the reserve.

HEALTH HAZARDS

Take precautions against malaria. Beware of potentially dangerous animals.